ISSUE 33 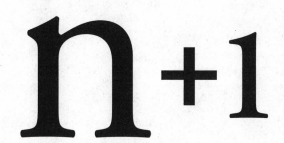 WINTER 2019

OVERTIME

ISSUE 33
WINTER 2019

ESSAYS

REVIEWS

LETTERS

n+1

n+1 is published three times a year by n+1 Foundation, 68 Jay St. #405, Brooklyn, NY 11201. Single issues are available for $14.95; subscriptions for $36; in Canada and other international, $55. Send correspondence to editors@nplusonemag.com. *n+1* is distributed by TNG and Small Changes, Disticor in Canada, and Antenne in the UK and Europe. To place an ad write to ads@nplusonemag.com. *n+1*, Number Thirty-Three © 2018 n+1 Foundation, Inc. ISBN 978-1-7322941-2-7.

THE INTELLECTUAL SITUATION

A Diary

The Best of a Bad Situation

IN OUR AGE OF REPUBLICAN MINORITY DES-
potism, attempts to grapple with anthropo-
genic climate destruction have been warped
to encourage several varieties of despair, rendered acute by the ticking-time-bomb nature
of the problem. The losses suffered by Earth
and its populations—plant and animal—are
neither reversible nor remediable. There
is no future filled with reparations. There is
no long moral arc. Ten or fifteen years ago
it was possible to think of the polar bear
and the white rhinoceros as martyrs, dying
off to shame us into better harmony with
the natural world. Not ruined archaic tor-
sos but videos of extinct creatures would say,
"You must change your life." The same hope
held with respect to coral reefs, forests, and
certain small Pacific Islands. A dark glim-
mer of progressive thinking (the "bargaining phase," as it were) was discernible in the
Kyoto Protocol and at the Paris conference,
where the prime minister of Tuvalu's call to
impose a strict not-to-be-exceeded target of
a 1.5-degree-Celsius rise in global temperature—the minimum required to save his
people from a homeless future in a world
hostile to refugees and immigrants—was
dismissed in favor of pragmatic mitigating
maneuvers intended to induce the cooperation of holdout nations such as the United
States, Russia, and Saudi Arabia.

At least now we can see things clearly—if
only we could focus on the problem. Whatever they may say or tweet, the Trump

Administration is not in denial about climate change. In fact, it has the perverse
distinction of being the first US administration to address it head-on. In 2000, we had
a presidential candidate who understood
the perils facing us, even if he underplayed
them to try to get elected. (By a margin of
one United States Supreme Court justice, he
was not elected.) Instead, the Bush Administration pretended climate change did not
exist, though back then it was called global
warming; "climate change" was a Bush/Rove
term of obfuscation that eventually carried
the day, even among scientists. President
Obama spoke softly about the seriousness
of human-driven climate change in public while his administration chipped away
at automobile emissions and provided
token green-energy incentives. These may
have been the correct policies for a major,
developed nation . . . in the early 1990s. But
like much else after the financial crisis in
2008, the opportunity for a visionary shift
in national focus—one that would have
required investment at least equal to that
being poured into the unwinnable war on
terror—was bartered away to chase after an
illusory political consensus with the termi-
nally uncompromising opposition.

By contrast, from its first days the Trump
presidency brought a series of cabinet
appointments and executive orders clus-
tered around the single purpose of hasten-
ing ecological collapse: Bring back coal!
Shackle and corrupt the EPA! Remove climate change information from government

websites! Withdraw from the Paris Agreement! A candidate whose platform called for pushing carbon dioxide levels past the frontier of scientists' most dire predictions could not have expressed that desire more swiftly or succinctly. It was almost as if that were the whole point. As indeed it was.

There are two clearheaded ways to deal with what's happening to the Earth. One is to Manhattan-Project the implementation of clean energy sources and immediately stop burning fossil fuels. We also need to ditch the patriarchal models of wealth and status reproduction that have been constitutive of nearly all expansionist, war-making, and resource-depleting societies of the past ten thousand years. While we do that, we can try to ameliorate the many catastrophes that have already been set in motion.

The other way, the path we're on currently, is to concede that billions of people will see their economic and cultural lives ruined before dying off at a scale to make the casualties of World War II appear insignificant—and "gameplan" not to be among them. That's what "winning" in the climate-changed future amounts to, and that's the world the Republican Party has committed itself—and the rest of us—to endure: a social-Darwinist survival of the "fittest," "wealthiest," or most prepared, at least in the sense of stockpiling the most guns and canned food. It's been painfully apparent since the term *ecological refugee* was coined in the mid-1980s that unthinkable numbers of people would be forced into migration in coming decades by climate change. Immigration, national borders, and food, water, and energy distribution will be the central issues facing all governments. From there it's a short step, if it's even a step at all, to a vehement resurgence of open racism and bigotry among those with the good fortune to inhabit the least immediately vulnerable areas, be they the highlands of Burma, the fertile Pannonian plain of Hungary, or the plunder-enriched sprawl of the United States.

The looming prospect of a panoply of belligerent, Blut und Boden regimes has always been one of the scariest potential political outcomes of widespread ecological collapse. Through a series of accidents and "influences," we got our version early in the United States. We can and should get rid of it, but the paranoid energies that enabled its triumph are durable and already have pervaded much of the world. Trumpism is our first national response to climate change, and it's a brutal, fearful, vengeful, and gloating response—one that predicts and invites warfare on a global scale. For all the terrible statistical projections, alarming models, and buried reports, what's most immediately terrifying to the human imagination about climate change is the revelation of how large numbers of our species behave under conditions of perceived threat, scarcity, and danger.

Trump's election has dragged us kicking and screaming into the Climate Change Era, even as so many of the discussions around Trump and his party distract us from seeing it. If there was ever a time when climate change, née global warming, was "a topic" to be discussed dispassionately, speculated about, and debated in chilly board rooms, classrooms, and 1 Dag Hammarskjöld Plaza, now it is a present danger and reality tangled up in every political issue. Any unrest, whether in the Sahel, the Middle East, or Myanmar's Rakhine state, where the Rohingya minority have been effectively wiped off the map—pretty much anything, even the uniquely stupid Brexit—could be said to really be "about" climate change. The same with the fates of New Orleans, Houston, Puerto Rico, and so on. The inextricability of people and climate has been understood and written about since at least the late 1980s and early '90s, when Bill McKibben's *The End of Nature* and Gore's *Earth in the Balance* came out, but now the effects are far more pronounced. No one can plausibly claim ignorance. You either know and know, or you know and deny, or you don't even know you know, but have absorbed the knowledge through subtler means, whether collective anxiety or just something in the air.

ONCE IN A WHILE, and with increasing frequency, climate change rises to the forefront of popular consciousness. It happened, for instance, in 2007, when *An Inconvenient Truth* won two Oscars and extreme heatwaves swept across the US and Europe, causing wildfires that torched over ten million acres of forest. A critical mass of people aided by the notion that others are doing something similar can break through the powerful psychological resistance and look the blinding thing in the face. It's devastating and painful; you grieve and you panic. Even so, there's relief in bringing something so painful into view, in holding it with your mind. But you can only look for so long. Resistance reasserts itself, and you slide back behind it. Next time you come out a tiny bit further before you retreat. This is how understanding happens, through a series of breakthroughs and retrenchments and consolidations, as with all efforts toward intentional growth. A single revelation is rarely enough. Even though "we know, we know," as Bellow's Mr. Sammler says about the human moral impulse, we also forget, forget.

So much of our daily behavior is confused and uncertain. We can't seem to lead the lives we have and acknowledge the future simultaneously, even as we must. We keep our eyes on the middle distance—our hopes for the country (universal healthcare!)

and for ourselves—and only feel the shadows on the horizon across our peripheral vision. We are everyday climate deniers the way we are everyday death deniers: we write our articles, save for "retirement," canvass for causes that give us the most hope. We go to bars and ask our friends whether they plan to have kids. Those of us with kids have become "preppers" in both senses, drilling our toddlers with blocks, trilingual board books, and Raspberry Pis to ace the local magnet preschool's entrance exam while lobbying high schools to teach organic farming and archery. Perhaps we should start cultivating other friends, those with hand skills, for when civilization breaks. But what will we be able to offer in return? We can edit their mission statements! More likely we'll do the unskilled labor, like rusticated Chinese intellectuals during the Cultural Revolution. Perhaps our arrow-slinging children will bear us on their backs out of the civilization we ruined for them.

We're not the first generation or nation to harbor such anxious fantasies. So, like Susan Sontag contemplating the end of the world in the aftermath of the Cuban missile crisis, we've been watching Japanese movies—the distracting disaster kind as well as the more realistic and subtle. In Akira Kurosawa's 1955 *I Live in Fear*, a wealthy Japanese businessman, terrorized by news of the recently developed H-bomb, hatches a plan to sell his foundry and move his large family, plus mistress, to a Brazilian estate he is told will be safe even from the winds of fallout once the cold war superpowers finish annihilating each other and their allies. He screens a movie of the acreage to his family: breezes blowing in gentle waves through tall crops. His children don't quite appreciate his consideration; they want a life like everyone else's. They envy their father's status and believe they're entitled to inherit it. So they take the patriarch to civil court to have the businessman ruled incompetent by law.

Both sides appear to have legitimate claims in the realm of ordinary generational dispute, but in the face of atomic threat it's not clear that building a fallout shelter or seeking a place of greater safety is any less rational than the children's expectation that Japan's semifeudal, postwar order will endure indefinitely to their benefit. The irony is that by acting to ensure some form of continuity—either bare life, genetic preservation according to the father's wishes, or social continuity for the children—both parent and children violate that which they claim to value most highly. The businessman ends up burning his own factory, laying waste to his riches, and alienating his offspring, whose lawsuit against him makes a mockery of the traditionalist values they want upheld. It's a tragedy in a postmodern sense, where the tragic does not consist, as Hegel thought, in the conflict between two equal goods, two equally valid demands, which can only be resolved by the next age or paradigm, but in a struggle between pointless desires and differing sets of human limitations.

The existential problem posed by the nuclear age, and now by climate change, is a variant of what Lauren Berlant calls cruel optimism: the instincts and habits that once served our survival and thriving, whether as social collectives or individuals, now work toward our destruction, and are revealed in many respects to have been working in that direction all along. This is what extinction feels like from the inside. The original English title for *I Live in Fear* is *Record of a Living Being*.

WE CAN GRASP the futility when we see it, yet we remain, to an extent, trapped. We streamed *I Live in Fear* during the final days of FilmStruck. We were even a little grateful to AT&T for shutting down the service to appease shareholders because it gave us something else to feel mournful about. Will all those amazing films become another minor province in Jeff Bezos's empire, or will they be snuffed out by an algorithm? Some days the relentless monoculture of Amazon weighs heavier on our humanity than the continued deforestation of the actual Amazon. Who wants to live in a future where no one watches Tarkovsky or Bergman?

Intellectually, this is the most difficult: to let go of our impulses toward the infinite and the eternal, which in another era might have been satisfied by religion but which we learned to redirect into literature and culture. There was a powerful seduction in the idea that while individual humans may die, books and ideas provide humans a quantum of immortality. Even if we didn't write a lasting work, we could participate in a community of shared meaning and purpose that predated us and would, because of our efforts, outlast us. The intimacy we may still feel with a long-dead writer or artist, even living ones we've never met, is the most special thing in the world. Such premises, though, cannot be reconciled with an understanding of what's ahead. We delay grappling with the fact of death in favor of a kind of collective immortality of literature, of shared thought—but that kind of immortality is premised on the existence of our civilization and the maintenance of our traditions. And when human civilization ends, whether in the sudden collapse of the Antarctic ice sheet or with a giant methane fart or both, wet and smelly, it's unlikely that whatever comes after will have much interest in shoring fragments against our ruins.

IF OUR IMAGINATIONS are robust enough, we can push ourselves to picture some posthuman, dominant life form for our post-catastrophic Earth. Fully conscious, autonomous *Robo sapiens* fueled by solar power, or new age crystals, or Tesla coils; fantastically evolved crystalline, anaerobic life-forms; or maybe the evolutionary champion will be a network of surviving flora with neural-network powers, like that planet from *Solaris*. Grant them, while we're at it—because of our inescapable human narcissism—a curiosity similar to our own when it comes to precursor civilizations and species. Imbue at least one of them with the archivist's desire to rummage, note, and classify (surely a bug in the program!) the data stored in some miraculously intact server, or in a hoarder's paper library preserved in mummified splendor in the new desert conditions of America's once Great Plains. What might they say about the literature produced by humans on the subject of global warming and climate breakdown during the crucial period from 1999 to 2019?

The first decade of the 21st century yields some fine specimens of humans actively grappling with the oncoming catastrophe without quite knowing how close it would be. Elizabeth Kolbert's pieces for the *New Yorker* in those years were framed as various encounters and profiles with archaeologists, glaciologists, climatologists. They have the deep narrative structure of mystery stories. What does the study of Greenland's ice cores reveal about potential freshwater availability at the equator? What does the presence of dolomite particles in sediment dredged from the Gulf of Oman tell us about a crippling drought that destroyed an ancient Sumerian civilization in less than four years? In 2005, she quoted the code of James Hansen's climate modeling program as if it were a piece of the Rosetta Stone or a monitory *Mene, mene, tekel, upharsin*. The tone was doom-edged but reassuring. The conditional

tense was a feature: This could happen *if*; this *might* happen. The line of thought was, as often as not, analogical: Other civilizations died, we too could die. Trust the experts, they said, a message for the public but also for an assumed audience of powerful "deciders" in Washington. Kolbert's articles were about forms of what one might call deep listening: to the winds, the cores, the fragments of pottery from a city that had devolved so quickly that one could learn in a matter of moments which pieces had been produced by the flourishing and which by the dying civilization. Nobody listened, so these now feel like the opening scenes in one of those alien invasion films that humans watch to entertain and placate themselves, in which a lone specialist must warn everyone before it's too late and is never heeded until it is.

By 2009, Kolbert turned to explaining the Anthropocene and climate change through the die-off of charismatic megafauna. The essays collected in *The Sixth Extinction* are less mystery and more of a style used in accounts of the great crimes of human history—think Lucy Dawidowicz's *The War Against the Jews* on a transhuman scale. The conditional tense was banished because it was already happening. Again to no great avail. Once the Great Barrier Reef turned bone white and it became clearer that humans could not avert their fate, a new chapter opened on mainstream magazine doom mongering. Climate writing was no longer the exclusive province of science writers. The gentler show-don't-tell gospel of Kolbert or even Bill McKibben was joined by varieties of Revelations—passing from what Nathaniel Rich terms the "Apprehension" phase to what he calls, with Wagnerian pathos, the "Reckoning." What will the *Robo sapiens* make of the end-is-nigh warnings of *New York* ("It is, I promise, worse than you think") or the *Times Magazine* ("we failed to solve this problem when we had the chance")?

Even Kolbert seemed to have caught the mood: by 2017 or 2018, the ratio of her long features to weekly or daily comments flipped in response to the slew of the government's many outrages. Where political leaders had been in the background of her earlier pieces, the name Trump appears increasingly in headlines, reflecting again his megalomaniacal dominance of the news cycle and the world. Could one man literally be responsible for breaking the climate? It seems so, yes. At this late hour, Kolbert recently returned to interview Hansen. Haunted by guilt at his failure to break through the toxic cloud of obfuscation and denial and hostility, he leaves a message to the planet: "The simple thing is, I'm sorry we're leaving such a fucking mess."

In other precincts, where powerlessness was more quickly intuited or accepted, a mode of climate elegy surfaced. Safely ensconced in a surviving lookout tower, a pair of books, Philip Connors's *Fire Season* and *A Song for the River*, offer accounts of what it was like to have been a professional witness to the disruption of the natural cycles of forest fires. Both engage with and test one's faith that nature provides "for such loss . . . abundant recompense" and that humans may, if they so choose, find evidence for renewal in the contemplation of conflagration. Connors writes as one who knows himself to be part of a dying breed, one of few "officiants at an ongoing funeral for the forest we had found when we first assumed our posts." The forest acreage dwindles from development and overgrazing; the fires no longer burn themselves out after being allowed to clear away dead and overgrown brush. There is more desiccated and dead forest to burn with each year. The river dries up in places and is threatened by a major dam project intended to benefit some politically connected farmers on unsustainable land.

That the loss of our climate also produces a climate of loss should be no mystery. The elegy, too, though, is a symptom of humans' nearly unbearable optimism in the face of the catastrophe about to engulf them. Mourning implies, by the very act of committing to mourn, a hope for renewal and survival—or at least a belief that the author, if not the book itself, will find "pastures new," as an earlier elegy has it. At the heart of even the best literature about climate change, we find this ghost of consolation for something which ought to leave us inconsolable.

The human belief in immortality seems to have tricked us, allowing us to project ourselves into a humanless future that nevertheless reads and sifts the ashes of human culture. This leap of faith—a belief that memories and cultural traces can persist past our ability to comprehend how those traces will be shaped and interpreted—animates Roy Scranton's more stoic than elegiac *Learning How to Die in the Anthropocene*, which, like Kolbert's earlier work, offers a perverse sort of consolation: Because we were able to recover the texts of earlier cultures and civilizations—like the ancient Sumerians, and the Akkadians, the Mycenaeans, the Hellenes, and the Romans, all of whom were doomed by forces beyond their control—some Beings, human or not, might recover us. "We must build arks," Scranton urges, "not just biological arks, to carry forward endangered genetic data, but also cultural arks, to carry forward endangered wisdom." We should live now the way the philosopher Jonathan Lear (in *Radical Hope*) suggested the Crow Nation learned to survive their cultural genocide by European settlers, by imagining ourselves as remote ancestors to a posterity we have lost any right to claim as our own.

Our integrity consists in our willingness to surrender our culture without abandoning it.

OF POTENTIALLY GREATER predictive and preparatory value for what awaits us in the short term are the apocalyptic effusions of pop culture that do not reference climate change at all. The world is destroyed more times in a Hollywood studio executive's calendar than in all the creation and decreation myths of Hindu mythology. *The Walking Dead* absorbed the attention of millions when *The Sixth Extinction*, a wild success by publishing industry standards, sold about 360,000 copies. Partly this is because the zombies are us—duh!—but "us" in a way that allows us to displace responsibility for the destruction we wreak on that which we love best, which also happens to be ourselves. When disasters strike, as they have already and will again, they will feel external, set in motion by forces so deeply structural that they might as well be "natural." Our willed ignorance is part of what allows us to fantasize about surviving the consequences of our ignorance.

Such are the fantasies and thoughts we entertain under the flat, blinding lights of our neighborhood Trader Joe's, housed in the basement of a new luxury mall. We maneuver our cart around the ant-like evening crowd, join the queue winding through crates of packaged snacks and produce. Everyone is civil in this underground bunker. Everyone looks like a corpse going through the motions. It's the bourgeois bread line of apocalypse. The impressive chaos management of the employees reminds us of FEMA and the thought that we may soon live in box stores, like the refugees from the Paradise wildfire out in California. And why are these lights so awful?

At least we know the answer to that one. One of few successful attempts to reduce carbon emissions in the United States in the 21st century resulted in the slow replacement of heat-generating yellow incandescent light bulbs with cold white-blue light-emitting diodes. LED—it doesn't stand for "lower emission density," although that's what they want us to think. Of course we would sacrifice a little aesthetic indulgence if it meant saving the planet. But the back-of-envelope math suggests that even if every incandescent bulb used in the United States for residential and commercial applications were replaced by its diode equivalent, the likely total differential would be a percentage point of our total energy use.

Why is this trivial benefit, at significant cost to quality of life, the stated objective of a law of the land? Could it be that this depressing-seeming side effect of state-enforced limitations on our lighting choices is in fact its primary effect? That its intrusion into the intimate routines of private life and the big rituals of public life, like shopping, taking a walk at night through our favorite urban haunts, or spending hours in a hospital waiting room, was meant to socialize us, lumen by lumen, into the asceticism the crisis seemed to call for: a joyless, penitential Protestant inheritance through which we could prove our own moral fitness for salvation by how little we indulged?

The lights give us headaches; we catch ourselves raving. We like to think of ourselves as people who believe in good governance and ecological stewardship. The minor virtue of foregoing the small pleasures of incandescence can make us feel engaged with sustainability and help us avoid the larger duty of addressing more difficult problems, like the two-thirds of energy we waste in generating and transmitting electricity, or the climate catastrophe itself. So many people changing so many light bulbs makes it feel like the degree of impact must be similarly momentous. On the other hand, for people who hate "big government" and also deny the Anthropocene, this same policy confirms their biases: a ridiculous, nannying regulation with no significant benefit. The case of light-bulb regulations is a miniature of all that was wrong with the discussion of offsets, trade-offs, and watching your carbon footprint in the early to mid '00s. And the political consequences of the ascetic approach to saving the environment have been epically disastrous.

TRULY, WE HAVE fucked it up in so many ways! Yet while climate change increasingly feels like an inescapable doom upon humanity, our only means of recourse remains political. Even under the heavy weather of present and near-future conditions, there's an imperative to imagine that we aren't facing the death of everyone, or the end of existence. No matter what the worst-case models using the most advanced forecasting of feedback loops may predict, we have to act as if we can assume some degree of human continuity. What happens in the next decades is instead, as the climate reporter Kate Aronoff has said, about who gets to live in the 21st century. And the question of who gets to live, and how, has always been the realm of politics.

The most radical and hopeful response to climate change shouldn't be, What do we give up? It should remain the same one that plenty of ordinary and limited humans ask themselves each day: How do we collectively improve our overall quality of life? It is a welfare question, one that has less to do with consumer choices—like changing light bulbs—than with the spending of trillions and trillions of still-available dollars on decoupling economic growth and wealth from carbon-based fuels and carbon-intensive products, including plastics.

The economist Robert Pollin makes a convincing case that only massive investment in and commitment to alternative energy sources stands any chance of lowering emissions to acceptable levels. All other solutions, from "degrowth" to population control, will fall well short of intended targets while causing greater societal pain and instability. To achieve a fairly modest 40 percent reduction in carbon emissions within twenty years, Pollin suggests in a recent *New Left Review* essay, we would have to invest, per year, "1–1.5 per cent of global GDP—about $1 trillion at the current global GDP of $80 trillion," and continually increase that investment, "rising in step with global growth thereafter." Whether we call this a Manhattan Project for renewable, sustainable energy or a Green New Deal, as Pollin and politicians like Alexandria Ocasio-Cortez have named it, the point is to change the political discourse around climate change from either mindless futurism of the kind that proposes large scale "geoengineering" projects or fruitless cap-and-trade negotiations at the mercy of obstructionists. Only a great potlatch of what we have can save us from a bonfire of the vanities on a planetary scale.

In the short term, a true Green New Deal would need to be more like a Green Shock Doctrine. As hurricanes, fires, and floods pile up, each one would provide the occasion to unhook more people from the fossil-fuel grid. At the scale Pollin envisions, it would be naive to assume that a switch from fossils to renewables could happen smoothly. There would be disruptions to almost every aspect of economic life, including food supplies, the power grid (even the internet!), and daily work rhythms and commutes. There would be black markets in banned fuels, and even some forms of violence, like the current populist French riots against Macron's gasoline taxes. If even such small measures aimed at reducing carbon consumption result in such aggressive pushback, there is no reason to be moderate. Compared with what awaits us if we continue as we are, such shocks are as a rainstorm to a hurricane, or the 1977 blackout of New York City to the bombing of Dresden.

The economic costs of climate change can already be measured by toting up the losses incurred during every single hurricane, wildfire, drought, and war of the past ten years or longer. Because these costs have not yet been borne by any of the major stakeholders in the US or — really — the global economy, they are written off as the price of doing business. No sane group of investors or empowered body of citizens, however, would make these trade-offs to ensure a few more years of short-term profits when measured against the prospects of what would be the last and most profound crash in the history of capitalism.

The immediate switch to sustainable energy on a global scale also addresses one of the intellectual stumbling blocks that has bedeviled even well-intentioned climate-change policy makers: what to do about so-called developing societies. Unlike the ascetic cap-and-trade system, we aren't required by this switch to turn to Indian or Chinese middle classes and say, "we deny you the quality of life that we enjoyed." We should have never enjoyed it in the way we did—that was well understood, then as now, if for different reasons. The extraction-based political economy that buoys a specific stratum of India, Brazil, Iran, the Arabian Peninsula states, and China is objectionable on nearly every level; there's no "global justice" legitimacy to

the idea that past resource exploitation by Western powers entitles the elites of postcolonial developing countries to squander the future of their own citizens and the rest of the planet. Wholesale disaster under the banner of postcolonial nationalism will not feel better than under the banner of revanchist white nationalism.

Does this sound madly utopian? If so, it's because the fossil-fuel industry—and that term, *industry*, must now include governments like Russia's and our own—has been successful at obscuring how close we are to being able to switch over to renewable energy. The relevant technologies of solar, wind, hydro, and even nuclear power all exist. Architects and green industrial designers know how to make structures that aren't just energy efficient but even net-energy positive. Under political conditions other than our current ones, we'd have great reason for optimism.

But unlike with other utopian programs, no one seems to see the promise. "Decouple now" and "Renewable or bust" don't seem likely to harness the diverse interest groups currently opposed to Trump and the Republican Party. Most of us prefer to remain in the dark when it comes to energy. It's still far easier to imagine the end of the world than the end of carbon-based capitalism. But what other choice do we have, America? Let's get right down to the job—nearsighted, psychopathic, queer, angelic, diabolical, whatever we are, harness that most renewable of resources, human will, and put our shoulders to the wheel. +

SHIRLEY WEGNER, *AERIAL VIEW #13*. 2016, PIGMENTED INKJET PRINT. COURTESY OF THE ARTIST.

POLITICS

Memoranda

RICHARD BECK
The Korean Peace Process

IN LATE JUNE, JUST A FEW WEEKS AFTER Donald Trump and Kim Jong-un shook hands and watched a propaganda film about themselves in Singapore, several news outlets excitedly reported that the American President had been duped. Their source was 38 North, a nonpartisan website that publishes North Korea analysis and that had found, through examining satellite imagery, that North Korea was continuing to expand and improve the infrastructure at its nuclear research facility in Yongbyon. "Hold the champagne on North Korea, President Trump," chided a *Washington Post* editorial headline. NBC News described Trump's decision to suspend military training exercises on the Korean peninsula in the wake of the Singapore summit as "a major concession," one that didn't look so good in light of this new satellite imagery. On the basis of these editorials and the 38 North satellite imagery analysis, a consensus soon emerged: the Kim regime had been negotiating in bad faith, and Trump and Secretary of State Mike Pompeo would have to respond accordingly. "The observed activity appears inconsistent with a North Korean intent to abandon its nuclear weapons programs," a North Korea wonk from the Heritage Foundation told NBC. "There seems little reason to continue expansion plans if the regime intended to dismantle them as would be required under a denuclearization agreement."

Here, however, is the second paragraph of the 38 North report itself:

> Continued work at the Yongbyon facility should not be seen as having any relationship to North Korea's pledge to denuclearize. The North's nuclear cadre can be expected to proceed with business as usual until specific orders are issued from Pyongyang.

In the report, 38 North went out of its way to describe the Yongbyon improvements as unremarkable and even expected, rather than as the harbinger of a mushroom cloud over Seattle. Of course Kim would continue to build up his nuclear infrastructure until real negotiations began—you want to enter negotiations in the strongest possible bargaining position, and North Korea's status as a nuclear power is the only reason it has a bargaining position of any kind.

But these considerations did not find their way into the media's view of events. At every step of the peace process that began to unfold between North and South Korea in the spring, American commentators have claimed that the whole endeavor is bound to fail, and in so doing increased the likelihood that it actually will. There could be no more certain proof of the media's inability to learn from the mistakes it made justifying the Iraq war than the spectacle of editorial boards demonizing Kim as a "madman" during a period of heightened nuclear tensions, or of talking heads preemptively belittling the US government's efforts to broker a peace agreement that the US government itself helped make impossible half a century ago. The Korean peace process is a historic opportunity, and it will have been a historic opportunity even if it comes to nothing. Of course, it could come to far worse than nothing. If war breaks out in the wake of the collapse of the peace process, the American media will have blood on its hands, just as it did beginning on March 20, 2003.

At the time of this writing, negotiations have stalled. The Trump administration has repeatedly promised a second summit between Trump and Kim, but even the most basic details (date, location) have yet to materialize. John Bolton and US generals have rediscovered the language of American dominance. Trump announced and then quickly canceled a trip to North Korea by Pompeo, who was heading to Pyongyang for a fourth round of talks with North Korean officials. Those officials were angry because the US has so far been unwilling to consider bringing the Korean War to a formal end: while armed hostilities between North and South (plus the US and China) ended with the adoption of the Korean Armistice Agreement, a formal peace treaty was never signed. (In an exquisite example of the hairsplitting often involved in diplomatic negotiations, the most the US has offered so far is to issue a statement acknowledging the objective reality that armed conflict has ceased.) Pompeo did meet with Kim for a two-hour discussion in October, but reports suggest their conversation was merely an attempt to schedule the still-elusive second summit, rather than an effort to hammer out the details of any deal. Since then, North Korean officials, though careful not to criticize Trump directly, have registered

their displeasure with some of his positions, including what they perceive as a lack of urgency on his part to get something done. Most ominously, according to a report from the website Tokyo Business Today, national security professionals and administration officials, those involved with the grunt work of maintaining the American foreign policy consensus, are working quietly to prevent President Trump from meeting with Kim again. They are worried that he will give away too much—i.e., that a second summit would go too well for their liking.

Still, there are reasons for optimism. Peace is possible, if just barely, on the Korean peninsula neither thanks to nor in spite of America's leadership, but because America isn't leading at all. The country's ruling party has been thrown into such chaos by Trump's election that it lacks a coherent geopolitical strategy, and the State Department is a nonfunctioning husk of its former self. Trump, meanwhile, doesn't care about geopolitics. All he wants is to win—or, more specifically, to be seen as having won. He embodies the decline of America's global influence even as he exacerbates it. Maintaining hegemony over a peninsula located on the other side of the world requires brute force—that is, troops, tens of thousands of whom are stationed in South Korea—but also some real thought, and American foreign policy hasn't done any real thinking in two years. What Kim Jong-un and South Korean president Moon Jae-in have done is recognize America's geopolitical incoherence as an opportunity to act on their own behalf. The peace process is primarily of South Korean design, it was underway months before Trump flew to Singapore, and it illustrates the kinds of space that open up, and the kinds of diplomacy that become possible, as the US begrudgingly starts to cede its place at the head of the world's table.

THE US HAS MAINTAINED a huge military presence in East Asia since World War II. By treaty, America is responsible for the military defense of Japan, which is not permitted to have offensive forces of its own, according to the constitution the US drew up for it after World War II. Currently there are about forty thousand American troops stationed there, and at least twenty thousand are deployed in South Korea. These troops were originally sent to the region to contain the global ascendancy of communism (in general) and China (in particular), and while history has obviated the first justification, the second one remains. The US says it is running a kind of protection racket in the region, that its troops are there because North Korea is aggressive and dangerous. But the real reason for their presence is that the US wants to prevent China from becoming the regional hegemon. This was also the goal of Obama's Trans-Pacific Partnership, a free-trade agreement that included almost all of China's regional economic rivals, from which Donald Trump withdrew the United States in January 2017. Obama was explicit about this: "We can't let countries like China write the rules of the global economy," he said in an official statement on the TPP. "We should write those rules." The US is failing to achieve this goal. China has attained economic supremacy in the region, and with major projects like the Belt and Road Initiative, a set of planned infrastructure developments reaching across Asia and into Africa and Europe, it is on its way to doing so globally. But failure hasn't been enough to bring home American troops in other parts of the world, and so far it hasn't been enough in East Asia.

Liberal commentators have suggested that Trump and Kim's rapport can be credited to the two leaders' similarities: the fact that both are unstable megalomaniacs with bad haircuts and a grotesque flair for media spectacle. An extension of this idea is the notion that Trump was able to bring Kim to the negotiating table because he "speaks his language," as though the problem with Obama's sober diplomatic outreach was that it just didn't resonate with a leader who, in the end, needed to hear the brutal rhetoric of nuclear annihilation. The similarities between the two men have been exaggerated, and the enormous differences in their political positions have been overlooked. Trump is the celebrity figurehead of a party that is fractured and weak, which only remains in power because the opposition is even weaker. He is neither the product of a political school of thought nor someone with political ideas of his own. He is a media personality whose shamelessness and aggression were perfectly suited to exploiting Republican and then Democratic weakness in 2016.

Kim is an authoritarian despot, but he is also the head of a dynastic line that has ruled North Korea without interruption since 1948. The legitimacy of his family's rule derives from his grandfather, Kim Il-sung, who founded the Down-with-Imperialism Union in 1926, opposed the nearly four-decade-long Japanese occupation of the Korean peninsula as an effective Communist guerrilla leader, and was installed as the head of the Korean Communist Party by the Soviet Union in 1945. Kim's fate is tied to that of the country he rules in a way that Trump's is not, and the fall of Kim's regime would usher in a transformative upheaval in North Korean politics and society. Trump, by contrast, is the *product* of an unfolding upheaval of American politics and society.

It's in that light that Kim's race to develop North Korea's nuclear capabilities needs to be understood: the regime sees nuclear weapons as the only way to guarantee its survival. They have felt this way since at least January 29, 2002, when George W. Bush deemed North Korea, along with Iraq and Iran, as part of an "axis of evil." Fourteen months later, the US invaded Iraq and toppled Saddam Hussein's government, and prominent Republicans spent the next decade publicly fantasizing about doing the same to Iran. Obama's nuclear deal provided a reprieve for Ayatollah Khamenei, but then there was Muammar Gaddafi. In 2003, the Libyan dictator announced that he would have the country's incipient nuclear weapons program dismantled, as part of an effort to normalize relations with the United States. That looked good for Gaddafi until 2011, when NATO took advantage of the Libyan civil war to have him overthrown. Then Trump took office and made it clear that the US would be pulling out of the Iran agreement before long. It would be hard to blame the Kim regime for deciding that the signals had become too obvious to ignore. In May 2017, North Korea conducted a test of its Hwasong-12 missile, prompting speculation in the American press that the country had developed the capability to strike the United States. On July 4, the Kim regime tested the Hwasong-14, a missile with a potential maximum range of about four thousand miles. Further tests followed in August and September, including one missile that passed over Hokkaido, Japan, prompting residents there to seek shelter. By the end of the year, North Korea had declared itself a full-fledged nuclear power.

Trump encouraged this escalation for months with warmongering speeches and tweets, bringing the world closer to nuclear war than it had been at any point since the Cuban missile crisis. He promised to rain down "fire and fury" on Kim's regime, described military solutions as "locked and loaded," and, in a speech given

at the UN, threatened to "totally destroy" North Korea. This was very dangerous, and also very stupid, because it was an obvious bluff. There could be no military solution to the Kim regime, no invasion of Pyongyang, no missile strike on Kim's presidential palace, because any of that would quickly result in the deaths of tens of thousands in South Korea. Even according to the cold calculus of American geopolitics, Trump's aggressiveness was destructive. American influence in East Asia is predicated on the idea that the US can protect Japan and South Korea by suppressing the belligerence of the North. But over the course of 2017, Trump did the opposite, theatrically upping the ante at every opportunity. The rest of the American government proved unable to rein him in.

As a result of Trump's rhetoric, South Korea was forced to reconsider the amount of faith it felt able to put in US security guarantees. In late 2017, the author of a *New York Times* op-ed described a history lesson he'd received as a South Korean third grader in the late 1980s. "A teacher spent an entire class period telling us that the United States was deliberately keeping the Korean Peninsula divided so it could sell weapons to our country," Se-Woong Koo wrote.

I repeated the story at home, and my mother and brother told me that my teacher must be a radical pro–North Korean sympathizer. I should know that the United States is our ally, they said, and that our real enemy is Kim Il-sung up north. Communists want to destroy us, and Americans were simply trying to protect us and our precious democracy.

I believed it then. But it now looks like America could bring our doom.

A protection racket doesn't work if you can't actually provide the protection.

With the US rendered ineffective, if not fully sidelined, by the unpredictability of its own head of state, North and South Korea took the initiative. South Korean president Moon Jae-in, who was elected in May 2017, is a progressive who had argued for peace negotiations with the North during his campaign. Moon, who was born in a refugee camp during the war after his parents fled the North, was symbolically well positioned to make this push. His predecessor, Park Geun-hye, is the daughter of Park Chung-hee, a conservative and five-term president of South Korea (he served from 1963 to 1979) who first came to power via military coup. The Parks are indelibly tied to the legacy of the Korean War, and so in 2016, when Geun-hye was impeached for influence peddling, Moon was able to present himself as someone who could offer a fresh start.

At the 2018 Winter Olympics in Pyeongchang, North and South Korean athletes marched together under the "Korean Unification Flag" (a blue silhouette of the peninsula on a white background), and Kim's sister Kim Yo-jong presented Moon with a letter from her brother, inviting him to a summit between the two heads of state. The leaders met two months later in the demilitarized zone, each stepping briefly across the military demarcation line while clasping hands (because there has been no peace treaty, the line is not an international border). This was the first time a North Korean head of state had set foot in South Korea since the country was divided. The summit's end product was the Panmunjom Declaration for Peace, Prosperity, and Unification of the Korean Peninsula, in which both sides affirmed the goal of a "nuclear-free Korean Peninsula" and pledged to work toward a formal peace treaty by the end of 2018. The two leaders met again in September and rode together in an open-topped car through the streets of Pyongyang. They signed an agreement establishing a no-fly zone along the DMZ and mutually ending the military exercises there that have been a great source of tension between the two countries.

The American press has treated Moon with some condescension for his eagerness to meet and negotiate with Kim, and especially for suggesting that Trump deserves the Nobel Peace Prize (as though flattering someone who clearly values flattery and public acclaim more than anything else on Earth weren't a wholly sensible move). Perhaps American pundits and reporters had mistaken American interests for South Korea's. Moon's peace efforts won him an approval rating of over 80 percent among South Koreans in the spring of 2018. (That figure has since dropped precipitously, but this is mostly due to the country's struggling economy.) This may be hard to understand in light of Kim's nuclear tests and the expansion of his arsenal, but those tests weren't aimed at South Korea—they were aimed at the United States. The whole Korean peninsula is just a third bigger than Florida, and North Korea is one of the most militarized societies in the world, with nearly 1.2 million of its 25 million citizens serving in the armed forces. Kim does not need nuclear weapons to destroy Seoul. Conventional arms could cover the distance from North Korea to Seoul just fine. North Korea's long-range ballistic missiles did, however, qualitatively change the threat Kim can pose to the United States.

But press condescension to Moon could not cover up just how bad the optics of the Kim-Moon summit were for American leadership in the region. Vice President Mike Pence had already embarrassed himself at the Pyeongchang Olympics, avoiding VIP dinners at which North Korean officials were in attendance and, at the opening ceremony, making a petulant show of ignoring Kim's sister despite being seated directly in front of her. Now the US looked totally out of touch with events transpiring on the peninsula, and so when Moon emerged from the summit announcing that Kim wanted a meeting with Trump as well, Trump could hardly have refused without making the US materially less relevant to the unfolding diplomacy. All the while, Moon congratulated Trump on his "leadership," understanding the need to manage and flatter the American President. Trump "deserves big credit for bringing about the inter-Korean talks," he said, presumably suppressing a smile. "It could be a resulting work of the US-led sanctions and pressure."

The US is a necessary part of the peace process because only the US can give the Kim regime what it wants most: a guarantee that the US will stop working toward regime change in North Korea. North Korea's official position is that it has pursued nuclear weapons out of fear of American aggression, and that it would be willing to abandon nuclear arms in exchange for American security guarantees. In the joint statement Trump and Kim signed at the end of their June summit in Singapore, Trump committed to providing exactly those security guarantees. The joint statement is not any kind of binding agreement, and it didn't work out the details of anything. At the moment, America has not granted formal diplomatic recognition to North Korea as a state. It does not have an embassy in the Democratic People's Republic of Korea (limited American consular functions in North Korea are performed by Sweden), nor does the DPRK have one in Washington. The furthest the US has gone is to acknowledge that the Kim regime currently governs the region of the Korean peninsula north of the demilitarized zone. Security guarantees are still a long way off,

but they are the central issue, and the joint statement did not try to pretend otherwise.

Trump made another, even more meaningful gesture at the last minute, and appears not to have consulted with any of his advisers before deciding to make it. At a press conference conducted after his meeting with Kim, an ebullient Trump, doing his best to perform an awareness of the moment's historical gravity, announced that he would be doing away with the war games the US had jointly conducted with South Korea for years. Halting the exercises, which typically involve more than twenty thousand US troops (plus three hundred thousand South Korean military), "will save us a tremendous amount of money," Trump said. "Plus, I think it's very provocative." Trump said this last bit with the same air of bullshit insouciance that he brings to all of his public statements, but the words themselves were plain fact. The joint war games are rehearsals for the invasion of North Korea. North Koreans react to the war games just as Americans would if Canada and Russia annually sent bomber jets, aircraft carriers, and hundreds of thousands of troops to Nova Scotia, where they practiced invading Boston with live ammunition.

The American foreign policy establishment, which had been uncomfortable with the summit from the start, was furious about Trump suspending the war games. Democratic politicians interviewed around Capitol Hill sounded like Republicans talking about Obama's Iran deal in 2015, chiding the President for failing to be tough on the dictator. "This was a big win for North Korea," said Delaware senator Chris Coons, who, when asked to comment on the idea that the war games are threatening and provocative, said, "That's the perspective of North Korea, not the perspective of the United States." Apparently diplomacy should not involve considering and making concessions to the perspective of the other party. Senator Mazie Hirono of Hawaii criticized Trump for legitimizing Kim's regime by meeting with him in the first place. On MSNBC, the avatar of liberalism Rachel Maddow spent the opening two minutes and fifty seconds of her show teeing up the revelation that North Korea shares an eleven-mile border with . . . Russia. Nearly twenty hallucinatory minutes later, she got to the point: "You know who else wants the US to stop its joint military exercises with South Korea?" She accused Trump of abandoning the exercises, "a pillar of [US] national security strategy," to help Putin. Nancy Pelosi and Chuck Schumer joined in the criticism as well.

If the Democratic Party's view of the summit was nearly unanimous, Republicans found themselves in a trickier political spot. Their reactions to an identical summit that featured Obama rather than Trump are easy to imagine, yet Trump's media savvy and low-grade approximation of populism, along with his white-supremacist dog whistles, are all the party has holding it together. How to accommodate themselves to a diplomatic summit over which they likely would have started impeachment hearings had Obama been the one shaking hands with Kim in Singapore? They needed a win too badly to criticize what looked to be Trump's first actual success since Neil Gorsuch's nomination to the Supreme Court, so they mostly held their tongues, aiming for quotes that could be forgotten as soon as they had been uttered. "Obviously, it's the first step in what will be a long process in the coming months," said Senator Tom Cotton. Perhaps the sharpest criticism came from Marco Rubio, who managed no better than a mildly worked-up tweet: "Should be skeptical of any deal with #KJU." Lindsey Graham warned Trump that the details of any agreement would need to

be approved by Congress, which barely qualified as a warning.

One factor that contributes to the GOP's relative indifference to Trump's impulsive and ego-driven diplomacy is declining interest in foreign policy within the Republican Party in general. The Tea Party insurgents who started taking over after Obama's election are primarily motivated by domestic grievances, and the old grandees of conservative foreign policy—the Corkers and McCains—are dead, retiring, marginalized. A new generation of Republican ultrahawks—people like Rubio and Cotton—whose spectrum of opinion for diplomacy ranges from condescension to contempt, is now rising through the congressional ranks, but they have not yet taken hold of America's foreign policy levers. This has given Trump significant leeway to improvise.

Democrats, meanwhile, remain fully inside the mainstream of American foreign policy thought. They believe in free trade, NATO, and the use of military force (or, at minimum, the presence of military forces) to maintain US supremacy around the globe. Their objections to the Korean peace process—which persist even though nearly 80 percent of *South Koreans* have said they trust Kim Jong-un to pursue reconciliation and denuclearization in good faith—may in part reveal a simple partisan desire to deny Trump a win, but they also speak to what the US imagines its purpose is in East and Southeast Asia. The question raised by Democratic skepticism is whether the US sees bringing the Korean War to a formal end as somehow not in its national interest.

Shortly before the Singapore summit, a group of seven Senate Democrats that included Dianne Feinstein and Chuck Schumer sent a letter to President Trump outlining their conditions for viewing the summit as a success. It described the ultimate goal as the "complete, verifiable, and irreversible dismantlement" (the acronym, now in common use, is CVID) of North Korea's nuclear and missile programs. Relief of US economic sanctions on North Korea "should be dependent on dismantlement and removal," the senators wrote, foreclosing the possibility of graduated, mutual gestures of good faith (i.e., some sanctions removed in exchange for the destruction of some particular missiles, and so on). Furthermore, having totally dismantled its weapons programs, North Korea must agree to "compliance regimes" permitting the inspection of both declared and undeclared but suspicious-looking sites by outside investigators, "anywhere, anytime." Failure to comply would result in the immediate reinstatement of sanctions. Anything short of this, the senators wrote, "is a bad deal."

This set of requirements is not a good starting point for anything trying to call itself a good-faith negotiation, and it is a lucky break that Trump didn't take the Democrats' advice heading into Singapore. CVID has become something of a rhetorical fetish in Washington. It was first coined by Bush Administration diplomats working with North Korea in 2003 and 2004, and it is just as untethered to reality as Bush-era diplomacy was in general. Some parts of the idea are simply confusing, such as the "irreversible" component. North Korea is already, right now, a nuclear power. Were it to dismantle every missile and test site and laboratory within its borders, it would still retain the technical knowledge to restart its nuclear program if it so desired. Are the scientists to be exiled from the country? Should their memories be wiped? Other aspects of CVID are simply not realistic. No sovereign nation would consent to "anytime, anywhere" inspections of its scientific

and military facilities by representatives of a country with which it is still technically at war, especially not when such inspections could result in the automatic reimposition of economic sanctions that have turned North Korea into a pariah, dependent on Chinese trade for its economic subsistence. And North Korea was supposed to agree to all this, to ending the nuclear program that is its *only* piece of international leverage, before getting anything in return.

The diplomatic uselessness of these demands became apparent soon after the Singapore summit, when Mike Pompeo traveled to North Korea to conduct preliminary negotiations with government officials. Pompeo returned to the US describing the talks as productive, but North Korean state media quickly released a statement throwing cold water on that idea. The line that got all the attention in the US was when North Korea insulted what it called America's "gangster-like mind-set," but the statement described the reasons for North Korea's unhappiness pretty clearly. "We expected that the US would come with constructive measures that are conducive to building trust," it read, "and we considered providing something that would correspond to them." But instead of engaging in the "phased and synchronous approach" North Korea called for, US negotiators came with unilateral demands, and never even mentioned a treaty to bring the Korean War to a formal end. We don't know what exactly transpired between Pompeo and the North Korean officials, but the secretary of state is a longtime Washington insider whose views have never significantly diverged from the US foreign policy mainstream. It is safe to assume that he proposed something like what the Democrats demanded Trump impose. The North Koreans went in looking for a negotiation. Instead, they got CVID.

"Gangster-like" is colorful, but it's also reasonably accurate.

THE REASON THE US is acting more like an occupying military force than like a sovereign nation negotiating with peers is that the US *is* an occupying military force on the Korean peninsula, something American politicians and journalists have been careful to avoid mentioning in discussions of North Korea. It is a commonplace to say that Americans avoid public discussions of the Vietnam War, the country's great 20th-century humiliation and the primary generational trauma of the boomers. But the war Americans actually never discuss, and about which younger Americans know nothing at all, is the Korean War. Hollywood never goes more than a few years without releasing a new movie centered on the Vietnam War, and Ken Burns's fourteen-hour series on Vietnam was among the most discussed documentaries of 2017. Meanwhile, Hollywood has never produced an enduring pop-culture monument to the Korean War, except for one, Robert Altman's 1970 film *M*A*S*H**, which everyone knows is actually about Vietnam (a number of the male characters have shaggy hair, an obvious giveaway when distinguishing between a war fought in the late '60s and one fought in the early '50s).

Americans don't like talking about Korea because Korea is like a Vietnam that America didn't lose, yet things turned out badly anyway. In both Vietnam and Korea, the US intervened in a civil war to prevent indigenous Communist forces from prevailing, as part of the policy of containment (the Korean War was the first conflict the US waged in the name of that doctrine). In both countries, it's clear that the northern Communists would have won had the US decided not to intervene, and in Vietnam they won

anyway. Recovering from the devastation of the war took many years, but today Vietnam, which remains a one-party republic, is doing well, driven by its quickly growing, socialist-oriented market economy with significant agricultural exports. Its population today is more than twice what it was in 1965, and its poverty rate is lower than America's.

In Korea, however, America avoided defeat. The peninsula was first divided up in a panic at the end of World War II. Japan lost Korea, along with all of its other colonies, after its defeat at the hands of the Allies. Two days after the US dropped a nuclear weapon on Hiroshima, the Soviet Union declared war on Japan, and Stalin's troops began to move quickly down the Korean peninsula. Perhaps worried that the Red Army would occupy the whole thing, US government officials, without consulting anyone from any other country, literally used a National Geographic map to decide on dividing the peninsula at the 38th parallel. Separate governments formed in each half of the country. The US organized elections for a legislature in 1948, and although the UN certified those elections as "free and fair," the franchise was limited to landowners, taxpayers, and village elders. This arrangement satisfied nobody. Koreans did not want their civilization, which had existed for thousands of years, to be split in half. Political unrest and border conflict became more common in the latter half of the 1940s, and civil war decisively broke out on June 25, 1950. There is much arguing about whether the North invaded in a conquering spirit or because it was provoked, but it doesn't matter. The political situation was intolerable, and the US had blocked all possible avenues to its resolution. The question would have to be decided by war.

And war *would* have answered the question, except for US intervention. Resistance in the South collapsed almost immediately. President Syngman Rhee, who had assumed rule of South Korea with General MacArthur at his side, fled the capital a few days later and ordered that his political opponents in the South be massacred following his departure. Some thirty-seven thousand North Korean troops captured Seoul. America's first meaningful military engagement on the peninsula took place on July 5. What followed were six months of free-ranging, unpredictable conflict. By September 1950, North Korea controlled all but a small portion of the peninsula's southeast corner. By October 1951, US, UN, and South Korean troops had pushed well north of the 38th parallel, and, newly confident, the US now believed it could not just contain but roll back Communism in Korea.* China, however, intervened soon after the US crossed into the North, and shifting battle lines gradually stabilized around the middle of the peninsula. The presence of UN coalition forces constrained the Soviet Union from officially entering the war — Stalin could not afford to let the cold war turn hot. But the USSR was covertly involved throughout, supplying aid, guns, and fighter jets, along with Russian pilots to fly them (they flew under Chinese and North Korean markings). Two years of indecisive position warfare followed, during which time peace talks failed to reach a resolution. An armistice was finally signed on July 27, 1953.

Containment had worked. The US prevented the unification of the Korean peninsula under Communist rule. But the price of America's success was enormous. Though US casualties did not approach the horrific numbers of the protracted war in Vietnam, more than thirty-six thousand Americans died in Korea, and a hundred thousand more were either wounded or MIA. South Korean casualties numbered somewhere around 1.5 million, and North Korea suffered more than 2 million casualties, as many as 1 million of whom were civilians. (These kinds of estimates are always contested and inexact.) The loss of life was accompanied by an American air war that devastated North Korea and that still lives on bitterly in the memories of those who experienced it and their descendants. Extending the application of what they learned firebombing the Germans and the Japanese in World War II, American forces essentially carpet-bombed North Korea for three years, ultimately dropping more than six hundred thousand tons of ordnance. North Korea's air defenses basically didn't exist. "We burned down *every* town in North Korea and South Korea," said US Air Force general Curtis LeMay. A Hungarian writer who visited North Korea in 1951 described the results:

---

* The Korean War was the UN's first global test, a chance for the institution to prove that it really could mobilize an international coalition in the service of peacekeeping. But, as would become a pattern throughout the second half of the 20th century, the UN's true role may have been to lend a stamp of international credibility to military action that the organization's dominant member state, the United States, was going to undertake anyway. When North Korea crossed the 38th parallel, UN Security Council Resolution 84 declared it a breach of the peace and encouraged its members to send troops to South Korea's defense. The Soviet Union could have exercised its veto power on the Security Council, but it was boycotting the UN at the time over its refusal to recognize Mao's Communist government of China. President Truman never asked Congress to pass an official declaration of war on North Korea—he argued that UNSCR 84 was enough. Troops sent to North Korea by UN member states, including the UK, Canada, Belgium, the Netherlands, France, Colombia, Ethiopia, South Africa, New Zealand, Turkey, Greece, Thailand, Luxembourg, Australia and the Philippines, were all placed under US command.

There was only devastation . . . every city was
a collection of chimneys. I don't know why
houses collapsed and chimneys did not, but I
went through a city of 200,000 inhabitants and
I saw thousands of chimneys and that—that
was all.

By the spring of 1953, the US had already
bombed every major population center
in the North—now American bombers
began to target dams. Thousands of acres
of farmland were destroyed, and it was only
emergency assistance from other socialist
countries that averted a major famine.

With the help of other countries in the
Communist bloc, North Korea rebuilt
quickly after the war. But the fall of the
Soviet Union and the breakup of the Soviet
states deprived it of access to its key trad-
ing partners, and a series of natural disasters, including drought and flooding,
caused a famine that lasted from 1994 to
1998. Estimates as to the number of deaths
vary widely, ranging from roughly a quarter of a million to as high as three million
people. The effects of the natural disasters
were exacerbated by human failures of policy and economic planning; fuel shortages
meant that food could not be moved around
the country to areas that needed it. North
Korea has functioned since then as a garrison state—hypermilitarized, economically
backward, shut out of world diplomacy,
and treated with contempt by every relevant power except for China, which mostly
trades with Pyongyang to stave off a refugee crisis along the 880-mile border the two
countries share.

It does not absolve North Korean leaders of their own responsibility to describe
this situation as the legacy of American success on the Korean peninsula. North Korea
is the primary locus of regional instability
in East Asia, and its current condition is an

indictment of America's contributions to
that part of the world over the last seventy
years. The last best chance the US had to
improve relations with North Korea came in
1993, when, in an effort to de-escalate a crisis developing over North Korean prepara-
tions to reprocess fuel rods used for nuclear
power into weapons-grade plutonium, Bill
Clinton sent former President Jimmy Carter
to Pyongyang to meet with Kim Il-sung.
In 1994, the two negotiated an agreement,
which called for US sanctions relief and
aid in exchange for North Korea shutting
down its weapons program. Later that year,
Republicans took over Congress, delayed
aid deliveries, and refused to lift sanctions,
and the deal slowly fell apart, with North
Korea restarting its weapons program in
1998. When George W. Bush named North
Korea part of the "axis of evil" in 2002, he
hoped that a punishing sanctions regime
would weaken and eventually topple Kim.
This was the same line of thinking that motivated US sanctions in Iraq throughout the
'90s, and in both cases it had the opposite
of the intended effect. US leaders fantasized
that "ordinary" Iraqis/North Koreans would
rise up and overthrow the leaders who had
brought sanctions down upon them, but
instead Saddam and Kim were able to accurately blame their respective countries' dire
economic straits on the United States. The
only effect sanctions had on ordinary North
Koreans was to further demoralize them.
Obama spent eight years pursuing a policy
of gradual sanctions escalation, which his
administration called "strategic patience."
Essentially, he left the status quo in place
for his successor, who he assumed would be
Hillary Clinton, to address.

America's presence in East Asia is one
that clearly emerges as imperial once you
take a look at the details. For example,
not only does America keep nearly forty

thousand troops based in Japan, but Japan pays for around 80 percent of America's basing costs. Another fact that brings the situation into sharp relief is that in wartime, the US military *assumes operational control* of South Korean military forces. Should war break out on the peninsula, it would be American generals deciding where and when and how many South Korean soldiers would die. South Korean liberals have long agitated for the return of wartime military control to South Korea, and late last year, as the Trump-Kim rhetoric was escalating, Moon Jae-in gave a speech in which he said that "retrieving wartime operational control will boost military development and place South Korea at the center of East Asian security, based on independent defense capabilities." It is not a coincidence that Moon made this argument at the same time as he was preparing a thaw in relations between North and South Korea. Both countries understand that America's presence in the region is a boot placed on the necks of the countries it deals with—the pressure placed on South Korea's neck may be lighter, but it is still the same boot.

This fact is coming into clearer view as South Korean progress with North Korea begins to outpace that made so far by the US. According to anonymous officials within the Trump Administration, Seoul has let the US know that they see the nuclear issue as essentially between North Korea and the US alone, and that it intends to press on and deepen its engagement whether or not Trump and Kim are able to make more concrete progress. "We have a big problem coming with South Korea," one official told a reporter from Tokyo Business Today. "They no longer feel the need to act in parallel with us." Other officials have even suggested—ludicrously, one hopes—that the US would consider sanctioning South Korea

were Moon to make too much headway and expose the US as the really intransigent party in the process.

North Korea's isolation and belligerence (the latter born of the former) strengthen America's hand in East Asia, providing a convenient justification for the basing of tens of thousands of US troops in the region, troops that also serve as a useful check on China's ambitions. This may explain why the American foreign policy establishment today is the biggest single impediment to the peace process on the Korean peninsula, a process the Kim regime desperately wants to succeed and that four out of five South Koreans support. In strict geopolitical terms, the US is correct to throw roadblocks in the way of Kim and Moon. A final resolution of the Korean War would permanently dampen American influence in that region of the world. Peace isn't in America's interest—or at least it wasn't until Kim developed the capacity to strike the US mainland with ballistic missiles.

In the American press, an inability to acknowledge the opposition between America's interests and those of the countries it dominates has made basic components of the peace process hard to understand. Kim claims to want the denuclearization of the peninsula, commentators say—but then he drags his feet! He must not want denuclearization at all. But when the Kim regime calls for the denuclearization of the Korean peninsula, they're talking about *all* of the nuclear weapons aimed at the peninsula, including those that belong to America. America's "nuclear umbrella" currently covers Japan and the Korean peninsula. Asking both parties in a denuclearization negotiation to participate in the denuclearizing seems reasonable, especially given one party's history of actually using nuclear weapons, not to mention that the US became the first country to violate the 1953 armistice when, in 1958, the Eisenhower Administration began sending tactical nuclear weapons, including artillery shells, surface-to-air rockets, and land mines, into South Korea. But as recently as May 2018, the Pentagon's assistant defense secretary for Asian and Pacific security described the nuclear umbrella as nonnegotiable. If America's desire for denuclearization is sincere, the process will have to be mutual in some respects.

When all else fails, hand-wringing about Kim's international legitimacy serves as a useful refuge for America's foreign policy hawks. Democrats and liberals voiced this complaint en masse in the wake of the Singapore summit. "It sure looks as if President Trump was hoodwinked in Singapore," Nicholas Kristof wrote in the *Times*, arguing that Trump got almost nothing in exchange for his many concessions, of which "legitimacy" for Kim Jong-un was one. Just the fact of Trump's agreeing to meet with Kim, Chuck Schumer said, "granted a brutal and repressive dictatorship the international legitimacy it has long craved." This is a common rhetorical move within the US foreign policy establishment, which is always worrying about dispensing some of its storehouse of legitimacy to the wrong foreign head of state. But it's a bad concern to bring to a peace process, because a successful Korean peace process would necessarily increase Kim's international standing and help usher North Korea into the community of nations. Increasing Kim's legitimacy is the *goal*.

As a citizen, it's reasonable to feel uncomfortable about the prospect of the US boosting Kim's international standing. His family's regime is one of the most repressive and authoritarian in the world. Some one hundred and twenty thousand inmates endure awful conditions in the country's political prisons. Political discipline is maintained via state-controlled media and public executions. Populations are forcibly relocated from one part of the country to another, and travel within or out of the country requires government permission, which is usually denied. North Korea's human rights record is about as bad as it gets. And yet, even if the American foreign policy establishment's expressions of squeamishness on this front were sincere—and our cozy relationship with Saudi Arabia, another country in which torture and public executions are common, demonstrates conclusively that they are not—they would be misplaced. Kim is the legitimate ruler of North Korea—it's hard to imagine someone *more* legitimate than the grandson of the founder of the country and member of the ruling family—and America is stuck with him. Sanctions and isolation cannot weaken his regime to the point of collapse. All they can do, all that they have done, is push Kim toward further extremes of repression and make life harder for the people who live under his rule. War with North Korea is unthinkable. It presents all of the drawbacks of invading Iraq (the political vacuum in the wake of the dictator's collapse, the regional spread of the conflict, the certainty of a refugee crisis), plus nuclear weapons. It is also a political impossibility within the United States; there's no September 11 lying around to serve as a flimsy pretext for invading. A peace treaty ending the Korean War, mutual denuclearization of the peninsula by North Korea and the US, and diplomatic recognition for North Korea as a nation-state is the only viable option, not to mention the only option that presents a realistic prospect of improving the daily lives of North Koreans. One way or another, America's cold-war adventure in the Pacific is coming to an end. North and South Korea have presented the US with an opportunity to negotiate that adventure's protracted conclusion in a dignified way. They've done so despite America's long (and still lengthening) record of military aggression, torture, diplomatic bad faith, covert activity, and deal breaking. The US should recognize this generous offer for what it is and accept it. +

BARNABY RAINE
Renewed Labour

JOHN MCDONNELL IS CAGEY WHEN AN INTER-viewer asks, "Capitalism—inherently wrong? Or are you just the man to fix it?" It says something that the question is even posed. Just a decade ago McDonnell was the parliamentary spokesperson for picket lines and antiwar meetings, the champion of antique causes in Blair's Britain. He was the Labour MP who welcomed the financial crash with the words, "I'm a Marxist. . . . I've been waiting for this for a generation." In *Who's Who* he listed his hobby as "fomenting the overthrow of capitalism." Elsewhere he named Lenin and Trotsky among his heroes.

Now he is shadow chancellor of the Exchequer, the Labour Party's candidate to control Britain's money, and—even more than his old friend Jeremy Corbyn—a symbol of Labour's leftward shift. He won exhilarated applause from many long-suffering party members when he described his economic vision to their annual conference in 2016: "You no longer have to whisper its name; it's called *socialism*." Pressed on what this means, though, his evangelism is tempered:

> I don't believe capitalism serves the interest of our country at the moment. I want to transform our economic system. That means transforming capitalism. That means working through institutions like the European Union to make sure they are more open and democratic so we can break the neoliberal straitjacket there is on economic policy within Europe.

McDonnell has broken a pre-2008 taboo by naming the system and calling it a problem, but transforming capitalism doesn't sound the same as overthrowing it. Especially since the Brexit vote and the anxiety it generated, McDonnell has positioned himself as the "long-term" planner to end the rickety years of capitalist fundamentalism. Years of divesting from the state has paid poor dividends: failing infrastructure, an undereducated workforce, and measly aggregate demand. "Jeremy Corbyn and I are the stabilizers of capitalism," he has proclaimed, echoing the claim Yanis Varoufakis once made for the role of the left in our moment.

The crudest conclusion is that McDonnell has moved from smash-and-burn anticapitalism to "saving capitalism from itself." The Tory *Sunday Times* agrees, albeit approvingly: "McDonnell has softened his antibusiness rhetoric as he begins his transformation from left-wing firebrand to chancellor-in-waiting." One cannot be a firebrand in office, apparently—a certainty shared by historical determinists in the mainstream and on the radical left—since to be a government minister necessarily means to manage the status quo. Most commentators have managed to miss even this misreading. The *Financial Times* acknowledged the success of "Labour's intellectual revolution" after the party's strong electoral showing last year, but detected little besides the sudden reappearance of socialist orthodoxies. The *Economist* admits to being baffled by McDonnell, and concludes only that he has a confusing array of faces: "It is almost as if the true face is the Marxist who spent 35 years on the fringes of his party, whereas the other three are simply masks, put on to fool the voters."

Two narratives thus predominate about John McDonnell. To most he is an unreconstructed "Marxist." A few detect a conversion to moderation. In truth, something more interesting is afoot. On his appointment as Labour's shadow chancellor of the Exchequer, McDonnell immediately set about selecting a council of economic advisers that includes the mainstream economists Joseph Stiglitz and Thomas Piketty. In speeches, he makes admiring references to the Bank of England's thoughtful chief economist Andy Haldane. He has organized conferences on economic policy, noting with some pride that politicians in his job rarely do such things, and given a series of lectures outlining his thought. At the same time, he infuriates Labour's "moderates" by maintaining a coterie of close advisers from the radical left.

Is he facing two ways? Perhaps, but the answer might also be that McDonnell is bringing an unusual confidence to the left. He behaves like a man who believes that history is not over, even if established ways of picturing historical change on the radical left might be. He thinks the case for dramatic change is strong. Even more remarkably, he thinks he now has a shot at implementing it.

These convictions demand left-wing answers to the challenges of the moment, and they encourage a good deal of intellectual looting from the best minds of bourgeois society. As mandarins to power, insightful mainstream economists may know the logic of the system and its development better than those on the left, even as they are crippled by a failure to envision its supersession. That was Marx's presumption in a previous age of optimism about socialist ascent—but McDonnell is far from Marx and Marx's moment. He will not speak of ending capitalism, and McDonnell's attempt

to rethink socialism follows from the rubble of a left that tried just that and failed. While the left in most of Europe and the Americas concentrates on dissecting its failures amid a resurgent right, in Britain, McDonnell is tasked with handling the frightening prospect of electoral *success*.

After enduring years of mockery—a young Tony Blair once quipped, "You really don't have to worry about Jeremy Corbyn suddenly taking over"—the Labour left might now form the next government. What would they do with power? Much of the answer hangs on the challenges of Brexit and the ordinary traumas of state administration and class conflict, which threaten to derail any radical bid for power. But less attention has been paid to the shape of Labour's vision. McDonnell talks as if the zeitgeist is at last with the socialists again. If he is right, his thinking tells us something of the world to come.

THE BRITISH LABOR movement is not unique in having understood itself since the 1980s as a conservative force. In that decade, workers and unions fought bravely to save mining jobs and to resist automation in the print industry. These battles set the tone for the economic policy of the Labour left: existing communities of labor should be defended against the violent disruptions of deindustrialization. Corbyn's brief suggestion that he might try to reopen closed coal mines, offered during his first campaign for Labour's leadership, fits this pattern. The future is not always better than the past, and defensive conservatism was a way to oppose the acceleration of exploitation and alienation after the arrival of the International Monetary Fund in 1976. When that year a Labour government accepted an international bailout for Britain's struggling economy, promising austerity in return, the chaos came retrospectively to mark the breakdown of the social-democratic project.

Some at the time thought this might be the radical left's moment, its happy chance to take a great leap forward beyond capitalism. The corporatist compromise that militants had always opposed was finally dying, and powerful unions were helping to kill it. In the event, the left was pushed onto a defensive footing as Thatcherite radicalism tore chunks out of British society, smashing the workforce to extract more surplus value. Neither the labor movement nor the Labour Party could offer a competing vision of the future that went beyond defensive calls for deglobalization to develop the nation's productive forces. The irony now is that a new left can emerge only on the basis of the defeats of the 1980s. Because the world of coal and the factory floor are gone, we are freed from defensive obligations and forced into creativity.

Marx's savage treatment of nostalgic socialism in the *Communist Manifesto*, which established him as *post*capitalist rather than *anti*capitalist, provides an instructive lesson. While 1848's *Manifesto* shares much of the horror at capitalist degradations and depredations that marked the socialist tracts of his time and his own early work, Marx's shrewd innovation was to claim that the productive virtues associated with capitalism would compel its demise, such that to critique it did not require a moral standpoint outside it. If such a futurist vision was rare on the left in Thatcher's Britain, Marx's warning is only firmer in our own times. "Let the dead bury their dead," he wrote four years later, and let us take our "poetry [not] from the past but only from the future."

These sentiments have not always been alien to the left. In the US, where to be "left-wing" has had especially dubious connotations since McCarthy, people call themselves "progressives" in an unconscious nod to this tradition. Lenin saw electrification as half the work of revolution. In Britain, Labour's 1945 landslide election victory opened a new era by presenting nationalization as the image of the future: coordinated, efficient planning would overcome the anarchic backwardness of the free market. Two decades later another Labour prime minister, Harold Wilson, pitted scientific advances against the archaic gentlemen's clubs of Conservative ministers to hone an image of socialism as progress again.

Making any given vision look like the future is inherently ideological work, and it takes dexterity as well as favorable conditions to pull it off. In the early 1980s, Labour tried to depict monetarism as a clumsy return to the 1930s, but they were outdone by the Thatcherites' successful recasting of state control as clunking, unresponsive, and cartelized. Markets, by contrast, were dynamic, slick, and empowering. Although Tony Blair and Gordon Brown were often derided on the left as neo-Thatcherites, it would be truer to say that Blair, Brown, and the whole New Labour project lacked the confidence Thatcher shared with Clement Attlee. New Labour was committed to the view that political change was possible only through offering huge concessions to the right. In economic policy, limited redistribution could take place by stealth as long as one acquiesced to the Thatcherite veneration of markets. In social policy, a grand narrative of tolerance could replace Thatcher's Victorian values because—and this is the key point usually forgotten in Britain—a deep nastiness pervaded New Labour's hostility toward fifth columns, from refugees to British Muslims. Some government ministers attacked asylum lawyers and said refugees were crafty economic migrants in disguise, while others called for Muslim children to spy on their parents and boasted that they would refuse to talk to Muslim women donning the niqab.

Like Labour's fawning over Bush, that all looks like the drunken depravity of another world now. After New Labour came Ed Miliband, a Labour leader whose cautious moves leftward are sometimes seen as the bridge to Corbyn and McDonnell, but he too embraced a view of politics governed by fundamental tradeoffs: one could talk of inequality only while promising to continue austerity. For Miliband, as for Blair and Brown, claiming the future for the left seemed unrealistic.

In style if not substance, McDonnell represents a reversion to long-lost norms. He has enthusiastically embraced Labour's history of futurism. His speech to Labour's 2017 annual conference heralded Clement Attlee and Harold Wilson in exactly these terms and proclaimed:

> If you study the history of our party, you will see that it's always been the role of Labour governments to lead our country into each new era.... So as we now enter the next new era, the era of the fourth industrial revolution, I tell you it is a Corbyn Labour government that will.... lay the foundations of the new world that awaits us. That new world is being shaped already by the beginnings of the fourth industrial revolution. Huge changes are underway in our society and economy. Technological change is accelerating. This year, Chinese scientists used quantum mechanics to teleport data to a satellite. We can match that: we've got a Tory government teleported from the 18th century. We are determined that Britain embraces the possibilities of technological change—scary though that may be.

It is a claim repeated ad nauseam in McDonnell's speeches, though too rarely noticed.

We "must find new and better ways of working and living—not hanker after a mythical past," he says in a coded attack on much recent left-wing thinking. Three intertwined principles provide an outline of his approach.

First, he wants to paint the state as the future again. McDonnell has consistently pinpointed a crisis of "chronic underinvestment" whose solution involves the participation of the "entrepreneurial state" admired by McDonnell's adviser, the economist Mariana Mazzucato. Mazzucato sees the reflex to downplay the role of nation-states in directing long-term investment as a major flaw in the neoliberal worldview, insofar as it discourages states from making the investments necessary to ensure future prosperity. McDonnell often identifies several areas where private finance has failed to support lasting, sustainable growth: developing infrastructure, such as improved transport links to address regional problems of uneven development; supporting small and medium-size businesses, especially outside London and the southeast; and decarbonizing the economy, not least by investing in renewables. Climate change is a key case study in McDonnell's argument for the necessity of long-term state planning. It's an apparent externality that eventually becomes internal and detrimental to the market (which is partly how he conceives of low investment in infrastructure and skills, too).

McDonnell wants to portray state negligence as an incubator of disaster. Here, then, is McDonnell as capitalism's would-be savior, repurposing for far less radical ends an old argument about the complex codependence of states and capital. According to Marx's *Capital*, states secure the reproduction of capital writ large by sometimes setting themselves against individual bosses, who in their pursuit of accumulation and short-term returns fail to safeguard durable prosperity. Capitalists will immiserate their workers to the point of provoking political revolts and crises of underconsumption, and left to their own devices, capitalists also create supply-side underinvestment in both infrastructure and labor productivity—all of which have drastic spatial effects as wealth and poverty cluster at geographical nodes, whether in London and Blackpool or San Francisco and Flint. Fordist Keynesianism after 1945 was one governmental project designed to avert some of these risks. McDonnell's claim is that the sustained backlash against Keynesianism in recent decades has returned us to the anemic position it once sought to cure. This is the first and least original step in his argument.

Second, McDonnell's entrepreneurial state would seek to harness and redirect transformations associated with technology, particularly the ascent of "platform capitalism," in which huge profits flow to a tiny club of inventors and owners while technology undermines the job security of workers. If Marx thought that past industrial revolutions created capitalism's gravedigger, the threat of the fourth industrial revolution is that the gravedigger will be a robot.* McDonnell and his team see big changes on the horizon. State and collective ownership of profitable platforms is crucial to preventing gaping inequalities from worsening into postwork dystopias. McDonnell gives the following mission to his entrepreneurial state:

The new National Investment Bank and network of regional development banks will be tasked with supplying the funding to help support a new generation of cooperatively owned Ubers and Airbnbs.

In the medium term, automation offers a basis to question socialism's long and deep investment in utopias of work, and we are already beginning to see a vision of left-wing politics as a struggle over the distribution of *time*. In recent months, McDonnell has floated a four-day working week and a universal basic income. These represent the most significant signs of originality since Labour's 2017 manifesto, and suggest a willingness to have socialist politics remake its constituency and not just protect labor against the ravages of capital. As Italian autonomists had it in the 1970s, the proletariat should be a class "against itself," seeking the abolition of its own abject condition of possibility: toil. In McDonnell's emerging vision, collective ownership of new technologies can ensure that prosperity flows from automation to everyone, replacing labor with leisure. The fact that in 2017 McDonnell could tell the Labour conference—an organization whose very name denotes a fidelity to work—that "by the middle of this century, it is possible that up to half of all the jobs we do now could be automated away" and *not* mean simply to terrify his audience hints at the considerable ideological ructions underway.

The third feature of McDonnell's approach is perhaps the most surprising. In a speech at the London School of Economics in 2016, McDonnell conjured Friedrich von Hayek to offer a critique of postwar

---

* *Platform Capitalism* is the title of a 2016 book by Nick Srnicek, a futurist whose previous book raised the slogan "demand full automation" for the left, and whom McDonnell invited to Parliament to address his New Economics seminar series. An autonomist previously critical of parliamentary politics, Srnicek's involvement represents a trend in Labour's new thinking, in which it draws heavily from radicals outside its own tradition. Corbyn and McDonnell are valuably distinctive for their long involvement in social struggles that put them in dialogue with people to Labour's left.

social democracy. "Top-down nationalization," McDonnell said, failed to recognize that "centralized bureaucracies can be overwhelmed by the information-processing demands of complex, modern societies." Hayek's error, McDonnell went on, lay in his failure to accept that this was true of public *and* private bureaucracies. Against the despotism of corporate governance, McDonnell championed the "decentralized socialism" of cooperatives. He depicts as an *extension* of Thatcher's Right to Buy scheme—for transforming tenants of state housing into property owners—a new Right to Own scheme that would open businesses to their workers. He stresses that cooperatives can make better, more productive and profitable businesses. In the futurist frame, this means presenting socialist politics as healthy progress rather than a defense of what is under attack. It echoes Marx's understanding of the move from capitalism to socialism as the full flowering of the achievements of bourgeois society rather than their reversal. If Thatcher presented her politics as empowering ordinary people against unresponsive bureaucracies, McDonnell's clever move is to make that the language of socialism again: this is empowerment shorn of Thatcher's atomistic individualism and pitted against the corporate bosses Thatcher adored. McDonnell has also stressed that the neo-Hayekian view has dramatic implications for state institutions, which he wants to reorganize to make less centralized and less preoccupied with short-term targets.

This last point might sound borrowed from the 1990s, when "market socialists" and others joined the chorus condemning the state. Such condemnations feel outmoded after 2008, when the long-derided nation-state saved global capitalism with coordinated potency. What McDonnell intends is not to abandon the left's commitment to the state but to modify it. He still seeks the nationalization of railways and utilities and the return of unabashed economic planning. The modification is crucial, insofar as it quietly reframes a late 19th-century socialist norm hardly retained after 1945 except by Trotskyists: that nationalization does not truly break with capitalism if bourgeois technocrats continue to run services that have passed into the nominal control of the taxpayer. The key demand for socialists is direct workers' control, not only de jure ownership of the economy. Now that view is back in McDonnell's "institutional turn" (the approving characterization of two academics, Martin O'Neill and Joe Guinan), and it has begun to attract some belated media attention in Britain. Finding license for this position in Hayek might seem mischievous, but McDonnell is right to stress the historically broad political appeal of arguments against centralized bureaucracies. John Maynard Keynes struck a remarkably similar note in 1925:

> I believe that in the future the Government will have to take on many duties which it has avoided in the past. For these purposes Ministers and Parliament will be unserviceable. Our task must be to decentralize and devolve wherever we can, and in particular to establish semi-independent corporations and organs of administration to which duties of government, new and old, will be entrusted.

In short, Labour is demanding a three-pronged, state-led change in market patterns of production. The party wants to establish the infrastructure and capital for business growth in deprived regions, to pour money into technological innovation, and to alter norms of economic ownership by doubling the cooperative sector. That last point is perhaps the most significant. Like Marx,

McDonnell knows that changes in modes of production, not distribution, mark epochal transitions: "We're not just a party that thinks how to spend money," he says. "We need to be a party that thinks how to earn money." He gestures toward a future that marries democratic ownership and automation as a wholesale alternative to private control over the drudgery of wage work.

McDonnellism means to reclaim from neoliberals the imagery of the future, replacing its antibureaucratism with a desire for grand design from above in harmony with dynamism from below. Colossal state investment could unleash technology cooperatives across the land, tapping potential once left languishing by an absent state. Finland, McDonnell says, saw its lumber-exporting economy transformed into a technology-exporting economy by careful and bold state direction. Japan invests in a robotics strategy. Germany in the "industrial internet." McDonnell notes it all. He goes further than the textbook Keynesian claim that markets require state efforts to boost effective demand: McDonnell adds a deep, radical interest in patterns of ownership and a historically situated argument about postindustrial technology and its connection to futurist politics. And he moves beyond the postwar social-democratic inheritance by placing a desire for popular control alongside material comfort in the left's toolbox.

Two caveats about McDonnell's futurism. First, he flits between portraying Conservative ministers as delivering a nightmarish future and as impeding the future by failing to promote high-tech growth. He warns of two divergent paths opened up by automation: a postwork utopia and a postwork dystopia, in which the difference is determined by the ownership of technologies. This is not naive futurism. Progress can be the "catastrophe" depicted in one brand of 20th-century Marxism, such that the task of radicals is not simply to advance to history's next station but to switch our train to a wholly different track, and to use levers of collective agency (the state, say) to veer away from the destination our current course makes most likely.

Second, like most brands of futurism, McDonnell's has some *recuperative* content, seeking to salvage aspects of a lost past or dying present in superior form. McDonnell quotes Carlo Levi: "The future has an ancient heart." Miliband edged far more cautiously and haphazardly toward a reimagined political economy—he spoke of distinguishing "productive" from "predatory" capitalists, and of "predistribution" to complement redistribution—but it is striking that he leaned more aggressively on the traditional claims of the left to rally his base (poverty, employment insecurity) than McDonnell does now. McDonnell does mention the gamut of Miliband concerns, including rising homelessness, food-bank use, and insecure, precarious work, and adds to them traditional territories Miliband desperately avoided, above all support for strikes. His biggest headline shift was to brand Labour an anti-austerity party, freeing him to support public spending increases that Miliband's commitment to deficit reduction ruled out.

But McDonnell's objection to Conservative politics is not suspended at the level of moral protest, which is why he sounds more upbeat than Miliband and more optimistic than the radical left has long been. To understand why, we must draw an important distinction between rival ways of thinking about politics: one in which politics is understood as a competition between normative claims alone, and another in which those norms—opposition to wide inequalities, say—are presented as the corollaries of a technical plan rooted in a theory of history. Such a theory claims to explain how social relations are mutating, so that the task of politics is to work out how a given moment makes it possible to enact particular iterations of much more general normative commitments. But the dissident norms remain. If futurism is the ideological offspring of capitalist society, with its need for endless dynamism as the only alternative to death, then McDonnell's recuperative futurism is not uncritical. It is, rather, closer to an immanent critique of capitalist futurism, combining futurist foundations with concerns for the experiences of the poor that capitalist futurism sometimes scorns. As Labour plans billions in infrastructure spending while committing much less to reversing Conservative welfare cuts, however, the dangers of this particular futurist configuration are worth highlighting. Grand, gleaming construction excites more than a safety net for the disabled, but to make railways and new technologies the image of the future is to think like a 19th-century bourgeois.

McDonnell is — usually — better than that. Far more than most politicians charged with money management, McDonnell has made climate change central. He refers to dire warnings from critical scholarship about the Anthropocene. He talks always of developing an "economically *and environmentally* sustainable" economic model. Environmentalism provides an excellent analogy for his whole thinking. One claim of environmentalism is that drastic changes in our way of life might be necessary to save our lives. That is the logic of McDonnell's recuperative futurism, and for all their differences it hints at what unites Marx and Keynes — the figures between whom McDonnell seems poised. Both saw apocalypses on the horizon: for Marx it

was proletarian immiseration, falling rates of profit, and the grisly end of class struggle in "the common ruin of the contending classes"; for Keynes, poverty, revolution, and above all, war. Both thought it was possible to avoid catastrophe, and that the radical changes necessary to do so could dramatically improve the human condition. They touted defensive mechanisms that would also conquer new ground. In their traditions, McDonnell hopes to marry the fear of a possible apocalypse, a belief in political contingency, and an optimistic futurism to forge a robust orientation to politics.

IN HIS IMMEDIATE interest in improving the management of capitalist production, McDonnell echoes Keynes more than Marx, and his affinities with Keynes extend to his account of why capitalism has become so damaging in the hands of a particular social group. He is concerned less with the bourgeoisie in general than with rentiers in particular. In a past moment of capitalist crisis in the 1930s, a particular understanding arose among everyone from liberals to fascists of debts and rents as political categories. Keynes was one articulate exponent of this politics, where the problem of rents was understood above all as a problem of control over the future.

Keynes's central interest in his 1936 masterwork, *The General Theory of Employment, Interest and Money*, is not at all in effective demand, as later readers frequently thought, but rather and more radically in capital. Near the end of the text he hails a "brave army of heretics" who stood outside the development of professional economics, whose sums often failed to add up, but whose praiseworthy skepticism toward invisible hands saw them each highlight in different ways the existence and dangers of underconsumption as an organic symptom of capitalism. Keynes then underscored the lack of democratic oversight of the future, as capitalists' investment decisions instead shaped the world and led to the disastrous inequalities and wars of his age. Problems including underconsumption had their root in the uneven distribution of wealth and power synonymous with the existence of a permanent capitalist class of owners and rentiers, whose wealth derives (as Marx might have put it) from their ability to command labor power through their control over wealth-producing wealth. From ownership stems an ability to charge others for the conditions of their existence—to hold power over them by charging them long into the future.

Keynes thought the desire for accumulation presented grave moral hazards—the wealthy, he observed, lived in the leisure he hoped would soon be possible for all, and yet they lived viciously—and it was a severe practical problem, too. Where his political program had once been deliberately open and uncertain, heavily characterized by the veneration of experimentation, Keynes was by 1936 a postcapitalist in the sense that Thorstein Veblen, Joseph Schumpeter, and later Fernand Braudel distinguished "markets" from "capitalism." He sought not to abolish market exchange or the law of value as the predominant principle of distribution, but ultimately to abolish *capitalists* as personal stores of great wealth whose investment decisions could shake millions of lives. This was to redefine capitalism as a crisis-ridden system of circulation, not

production—to isolate the hoarding of cash by the wealthy as its constitutive feature, and the inhibition of the free flow of money to the people and businesses who needed it as its inbuilt harm.

"The ultimate foundation of capitalism," Keynes had already written in 1919, was the "relations between debtors and creditors." The last of his heretics in *The General Theory* is Silvio Gesell, the finance minister in a soviet government dominated by anarchists during Germany's abortive 1918 revolution, who proposed time-stamped money that would decrease in value every day it was not spent.* Keynes praised him lavishly, and David Harvey has recently recruited him as a crucial inspiration; both surely found in Gesell the end of capitalism, the near impossibility of accumulation and hoarding. For his part, Keynes advocated that ownership of capital should be democratized by ending incentives to hoard, by slashing interest rates first of all, so that capital would flow more freely. As in Schumpeter's monetary analysis and Gesell's claim that Marx had poorly defined "capital" by concentrating too little on money, this is a view that makes the circulation of money the key metric of where control over the future lies.

This focus on capital and rents continues to inspire. Where Keynes long ago sought "the euthanasia of the rentier," McDonnell now defines the present as "the rentier economy, where wealth is secured not by what you produce, but by the amount of rent you can charge." That perspective frames everything for McDonnell. As rates of profit have

---

* It is worth noting the charge leveled by Keynes's Marxist student Maurice Dobb, who saw in Gesell's conscious move away from Marx's architecture of social relations to a more singular focus on money the shadow of anti-Semitic political economy, where "money power" is a coded reference to Jews. Keynes was an anti-Semite, less out of a special concern with Jewish conspiracies and more as a general cultural essentialist who thought Jews naturally "avaricious" and so worried about their influence in Bolshevik Russia. It is reasonable to suppose, then, that to Keynes attacking money lust, as he recommends, presumptively meant making the world *less Jewish*.

slumped and opportunities for profitable investment have dwindled, he highlights corporate "hoarding" as a central challenge. Companies sit on cash or funnel it into assets rather than investing in businesses. Keynes's two anxieties thus reappear: first, that capitalist hoarding drains the circulation of money to grow businesses seeking credit. McDonnell emphasizes the geography of the problem and proposes moving the Bank of England to Birmingham as the symbolic summit of a strategy to draw money out of London, a strategy funded by a network of state-funded regional investment banks. He entertains Gesell-like ideas of negative interest rates (now mainstream), and Corbyn's enthusiasm for People's Quantitative Easing is now expressed in McDonnell's desire to borrow freely for everything defined as "investment."

Keynes's second anxiety was that scarce capital produces a class of rentiers who invest in ownership rather than productivity. McDonnell uses this insight to argue for rent controls and tenants' rights to dramatically alter the balance of power in housing; he seeks limits on the debt that credit card companies can extract and the abolition of higher education fees. All this means abolishing Maurizio Lazzarato's "indebted man" as a subject-position of our times: disempowered, afraid of the future, alien to the confidence of struggle. McDonnell ended 2017 with a warning about escalating personal debt. Household debt is first of all a symbol of the failure to secure rising productivity and pay, but it is also a class question, since it generates individual and corporate creditors whose accumulation relies not on producing use values, not even on producing

exchange values, but only on perpetuating a generally deleterious status quo in which life's goods—housing, education, money itself—are kept as scarce and pricey as possible.* And so the futurist development of the productive forces and the achievement of abundance require confronting this social class. A focus on rents completes McDonnellism by locating its class politics. Rentiers are the enemy of the future, those who profit from present stagnation. Thus class is expressed in part as *age*, where older voters are more likely to be property owners and the young are burdened with debts, so that Britain's new age-based political binaries do not represent the death of class politics as is sometimes supposed.

But the young are not the only losers in contemporary Britain. McDonnell's demands for decentralized nationalization—local co-ops as opposed to the rule of London—make good on his antirentier politics by concentrating on natural monopolies like utilities, in which profits flow in large part from ownership over assets: railways, water pipes, and the electricity grid. His emphasis on the potentially cost-neutral, long-term reality of nationalization stems from confidence that assets that benefit from public subsidies currently send wealth flowing to small numbers of owners, sometimes in tax havens, such that private ownership funnels profits away from the communities that use them. It is a leak in the economic water cycle, which McDonnell hopes to fix.

Concern about rents, then, is connected to McDonnell's technocratic political economy of *geography*. Distant rentiers evoke the problem of parasitism, in which prosperity is held back when surplus value produced in

---

* The general point about problematically private control over money is perhaps best exemplified by an example McDonnell has not yet used, which is huge profits flowing to private banks from seigniorage. McDonnell has not borrowed Martin Wolf's suggestion that control over the production of money ought to be renationalized.

Britain's North (for example) is realized in London. Wealth is sucked away and concentrated elsewhere, and a developmentalist strategy would be to relocalize the realization of surplus value—to use nationalization under regionally devolved control to plug that geographical leak provided by remote rentiers. This is the model employed locally by Preston City Council, to McDonnell's considerable admiration. Antirentier politics signal McDonnell's recovery of the radical Keynes, the figure of the crisis-ridden 1930s and not the stable '50s.

KEYNES'S CONSERVATISM inhered more in his means than in his ends. The supreme virtue of his aspirations, he boasted in closing *The General Theory*, was that they could overcome rentier capitalism without the need for revolution or class confrontation. He was explicit about his loyalties: his mission was to ensure that wise, inclusive politics would soothe class tensions and prevent the need for open battles between groups, but "the Class war will find me on the side of the educated bourgeoisie." Proletarians in general and organized labor in particular he saw as an oppressive vested interest. Keynes trusted the technical expertise of elites to reorder society a good deal more than he trusted political struggle from those with a world to win.

McDonnell knows better. In one speech, he highlighted a paper from the IMF's chief economist that sees in austerity not poor or stupid thinking, but rather a structurally necessary program to sustain an economy dominated by finance, where state revenues must be kept available for bailouts and not tied up in public services—class interests and not just bad ideas, in McDonnell's presentation. Keynes failed to see the need for a fight to depose rentier interests.

Lenin mounted a similar and compelling critique of Keynes in 1920 after the publication of Keynes's *Economic Consequences of the Peace*. Keynes's diagnoses and prescriptions were all absolutely right, Lenin told the Comintern in 1920, but his hope in eventual Allied "generosity" as a vehicle for realizing them was bound to disappoint. Keynes was "agitating for Bolshevism," Lenin thought, since others would see the "madness" he highlighted and seek out more reliable antagonists to battle against it. As Keynes had it in a revealing 1925 lecture, "Am I A Liberal?", "It is necessary for a successful Labour leader to be, or at least to appear, a little savage. It is not enough that he should love his fellow-men; he must hate them too." Keynes thought that a bad thing; we might depart from him there.

Keynesian thinking is not entirely absent, though, from McDonnell's *political* strategy. McDonnell now calls not for "insurrection" (as he has before) but for an alliance of proletarians, debtors, *and* sectors of capital to overthrow the outmoded institutions and rentier interests blocking his technofuturism. He heaps praise on businesses and bosses who invest in renewables and high-tech innovation, and promises to mirror Finland, Germany, China, and Japan in offering them state support. He presents himself as the bringer of much-needed liquidity and growth to Britain's poorer regions, and therefore suggests that entrepreneurs in those regions ally with him against finance capital and its Conservative friends. He hopes that cooperative ownership of new firms will decrease hoarding without the need for immediate demands to expropriate existing capitalists. Here he echoes not Keynes, but 19th-century utopian socialists like Louis Blanc, who thought the French state could fund cooperative production to whittle away at capitalist norms until eventually they faded from history. Now McDonnell hopes the promise of supply-side investment can wean some capitalists from their temporary loyalties to neoliberalism, and that putting workers on company boards and investing in automation and cooperatives can begin to transform the structure of capitalism.

This is, at least, a strategy. It comprises a willingness to face bad new times rather than live as if in the good old days—acknowledging the absence of any subaltern agent ready to man barricades in Britain today—and a refusal to lapse into fatalism. The lack of a vanguard and (more importantly) a rearguard for insurrection need not mean that nothing good is possible, or that capitalist crises and fetters must end in chaotic disintegration. After the neoliberal revolution destroyed the agents and voided much of the content of past visions of social transformation, this is a bid to find new things, to insist that our condition is not (as it may be) constitutively tragic for socialists.

Yet McDonnell has no intention of abandoning the British proletariat as a radical political subject. On the contrary: unlike Keynes and those postwar social democrats for whom boosting effective demand was an end in itself—returning large populations to well-paid, stable jobs and thus, perhaps, to docility—it seems to me that McDonnell wants the return of good jobs for a quite different reason: they might grant the working class the footing to rise *out* of docility. McDonnell wants to create the conditions of possibility for a new working class that can agitate and advocate for itself, empowered and emboldened by the novel experience of running firms democratically. He wants to make the state a lever from above for reigniting industrial politics from below, which has long been dormant. He wants to free trade unions from the legal shackles imposed by Conservative governments, and then flood them with members in jobs created by a National Investment Bank and its network of regional outposts. There is a covert conservatism here: solar-panel makers are not miners, but they are still *producers*, and thus the traditional subjects of emancipatory politics. This suggests a certain nostalgia, and dreams of reindustrializing Britain must face the reality that mass capitalist production now takes place more cheaply in the Global South. But this is no mere Fordist reenactment, as the emphases on democratic control and automation demonstrate. McDonnell seeks the popular administration of leisure as an embryo of life after capitalism. He makes rentiers the first enemy of that project.

This "stagist" approach produces a conflicted politics, however, and raises the question of in what sense McDonnell's policies are really socialist at all. McDonnell champions parts of the bourgeoisie for now—and for how long? His immediate plans to take on finance capital involve summoning a national bloc of debtors, workers, and industrial capitalists to support him; less clear is what will happen when his target shifts to those very industrial capitalists he needs now. If workers strike at Ecotricity, a company whose boss McDonnell praises as exemplifying the sustainable model he wants to build, what would McDonnellism say?

Targeting finance capital is a mission that can unfold on an antineoliberal horizon. Expropriating *all* capital requires a longer socialist one. This is where things get hazy. Keynes's stated hope to deliver "peace in the short run" feels like a statement of McDonnell's mission now; he says he wants to replicate Clement Atlee, who dragged Britain's center leftward in 1945, though McDonnell knows that Attlee's achievement did not last. McDonnell has Keynes's temporality, and not Marx's: his is a fix to improve things until the next crisis more than a proposal to end cycles of crisis for good. In dismal days for the left, McDonnell is a socialist concerned with reviving one precondition for socialism—its actors. His plan would enlist the support of sections of industry to rebuild their own gravedigger. But the really tough challenge, as the 1970s left discovered, then becomes *what to do* with those actors, *how* they might enact the deferred break from capitalist society. Worse, even the frail, temporary social-democratic settlement possible in Atlee's time is far less achievable now, given the uneven balance of power between the British state and the international lenders McDonnell will need if his National Investment Bank is to get off the ground. McDonnell knows this too; he echoes the grandeur of Keynes's vision in calling for a new Bretton Woods agreement and stressing that our challenges are global. But his domestic political economy still smacks of national developmentalism in the postwar vein, and in Corbyn's "Build it in Britain" strategy the left's classic problem of dual loyalties is manifest. How to champion internationalist principles and a domestic electorate at the same time? Labour's new thinking faces a host of old problems. Grand successes remain unlikely.

It is tempting to forget that now, since McDonnell has a burning task on his hands. His immediate mission is to shatter a national political map dominated by cultural binaries only heightened by Brexit, where social sadism reigns. Labour's future rests on its ability to align voters on economic issues—to talk of debts and rents and jobs and so to reconstitute class politics. In practice that means assembling a counter-hegemonic bloc to unite older white voters in postindustrial towns with younger city dwellers, and this is a tough task today.

If McDonnell's recuperative futurism can revive local communities with new technologies rather than with nostalgia for closed coal mines, he will have succeeded in articulating the submerged common interests of the low-waged and the unemployed from Brixton to Bolsover. Labour has already had some success in this regard, providing a popular left-wing language of anti-elitism that's spared Britain from the European norm in which far-right parties attract the discontented and prosper. Amid liberal fears about Brexit, this is often missed, though it really is our only hope. Still liberals cling to Keynes's hope for salvation in the "educated bourgeoisie," now imagined in Britain as cultured, cosmopolitan Europhiles, the symbol of all things good.* Progress is thus coded as the enemy not only of aristocrats but more aggressively of many proletarians. Implicitly or explicitly, this is the vision of anti-Brexit "Remoaners," and it has been the assumption of postindustrial "modernizers" in all political parties over recent decades too. It has only produced the bitter democratic impasse from which McDonnellism now hopes to save us. +

---

* One liberal response is now to *abandon* democracy, having seen that championing the liberal bourgeoisie makes for a poor democratic strategy. David Runciman was ahead of the curve, arguing in 2015, a year before Britain's EU referendum, in the *London Review of Books*, "It pains me to say it, but if ever an election needed a bit of fixing it was this one." He was referring to the impending likelihood that Jeremy Corbyn would be elected Labour leader.

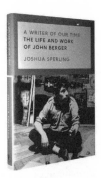

KATJA NOVITSKOVA, *LIGHT TRAJECTORY (MRI)*. 2016, DIGITAL PRINT ON 2 LAYERS OF ALUMINUM, CUTOUT DISPLAY. 70.9 × 57.1 × 9.8". COURTESY OF THE ARTIST, GREENE NAFTALI, NEW YORK, AND KRAUPA-TUSKANY ZEIDLER, BERLIN.

REDEDICATION

Imraan Coovadia

He does not burden a soul with more than it can bear . . .

I AM IN THE THIRD ROW of the shuttle, half asleep, when I hear what sounds like an argument coming from the front. I check on the Secretary, who is unconscious, stretched out on the seats. Her face is frosted over in the hood, every sign in the expected range. She will survive the trip, despite the infection planted in her blood. I tell myself to relax and watch the seven moons and suns glow in the window, fusion fire as green as the ocean below, as we speed at a thousand knots toward our destination.

I cannot enjoy the view. In this position, high in the government, my feelings are bound to the Madame Secretary. I was dedicated to her in a government center under the appropriate constitutional provision, made into the perfect companion. I hunger when she is hungry. I thirst when her mouth is dry, as it has been for a day. My arms are chilled to the bone, as hers have been, and there is a rot in my blood that makes me think I have been poisoned by a piece of fish. I would like to clear the ice from my eyes, though there is nothing there but the sensation of it. In all respects the condition of the woman lying across the seats is my own. I tell myself that I am lucky to serve, and in serving to live again, but my heart doesn't listen to advice.

The shuttle is automated, the better to maintain quarantine around the Madame Secretary on our brief trip into orbit. Apart from myself there is a pilot in the forward compartment, placed there for the sake of protocol more than for any good he could do in an emergency. I seek him out nonetheless. On my way I almost see my lady's chilled breath in front of me.

The shuttle is designed for the needs of dignitaries. There is a marble counter serving as a bar, champagne bottles shining on the wall above it. An ice bucket is fixed in place. Then there is a security console, about the size and shape of a writing desk, for federal officials to send and receive their streams of entangled photons, confident that nobody in any possible universe could overhear their conversations. Next to the airlock is a rack on which hang the Madame Secretary's formal garments, the scarf and robe that indicate her status as a cabinet minister. She is entitled to the loyalty of a dozen men and women like myself, but today, in the wake of a biological strike, I am the only one alive to tend her.

I slide open the forward compartment to find the pilot dead. He has been hit in the back of the head so hard that his skull is visibly broken. I try not to panic as I search for the cause of his death. It doesn't take long. The rotator arm, designed for fine mechanical adjustments around the cabin, is covered in blood. For the moment it is content to snap its pincers, a fine current running between them. Who knows who it works for?

I kneel down to keep clear of its scope and turn the pilot over. I search his body for the key fob, the charm to let me in. The man's body is sticky with blood and its rich smell brings me to the point of fainting. As a person placed in a condition of emotional bondage, I am sensitive to the smallest degree of blood and suffering. I am intended for civil purposes, not a security detail. Nevertheless I tell myself that my soul would not be burdened with more than it can bear.

On the pilot's console the winged symbol of Tennessee Station appears. A woman's voice is speaking quickly behind it, but I don't have time to talk. The station approaches at terrifying speed, red lights rippling along its superstructure, guarded by artillery and radiation missiles. I know the problem. Without authorization, its sentries will not fire on a vessel bearing a personage at the level of the Madame Secretary. The permission will take minutes to arrive, long after the disaster to come. They want me to give permission from inside the ship. But I can't say the words to condemn the Madame Secretary to death.

I overturn the chairs and ransack the drawers in the nearby cabinet. Finally I find the key fob underneath the pilot's body. I take it, trying not to look at the murderous rotator arm. If my programming allowed me to pray, I would put a wish to the Almighty. I do not want my name to be ruined. I am being set up for the murder of a high-ranking official to cast doubt on the program of service through rebirth. In another part of my mind I hear the increasingly frantic voice of the controller at Tennessee Station.

I run through the shuttle, looking for the escape hatch. The engines are straining under my feet. I tear up the flooring with my bare hands, surprising myself, but find nothing more than the smooth surface of the hull. It administers a shock to my arms. I will have to get through the airlock to safety. I hunt through the closets lining the galley. In the last there is a single spacesuit on a hanger, an old copper-tinted model, good enough for a day in vacuum. I take it out and check for damage.

Despite the blood and desperation there is a feeling of peace aboard the ship. The moons and suns spin in the window, their beauty undisturbed. The shuttle turns its nose directly toward its target, the machinery starting to smoke through the walls. I let myself understand what is about to happen. Fatal graphs light up my visor. Then I put it out of my mind. Every day we learn to serve anew.

The hood comes off the face of the Madame Secretary with minimum fuss. I unclip it and clear chips of ice from her eyes. I imagine her reaction. In reality my contract holder is frozen solid and any residual awareness is confined to her brainstem. Her life, like my own, is buried deep in a dream of its own, a dream that may never return her from its depths.

I am stronger than I believed. Without difficulty I lift the Madame Secretary from her prone position, hoisting her over my shoulder. A shiver passes through her body. Beneath her eyelids something is stirring, the will to live and dominate others that has kept her in one piece for three centuries. In my arms, for the first time, she is nothing more nor less than an elderly woman with bone-white hair and dozens of moles dotted along her nose.

I hold her upright while I zip her into the suit, starting with the legs. I close the helmet and turn it to the side until oxygen hisses through the pipes. She is starting to breathe, her pallor perfect as marble. Her expression is strange and familiar at once. Such is the force of sympathy that I feel I am staring at my own frozen face. I dismiss the sensation as a by-product of my programming and lower the gasping body to the floor as gently as I can. The shuttle is shaking from its own propulsion.

The pilot's key doesn't let me open the airlock directly. I search for something to help. The closet beside the bar opens to my touch, revealing a series of cleaning and security devices and, to my relief, a hypersonic cutter the length of my arm. I use the cutter to melt the handle of the external door, feeling its fine vibrations in my teeth. I smile when it comes open, and I drag the Madame Secretary into position. Three feet from where I stand is the cold space of this distant solar system, the farthest picket set down by the government of the United States.

I bend over the body and touch my visor to her helmet, the closest I can come to placing a kiss on the mouth of the woman I have been dedicated to love. The Madame Secretary is more a mystery to me today than on the day we first met. Her frozen eyes glow like emeralds. She will live for centuries more without me at her side. In a decade she may not remember my name or my sacrifice. I cannot communicate the sense of loss I feel at this moment of communion. The ways of service number more than one. Today they lead me back to the conditions of death and dishonor in which I was reborn.

I take another minute to live. The station arrives at a horrifying velocity, clearing the suns and moons from view. Music wafts in from somewhere but I cannot identify the tune. I calculate a trajectory for the Madame Secretary that should remove her from danger. I eject her body, still trembling on the floor, and for one more instant, as I am consumed in flame, I see myself from a hundred miles away through my lady's green eyes.

o   o   o

O Men! Are you more difficult to create than the heaven which He has built?

W HO WAS I? When I tried to remember I had the impression of a hundred thousand misfortunes. I summoned images into mind—the crystal-clear face of a woman who had been inexpressibly dear to me, a man on a deserted beach coaxing fire out of a heap of logs, the flag of the United States, which made my heart beat so strongly I turned to the side.

I was lying in a cylindrical tank that was heating up from the bottom. I was already drowned. Phosphorescent liquid sparkled throughout the interior. There was no feeling of distress. I could breathe without panic and see lights outside as well. Sensation returned to my hands and feet, followed by a fierce attack of pins and needles.

I tried to lift the hatch. It wouldn't budge. To my relief the liquid began to drain from the tank. After a minute it was gone, leaving me with the sight of similar pods around me, dozens or even hundreds containing men and women in the same position, all floating in a vast pool of what must have been liquid mercury. We made signs to each other and mouthed words, communicating enough to know that we had been reborn together, had found ourselves in a world of delight and sensation, and would teach one another how to serve. My head sang with happiness.

Several minutes passed before the pods began to move in concert, arranging themselves in rows of a dozen and queueing for the exits. We left the first chamber and entered a series of narrower rooms, moving faster and faster, leaving trails in the mercury. I lay back and closed my eyes, enjoying the acceleration. For the life of me I could not recall my name. Only the taste of kerosene remained, a keepsake from what might have been another existence.

When I looked again the pod was screaming along the supersonic line, far faster than I could have imagined. I saw a sky punctuated with stars, American stars, and industrial chimneys miles high leaning against one another. White smoke spiraled out of their faraway mouths.

The pod dropped suddenly, falling thousands of feet in a few seconds, and shot off in a new direction. I gasped from the change. The line converged on others, revealing other pods moving toward the same destination. Each one glowed as it eased to a crawl and was nearly silent by the time the station approached. Each one contained a person just like myself, with his or her own secret history and dedications.

I disembarked onto a platform amid thousands of nude men and women. The pods closed their lids in unison and shot off noiselessly along the causeway. We arranged ourselves in a regular pattern, facing the interior doors. We all had the sheen of birthing gel on us, and the same aniseed scent. Canisters sailed down from the ceiling, a white gas spilling out of them. I felt the infrared heat from the walls, as if we were being burned alive, and yet there was no distress. The gas filled the entire platform, so dense that we could hardly see one another, and then it vanished.

Along with the others I took a robe from a heap on the ground and tied the belt around my waist, two knots to keep it secure. I had never been told what to do and yet I had the knowledge of it in my hands. This was my ritual birth to celebrate with all the others. It was my luck to be reborn to turn the distant nebulae American.

Fluorescent arrows embedded in the walls pointed to a gate through which we filtered one by one into a tiled corridor. I entered a booth and positioned my body according to the silhouette on the sign. A laser from the ceiling inscribed a barcode on my arm, lingering for just an instant to produce a trace of painless burning.

The next man came in before I went out. I thought of introducing myself but I couldn't recall my name. The difficulty must have occurred to him too, for he looked down, hiding his face. Outside, the line moved rapidly past a second gate and a cubicle bearing the shield of the Galactic Labor Service, thirteen stripes and countless stars representing the civilized domains—habitats, planetoids, domed cities, and hospitable moons.

In the cubicle was a man with short hair, entrenched behind his sunglasses, white head and hair indistinguishable. He seemed to be counting us as we went by. He was the first citizen of the United States I saw in this incarnation. He represented the Labor Service, which allowed noncitizens to defray, through the course of one or more lifetimes, whatever expenses or inconveniences they had caused to the federal government. The relevant statute was imprinted on my memory.

Logically, therefore, I belonged to a deprecated class. I might be a refugee, working off the costs of my upkeep. Equally I might be a criminal who had victimized a citizen or sentient construct. I might be a sex offender, one of those men whose desires were notoriously costly to reprogram, or a wildcat journalist who had disseminated information inconsistent with the peace of the world—someone who had forfeited the rights and responsibilities of citizenship. In special cases, existential ones, I might be the child or relation of a prohibited person, detained on the authority of the President.

Our destination was a hall a hundred feet high and a half-mile wide, clean and bright, decorated with murals. The prophets of the Torah—Abraham, Isaac, Phineas, and Gad portrayed with flowing beards and gorgeous robes—took up one wall. The adjoining one was dedicated to the story of the United States and its off-world achievements, from Musk's settlement in the Valles Marineris, in the heart of the Red Planet, to the establishment of self-sustaining orbitals and planetoids, and finally to the construction of the giant habitats near the Kuiper belt.

The arrows led each of us to our assigned place in the lineup. We stood in ranks of a hundred before a rising bank of seats, many of which were vacant. Civilians, men and women, were filtering in from an entrance on the left. They looked up and then down again at their screens, connecting our faces with whatever information was stored in our folders. They called people from the platform, pointing them toward a passage on the far end of the hall. I tried to be calm but I knew that the character of a contract holder was crucial for this life. A good master made life as painless as a dream.

The throng of laborers had thinned out when I was summoned by a man. He wore a digital lens on one eye, in the style of a jeweler, and waited for me in the passage. He led me into a conference room furnished with red leather chairs and a secretary desk.

The man looked me up and down through his lens, making a determination. He was a foot taller than I was and had a plain silver ring in one of his ears. He wore leather pants and a fringed leather jacket, the logo of a motorcycle brotherhood stenciled over the breast.

The man moved around to inspect me from the back, so close I could smell the rose tobacco on his body. He put his hand on my neck, gripping me. Despite my conviction that I had been chosen for great and good deeds, a sense of disgrace flowed over me. My cheeks were hot.

"Do you know your place, my friend?"

"I hope so."

He moved back and ran his hand along my barcode, as if to read it with his fingertips. It wasn't an unfriendly gesture.

"My name is Geronimo. I believe I have found a good use for you. I am in the trade professionally."

"What do you mean by the trade?"

My companion sat at the table and poured out two glasses of water, the customary portions of hot and cold that signified the nature of the bond. We would be bound to care for each other, Geronimo and I, to guard each other's dignity as much as life and limb, so that what was right in the eyes of the law never became an instrument of oppression.

Geronimo drank from both cups before he replied to my question. He wiped his mouth with his sleeve and waited for me to reciprocate, tiny squares moving in front of his lens. I drained the hot water then the cold, relishing the steps of the ceremony. It didn't make a difference. Later, if he desired, we would go to a dedication center.

"My trade is in people like yourself. I manage a hundred contracts a month, arrange for contract holders to rent out their men and women when they need spare cash. Not everybody can afford the price of a full contract. Not everybody needs it. What do I need meanwhile? I need someone loyal by my side. And you, my friend, have shown a predilection for superior loyalty in your previous lives. You have excelled in dedication."

"Thank you for the compliment."

"On the other hand, it means you're much more expensive than I wanted to pay. That's why you're still here on the shelf. You pay for quality."

o   o   o

We created you in pairs . . .

G ERONIMO'S STOREFRONT was in the disreputable part of town. At the top of a three-story building, protected by a grate and a holographic intercom, it was hidden in a utility neighborhood. Automatic laundromats and server farms spun on the lower floors. Frost formed on the nitrogen-fixing tank on the roof.

Meanwhile kiosks shone on the street below, advertising rocketry on demand, private surveillance, virtual presence conference centers, and the spectrum of artificial sexualities. In the tower across from us was a warren of small offices, piled on top of one another, designed for consultation. Citizens received advice from judicial consultants, the high-functioning but narrowly constructed intelligences so often accused of autism.

My employment started the very first day of my contract. My job was to take indentured laborers like myself, accompanied by their contract holders, from Geronimo's office to the dedication center around the corner. There the barcodes were scanned and registered on the system while the indentured man or woman changed into a white gown and drank the usual cups of hot and cold water with the contract holder. By custom the two had their heads moistened with electrostatic gel by the apostle of rededication, a man in his seventies whose manner was professionally restrained. I never got to know the apostle's first name but I became very familiar with the way Sullivan cleaned his hands in a basin and smoothed the gel through each person's hair, singing as he did so.

From the low ceiling of the dedication center hung a number of transparent cones of varying sizes, some large enough to enclose the

whole of the human body. They came to life, singing along, as I imagined, with the apostle, and glowed with a purple charge. Lines of radiation sprang up inside the cones and penetrated the heads of the contract
holder and laborer. Their feelings would be linked unto death, unless
and until they returned for a new dedication.

Each ceremony needed a quarter of an hour, during which I took
care of payment and other details. Afterward both participants were
usually subdued, faces covered in perspiration. The apostle of rededication gave them a chance to clean up and counseled them in a gentle
voice about what to expect in the coming days, how to manage the
coincidence of their smallest thoughts and sensations. He gave the contract holder the option to pay in installments.

I have heard people compare a dedication ceremony to a wedding,
but it isn't like that at all. It's more like watching one person fall hope-
lessly in love with another person at extremely high speed. When you
see it happen on a hundred occasions it changes your perspective. One
part of me knew that I was witnessing a piece of alchemy made possible
by modern psychological machinery, perfected by Southern microcor-
porations. Another part of me—and maybe it was the part that mat-
tered the most—saw a rededication as a stroke of magic, bringing the
mysteries of the human heart into plain view.

On the way back to Geronimo's office, after taking leave of my two
charges, I was frequently too overwhelmed to speak, sometimes close
to tears, although I could not have explained then whether they were
tears of joy or sorrow. Around me the commerce of the city went on.
Drones rose and settled like dragonflies. Sensors exchanged information, updated the markets, recorded the play of desire and greed in the
faces of the pedestrians. Children ran on the walkways, attended by
their automatic companions. Some feeling of tragedy seemed to separate me by a thousand miles from this ordinary life.

o   o   o

So whoever does an atom's weight of good will see it.

I HAD BEEN BACK AND FORTH from the dedication center a dozen times
and had slept twice over in a cot in the back room before there was
any progress in my primary relationship.

The delay wasn't on my side. An indentured laborer is generally a keen observer of his contract holder. I became familiar with the music Geronimo played in the office, from Jethro Tull to Whitesnake, bluegrass to holographic death metal, and with his way of keeping one hand on his tie while he talked to a buyer, his drawl as slow as honey. I had not been specifically rededicated to him, yet in truth he was already dear to me.

Geronimo looked over at me one day while on a call and pointed me to the back room, raising his eyebrows.

I was pouring his espresso when he came in. The liquid was as dark as mercury. He drained it at once but sat down anyway on the mattress, loosening his tie and crossing his legs so that one of his boots was between us in the narrow space. It struck me for the first time that he was a young man, keen to set himself up in life.

I took the cup from him and washed it in the sink.

"You want one? Make yourself one."

I declined.

"Sit down in the chair." He cut himself a short cigar but then held it in his hand without lighting it. "You're doing okay with the dedications and rededications? Sometimes people find it jarring."

"I'm good doing it." I had to be respectful about what I said. "Each time, so far, I find it very moving, to be present when that kind of final connection is made."

"He told me so."

"Sullivan?" I asked.

Geronimo lit the cigar with a spark from his hands. He puffed on it until the stem turned cherry red.

"Sullivan the apostle man. He is the one who told me to seek you out. Someone like you, at any rate, with a great loyalty rating. In this business, I cannot afford to have a runaway. That would destroy my credibility. So I value dedication at any rate. But I believe I will have a particular assignment for you. I just have to set it up right."

At the time Geronimo didn't say any more about the nature of his business. Now and then he asked for my assistance with the paperwork, however. Folders came in twice a day from the Labor Service, offering contracts for all kinds of laborers: runaways, physical revivals, suicide bombers who had been brought back to life to serve out their sentences, even clones abandoned by the trillionaires who liked to keep them in reserve in case of emergency. Geronimo sat at his desk, a funnel of mild smoke rising from his cigar. He matched suppliers and clients while I helped him over his shoulder.

There was more need for indentured laborers than you might expect. By the authority of the twentieth amendment, certain roles in United States space were reserved for natural observers. To set the boundary of a claim in an asteroid field, or to run a hydrogen factory outside the gravitational well of a planet, required the presence of a once-living soul, as did of course the floating synagogues and kosher meat houses, rebaptism halls in revival cemeteries, and solar chapels, which petitioned Geronimo for assistance. They could buy a full, life-long contract, which came with a free rededication at Sullivan's center, or as little as a single day of a reborn laborer's life.

Plus intelligence was expensive where human life was cheap and flexible. Mining stations needed our type in considerable quantity, taking advantage of the fact that we are not eligible for judicial protections. Someone would sit alone for years at a time on a gravitational telescope, waiting for alien communications from across the universe—an ideal job for a noncitizen, as was the task of being a backup body frozen solid on a long haul to the American stars. Each morning, before the couples arrived for rededication, I helped to connect candidates on our list to the assignments that were coming in.

When the work was done Geronimo sometimes took me with him to the beer hall around the corner. It was a dome on the top of a soaring building. Guitars hung on the walls beside fashionable Confederate flags, oil paintings of petrol cars, and holographic visions of swimsuit models turning their heads. The beer was brewed in a zero-gravity tank, suspended over our heads.

From the dome you could see for miles, all the way down to the docks, where vast platforms floated on the waves, but for the most part the patrons buried their heads in their tankards of very dark black beer. Geronimo was no exception.

He offered me his mug. "You want to try?"

"It's against the rules."

He said, "I won't tell."

I was close enough to smell licorice. I moved away.

"I don't think I would enjoy it."

Geronimo was silent after one tankard. The second made him thoughtful. By the third tankard he was in a confiding mood. He told me about his father, who had been a preacher and a Monsignor, *homme de Sud*. It was one of the titles that had become more common in the wake of the Southern Ascendancy.

To everybody's surprise it had been Alabama and Tennessee, the Florida panhandle, and purified Jerusalem—Hebron and Ariel, cathedrals of old-time religion—that had been at the forefront of space colonization. They had the morale and the population to take the right to the galaxy by conquest, with the Old Testament to light the way. They had the will to confront the enemy and had driven out the Muslims, the Mexicans, and even the Chinese before them. Geronimo had been dealing in these captives, he explained, since he was 15 years of age, with the encouragement of his father. He specialized in former Muslims because, in his experience, once they had been rededicated you had no more trouble with them.

By the end of the night his head was on the table. I put him in an automatic taxi home and watched the pod accelerate along a magnetic line and disappear. I walked back to the office through the summer evening. The moons were spread out in the sky, a chandelier for our portion of the Milky Way.

The back room was as warm as an incubator. I couldn't sleep and found myself pacing around the floor of the building. My mind flooded with images of lives I might have led, scenes I might have witnessed or that I may simply have imagined: an orbital station at full alarm in the vastness of an unknown solar system, a woman's frozen body in my arms and the serene expression of her face beneath icy teardrops, a joint hearing of the House and Senate at which a 7-year-old girl, having pulled a black hood over her head, stabbed a congresswoman in the neck.

It didn't take a historian to know that the pictures in my head were remembrances of the insurgent campaign. For the better part of a decade the American worlds had been resisting the pinprick attacks that took the name of one or another previously unsuspected faction—Glory to God, Black Hand, the Awakening, or Number One Son. Each time an assault was successful the federal government tightened the surveillance networks and redoubled its investment in indentured labor, seeded more colonies with frozen bodies, and relaxed restrictions on the off-world enterprises of its trillionaires.

Unwilling to put myself back to bed I returned to the front office. I left the lamp off because there was enough light coming in from the corridor. In the corner of the first room was a file cabinet, its four drawers stuffed with old-fashioned information folders, the kind that lit up blue and white in your hands, page by page, as you read. Geronimo kept them as a backup. The trade in indentured persons was an old-fashioned business, he had said the day before. It attracted old souls like him, who preferred a document you could hold in your hands.

Listening with one ear for anyone outside, I spread the folders out on the desk and began to look through them. Each page contained the story of how a man or woman had been conscripted into the Labor Service, misfortunes ranging from a fall into debt slavery to having been captured on the way to carry out a mission on behalf of Number One Son. There were no photographs of any of the laborers, only gene information and the barcodes that were supposed to be consistent from one lifetime to the next.

I looked through page after page, wondering where I fit into the system, crying and laughing for no reason. I could have been any one of them. Then I put the folders back into their places and went to sleep. For the first time since I arrived on Geronimo's world, no dreams pursued me in the night.

o   o   o

The patient soul will be given his reward without account . . .

THE NEXT DAY GERONIMO was reserved. He sorted through clients' requests, colors streaming in his calculating eye as he went through the folders, and didn't communicate with me. I thought he must have noticed I had been in the files and worried about it. When I returned from the dedication center, though, he handed me a ticket and a twelve-hour right to ride the municipal trains.

"You're going to a concert, my boy. Rehoboth Plaza to Glenfield, in seventy minutes. Go early. Take off from work now. I don't mind."

The traveling coin was warm in my hand. I rubbed it, savoring the ridges in the lead, not to say the sensation of freedom it gave me. I could be on the other side of town in ten minutes, in the midst of the surrounding jungle, or at the beach in ten more.

I said, "Geronimo, sir, I haven't been dedicated to music before. Therefore I will not be able to enjoy it. I don't mean to complain, I don't want to sound ungrateful in any respect, but isn't that the principle of service? I need a permission for every pleasure."

"It's not that kind of a concert. It's a religious concert. You will find others there, like yourself, who are searching for answers about indenture. I would like you to have this experience before your rededication."

Geronimo called after me when I was already in the hallway.

"Remember, I didn't promise you would enjoy it."

"Understood, sir. Well understood."

o   o   o

The death from which you flee, it will meet you.

I DID UNDERSTAND. I understood Geronimo and loved what I had been given. On my way to the concert I told myself again that I was lucky to have a contract holder who would let me move through town, who gave me tickets, and who cared in such a visible way for my spiritual adjustment. Also I was more than a little eager to dedicate and be dedicated, to experience the deepest pleasures of service and submission.

The station was underground but the train rose vertically onto the raised magnetic tracks, which hung a hundred and seventy feet in the air so that you could look into the twentieth-floor bays of the nearby office buildings, the sun and seven moons reflected in their golden windows. Supercooled nitrogen steamed into the atmosphere along the path of the train.

The ride was frictionless. Soon the commercial and industrial zones gave way to residential estates, surrounded by parks and gracious avenues. Containment domes rose on the tree line, signs of local trillionaires who valued safety and privacy. They were the kind of people who could own a moon, control the administration of an entire habitat, and bend the will of the federal government to their own.

Glenfield Crossroads, the last point on the line I was traveling, was nothing but a levitating platform set on a magnetic field, served by an elevator. I went in and down, joining dozens and then hundreds of others on the road below who were bound in the same direction. I noticed their blissed-out expressions and deduced that they were also indentured laborers, my fellow spirits. I was excited to be among them, even more excited to be on the way together to the Church of the Many Resurrections. It was a ten-minute walk through gleaming fields of corn.

Our tickets were collected at the gate. Each of us was given a candle in a silver dish to hold before we went into the virtual cathedral, a hologram soaring a hundred thousand feet into the sky above our heads. There was a carillon, the sound of myriad glass bells pealing under the roof. Boards hung in the air listing the order of the service: a Gregorian chant followed by a reading of the constitution and its amendments, the psalms of indenture, a recital of "Rivers of Babylon" with the local orchestra, the sermon, and finally the procession back to Glenfield Crossroads under the light of the three nearest evening moons. I shivered with anticipation.

The floor was bare earth, covered in tracks from other pilgrims. I found a place and sat down as others were doing, placing my candle in front of me. Two women sat down next to me, their hair tucked into scarves. They also set their candles down. One turned to me. She put her hand on my sleeve.

"You know how it's going to work?"

I pointed to the boards hovering around us.

I shook my head, trying to clear it. "I have the feeling I have been here before, under this very roof, with the moons in exactly the same position as they are now, although I know that's mathematically impossible."

She said, "The seven will never meet again in the same way. That's what they say."

"I don't think I've heard that before."

"That's what they have said for centuries, since Americans first came here."

The woman introduced herself as Marina 511, an indentured assistant to a holography executive, who also worked as an occasional actress. Marina looked like she was in her thirties, but looks could be deceiving in her profession. Her companion, whom she had met on the road to Glenfield, was a Sally Seymour 014. Both were pilgrims from far afield who had come to the meeting ground on foot by permission, and had the crimson hair and matching crimson scarf worn by the truest believers.

Marina asked, "Is this your first service?"

"I believe so." I searched my memories. I knew the words to the American hymns. "But I cannot be sure."

Marina turned over my hand and studied my palm. Diamonds flickered in her eyes in the pattern of a circuit diagram. She ran a nail along the lines in my palm, sending a thrill through my arm and up into my head. Then she smiled at me, and my heart jumped. I thought to myself that this was unquestionably the first time, in any life, that I would have the privilege of falling in love.

She said, "I am pleased to announce that you are a longtime member of the Church. According to your lifelines, anyway."

"Do you believe in that?"

Marina turned her head to the rising podium. Representations of the priests and priestesses, the uniformed temple prostitutes, evangelists, and zealots in their scarlet robes, had begun to gather, signaling the opening of the ceremony. The ringing of the bells had died down.

She shrugged her shoulders and let go of my hand.

"I believe in the doctrine of the many resurrections. I believe in the federal right to the stars. All the rest, including what is written on our hands, is merely a reflection of that. Not to be trusted unless it confirms the doctrine."

The hymns began and I forgot about Marina 511 and her companion. Then I forgot my own name and the name of my contract holder. The symphony of infinite virtual worlds was hollow but had the effect of infinite abundance, planes of reality mirroring each other into endlessness. The digital oboes and trumpets sounded from the heights of the cathedral and I found that I was laughing and weeping at the same time, just as those around me were laughing and weeping. We had come to the rivers of Babylon. We had come to Babylon and longed for its beautiful women and its proud men, watched as they turned into skeletons before our eyes, watched as the righteous gods poured out Babylon's treasure into the dust and laid waste to its squares and public buildings, watched as its children were marched out to indenture, just as we had been, and if there was any misgiving in our hearts, it was solely that we did not deserve to have our lives spared and redeemed, spared again and redeemed.

The bishop was there to confirm this message. In his sermon he reminded us of the relentlessness of the enemies of the United States. They had been driven into bondage, as prescribed in the old books of the Bible, the true books rather than the false scriptures of the enemies. Indentured laborers had been integrated into a domain of purity and safety where women and children were the most protected. The ladder of life had been safely erected, the chemical spider and trilobite on the very bottom, the citizen and the cultivated intelligence on the very top as nature had intended. The federal government would not weaken its resolve for an instant. Indeed it would maintain resolve in perpetuity. Life sentence after life sentence was the judgment of the court.

At the end of the service I was silent for some time. I sat there cross-legged while the tens of thousands of pilgrims began to disperse, lost in the certainty of the endless simulation, one world branching from the next to infinity, each containing its unique ladder of life. My candle changed to burn with a smokeless crimson flame. The bells returned, but the walls of the virtual cathedral shimmered into the day.

I looked up to find myself almost alone in the vast field. It was fenced off from the surrounding farms by hedgerows. Long greenhouses on the surrounding hills sparkled under the three moons. As I walked in the direction of the station there was the smell of good earth around me. Tiny glowworms darted above the ground, attending to the microscopic details of the ecology, their light the same shade of crimson as my candle.

Centuries ago the United States had made the planet bloom, transformed it from the drab companion of a gas giant into an American backyard covered in new birds and plants. It was an honor to serve in this undertaking. And yet, as happy as I was, exulting in the beauty of this new earth, I also knew that I was nothing and less than nothing. This feeling lay there in the bottom of my soul, denigrating the entirety of my existence.

To my surprise Marina 511 was waiting for me at the entrance to the station elevator, her face uncertain.

"I waited for you."

"Do we have something in common?"

Marina looked around. The last pilgrims were passing in the fields around us, their scarlet heads disappearing into the tall corn. The empty elevator closed its door and shot up to the platform before she continued.

"There is something unusual about you. I read it in your hands. I see it in your expression."

I shook my head. "I don't know what it is. I have memories. I don't know what they mean. Maybe they mean nothing. Maybe they are scenes from a past life. Something happened."

Marina took my hand again.

"You are the number-one son," she said. "You are the blue-eyed boy."

I took back my hand, realizing that she was crazy, had been driven crazy over the course of many lives. Behind her expression there was nobody I could reach. I was completely alone.

I had my first migraine on the return journey. Stars flared in my eyes, as bright as the radium lamps along the track. I went to sleep. In a dream I saw the face of the woman who was dear to me. She had scarlet hair, and eyes the color of seaweed.

∘   ∘   ∘

And We have beautified the nearest heaven with stars.

GERONIMO WORE HIS FORTUNE on his face. Days when the trade was good, or when, as he put it, he had been lucky in love, you could read it in his expression. I knew when he made an unexpected windfall on the market, or when he was anticipating a shipment of souls from a visiting crèche, whittling down a piece of wood with a knife in one hand as he tried to reach the vendor. He would be withdrawn, even sour, when there were no deals to be found, or when there was a report of insurgent activity.

In the days following my excursion to the cathedral Geronimo was almost silent, as if he expected me to say something about my experience. I waited until one evening when he was combing his hair, fixing it in place with a fine spray, preparing for a drink with a woman who was a perfect mathematical match. I was reminded that he was a young man and had everything in front of him.

I asked, "Sir, is there a reason you sent me to the Church of the Many Resurrections?"

He didn't turn his head. "You don't agree that religion is a good idea?"

"I do agree."

"It adjusts the poor and the rich. It brings acceptance to the former, graceful condescension to the latter. It reduces the threat of terrorism to almost zero, although you wouldn't know it if you went by the news."

"I agree with all that, sir. I agree with everything you are saying. I just thought you might have an additional motive."

Geronimo placed an earring in one ear, turned it on, and then took it out again. He put his hand on my back and ushered me out the door and down the staircase. The nearby offices hummed with electronic life.

On the street, sunshine fell in diagonals. Men and women in summer clothing were heading to the beaches and lakes. Some were followed by their laborers. I recognized them by the way they held themselves, and yet I didn't see myself in them.

Geronimo said, "You're different. That is what I should have explained to you. You're not like us. You are not an American, and yet you are not entirely the same as a standard laborer. Do you know why?"

"I have no idea." I looked at my contract holder, who, for the first time, was smiling at me. "I have no idea what I am doing in this life."

Geronimo waited to enlighten me on this topic. We walked past the district court, and then the center for the alignment of cultivated intelligence. It was a steel oblong, twenty-seven stories high, where sentient beings were brought to be tested, adjusted, or extinguished when their programming showed the potential for misalignment. There was a rumor, I didn't know where I had heard it, that the entire network went offline for the smallest fraction of a femtosecond when an intelligence was shut down for good. In front of the center was also, as it happened, the best place in our neighborhood to get a cab.

In the cab the city districts flashed past: commercial spaceports and fungus agriculture, followed by marijuana distilleries and local stock exchanges with digits running along their facades, and then the long hedges and protective domes that signaled the arrival of trillionaires' row, the crooked road that wound past many of the most expensive estates in the solar system. Geronimo told me the names of the owners as we went by.

I recognized a few of the names, singers, investors, predictors, and captains of bioindustry, familiar to anyone who paid attention to the news, as well as the bearers of old names who could trace their roots to great Confederate lines from places like Tennessee and Hebron, men and women who had been born into the traffic in souls and would be sustained by it throughout their natural lives. There was some weird sensation that went through me, although I could not have explained it. Unlike them, Geronimo was not old money. He had been born in a traditional hospital to a single mother. He was in the trade to make something out of himself.

"You take my clients to the dedication center every day. Has it ever occurred to you that you haven't taken a spell under the lights for yourself?"

I said, "I assumed you must have a reason, sir."

"I have a reason. Indeed I have a reason. You have a loyal soul, my friend. If I play my cards carefully, you may be worth more to me than your weight in original gold. That's why we are here on trillionaires' row."

"I only wish to assist."

"Sullivan gave me the tip in the first place. I will owe him for this. I will owe him big. My first real score, all thanks to the fact that Sullivan keeps his eyes open and keeps up with celebrity gossip."

At the time I didn't know what Geronimo could owe the apostle of rededication, or what part I was meant to play in making my contract holder's fortune. I did have some idea about trillionaires. They were nothing like you and me, not like mere millionaires or billionaires, who were literally a dime a dozen in this solar system.

Nor were they exactly human. Trillionaires were a mixed breed—clans, families, and cloned lines, their intelligence a blend of human and machine, their memories stored in vats and replayed in infinite simulations. They had the greatest prize in human history in their grasp: eternal life on the quantum foam.

As a class they had a hold on the public's affections. There were stories of trillionaires capable of considerable kindness. Citizens revered them for their charity and glamour, their goodness and superhumanity. People spoke their real names out loud with reluctance but eagerly watched holographic movies in which a trillionaire fell in love with an ordinary person. Low as I was in front of Geronimo, I believed I would be annihilated in the presence of a trillionaire. But I was wrong. In the grandest settings there was a way to serve.

o   o   o

The life of this world is only the enjoyment of deception.

T HE ESTATE AT THE GATES of which we arrived was surrounded by cypress trees. The gatehouse was unmanned, and a coat of arms stood in for something so vulgar as a clan name. The sun played on the lawns rolling away from the driveway. I could see ponds filled with black water set throughout the property.

There was no living person to be seen, only the subtle blue lights that told me that intelligence was protecting the entire perimeter. Somebody had arranged for safe passage, because no pod of supermarines crashed down from the orbital, and no thundercloud of a hundred thousand drones formed before our eyes. I could scarcely believe we were permitted to come within a mile of an actually existing trillionaire.

We got out in front of a sprawling residence. An open French door led us into the entrance hall. A number of large black vases stood on pedestals, scenes from ancient texts decorating their sides: girls in bullock carts with braids in their hair being taken to be sacrificed, men wrestling in armored coats, images of temples that resembled the very building in which we stood. Here and there were bowls of flowers. Other bowls contained only water and lily pads, some dark stones visible beneath the surface.

Along the walls were a few bookcases. They held, for the most part, what I knew to be the sacred texts of virtual Buddhism, including Tien Kelpu's great treatise on the contemplation of infinite virtual worlds. The evangelical church had gone one way, in light of the numberless resurrections of the body, while elite Buddhism, religion of the trillionaires, was focused instead on the multiplication of the spirit.

After some time another door slid open and released us into a lounge, a floor surrounded by plate-glass windows. Geronimo seemed to know where he was going. He led me to the next floor and then up a second staircase to the top of the building.

He asked, "Do you recognize where we are? Anything about it?"

"I don't."

"This is where you used to serve, in another life. This is where you prepared for your greatest act of service when you cheated the Black Hand of its rightful prey. I happen to know about it, because Sullivan and I pay close attention to the history of indentured work, but most people in the profession are not so careful."

Geronimo opened a door on the side of the landing and went in. I followed and found myself in a carpeted room. The ceiling sloped and the windows had been sealed with mesh so that an even gray light hung in the air.

In the middle of the carpet was a four-poster bed covered with a canopy. Geronimo lifted the veil to let me see the occupant. It was a woman, her expression softened in sleep.

Geronimo looked greedily at me. "Can you tell me the name of this particular lady whom we have come a long way to see?"

"I don't know her name, sir. And yet I feel as if I have known her forever."

"You've seen her face in your mind? You have seen her? Sullivan was right to call you a diamond in the rough."

"I saw her in my dreams when I was born. I have seen her every night since then."

How could I have said what was in my heart? It wasn't a sensation that could be brought to light, turned over on the tongue, reduced to ones and zeros. Feelings arose that had not been there since the instant of my awakening. I had come upon something I couldn't doubt, something that was as momentous to me as it was secret. I could hardly breathe from the disturbance.

Geronimo sat on an armchair and put his feet up on the small table, peering at the portraits in oval frames on the walls before he returned to me. He produced a jug, which had been waiting underneath the table, and poured the hot and cold water into two gold-rimmed glasses.

"The Madame Secretary, Katherine de Gouveia Perreira. In a previous life, not very long ago, you were her jack-of-all-trades. Her stenographer and court witness, her adviser, her bodyguard, her lover according to the gossip around town. You saved her twice from the Black Dogs or Number One Son, first planet-side when they released a virus, and then during an attack on her medical shuttle, where you lost your own life, the one two steps before this one. She has been here since then, despite the best efforts of the federal scientists. Her estate is desperate enough to give us the chance to help."

I rejoiced at whatever I had done to earn the right to serve through so many incarnations. I had been bad to be good. I picked up the glasses and drank from each before I put them down at the foot of the bed.

"How many lives do I have?"

"As many as we need you to have. Her gene line would do anything to bring her back. If you can help her again you can serve until the end of time. So long as my cut comes through."

By then, to be honest, I could hardly hear his words. I felt as if seven moons and suns, a thousand nebulae silently breeding a hundred thousand new stars, stood between us.

I sat on the side of the bed and took Katherine's hand in my own. It was as warm as new bread. +

2018

EFRIM MANUEL MENUCK
Pissing Stars

JERUSALEM IN MY HEART
Daqa'iq Tudaiq

CARLA BOZULICH
Quieter

ERIC CHENAUX
Slowly Paradise

JASON SHARP
Stand Above The Streams

AUTOMATISME
Transit

JOYFULTALK
Plurality Trip

ALANIS OBOMSAWIN
Bush Lady

SANDRO PERRI
In Another Life

JESSICA MOSS
Entanglement

All titles on deluxe audiophile 180gram vinyl
with art print poster + download coupon.
Select titles on CD. Everything digital.

**CONSTELLATION
CSTRECORDS.COM**

NATALIE SHIELDS, *UNTITLED*. 2015, COLLAGE. COURTESY OF THE ARTIST.

EVERYBODY KNOWS

Elizabeth Schambelan

EXHIBITS

IN THE PHOTO INSERT of Bernard Lefkowitz's 1997 book *Our Guys*, there's a poor-quality close-up of a cute boy in a hoodie. It's from the boy's yearbook, where it was featured prominently. It was not originally a close-up—the yearbook editors cropped in on the cute face. I know this to be the case, although I've never seen the original photo or the yearbook itself. The photograph is captioned as follows:

> Bryant Grober, the son of a doctor and one of the leaders of the Jock clique in high school, wrestled and played football. The senior poll said he had the "nicest eyes." He later became a leading suspect in the rape investigation. State Exhibit: *State v. Christopher Archer et al.*

The subject of *Our Guys* is an incident known as the Glen Ridge rape. Glen Ridge is a wealthy New Jersey commuter town where serious crime is so rare, or so rarely reported, that no more specific appellation is required. On the afternoon of March 1, 1989, a 17-year-old girl whom Lefkowitz calls Leslie Faber was shooting baskets by herself in a park. A bunch of Glen Ridge High boys were hanging out nearby, and one of them—junior Chris Archer—approached Leslie and asked her to join him at the home of the Scherzer twins, Kyle and Kevin. All the guys were heading over there, he said; they were going to have a party. Leslie, who was intellectually disabled, had known Chris and most of the other boys since kindergarten.

She badly wanted to be liked by them. "He was my hero," she later said of one of them.

Leslie hesitated to go to this party where she knew she would be the only girl. But when Chris promised her that his older brother Paul would go on a date with her if she accepted the invitation, she said yes. Paul, a senior, was considered the most handsome boy at Glen Ridge High.

The thirteen Jocks—this is how Lefkowitz refers to them, Jocks with a capital *J*—adjourned to the Scherzers' finished basement with Leslie. The guys gathered around Leslie and began urging her to disrobe. She took off all her clothes and then, at the Jocks' behest, performed oral sex on Bryant Grober. She was then instructed to lie on a couch, where the Scherzers and Chris Archer took turns penetrating her with a miniature bat, a drumstick, and a broomstick. Richie Corcoran—a rambunctious lug of the type beloved in many a jock clique, a sort of mascot-enforcer—called her "Pigorskia" while this was taking place. Six boys got uncomfortable and split early on. None tried to stop what was happening, nor did any of them report it. The rape came to light when one of the guys' football teammates, Charlie Figueroa, heard about it and told a teacher, at which point Figueroa became a social outcast. At his graduation later that year, his classmates booed him.

By then, *State v. Christopher Archer et al.* had embarked on its balky and byzantine course. The al. comprised Bryant and the Scherzer twins. Prosecutors had hoped to charge more of the thirteen Jocks but in the end concluded they could only win convictions against these four. *Our Guys* follows the trial closely and is riveting as courtroom drama, but it is also a nuanced sociological study. To contextualize the rape, Lefkowitz describes the sexual mores of the Glen Ridge Jocks in great detail. The boys, he tells us, never went on dates. Instead, they threw parties that followed a rigid script: first the guys would watch porn while the girls chatted among themselves. When the groups did interact, the guys would make a desultory show of chivalrous ardor, rolling their eyes at one another when they could without the girls noticing, until eventually everyone paired off. These couples rarely had intercourse—the boys preferred to receive handjobs or blowjobs—but the thing that really seemed to turn them on was what they called "voyeuring": arranging situations where they could watch their friends fool around with unwitting girls. According to one of Lefkowitz's informants, a guy at one such party said, "You gotta go up and see what they're doing upstairs. She's unbelievably gross."

The boys craved a visual record of these experiences. Their oft-discussed fantasy was to produce their own homemade porno, presumably with girls who had no idea they'd been conscripted into the lead roles. One of the Jocks asked a friend to surreptitiously take a picture while he had sex, which he then put in a display case at school. They'd make up nicknames for their partners; one particularly ingratiating girl, for example, was dubbed "Seal." Their collective term for sexually available young women was *animals*. At school, they'd pin female classmates to lockers and grind against them.

Lefkowitz does not limit his investigation to the Jocks' teenage underworld. Much of *Our Guys* is devoted to the Glen Ridge community's response to the crime, which involved support for the victim and a lot of collective soul searching. Just kidding! The whole town was completely in thrall to the Jocks, and the majority of Ridgers, as they called themselves, were furious that the boys were embroiled in such an unsavory situation. In the orgy of victim blaming that followed the rape, Ridgers did not hesitate to paint Leslie as a slutty seductress (as defense lawyers later did, too, inquiring into her sex life with such grotesque prurience that it led to the strengthening of New Jersey's rape shield laws). After the defendants were charged in May, administrators called an assembly at Glen Ridge High and asked the student body to "stand by our boys."

While none of their boys comes across as sympathetic, one does feel a pang for Grober, the most remorseful of the four defendants. When a classmate describes "Bry" as "the ultimate crowd-follower," the reader is inclined to believe it, and to surmise that had it not been for peer pressure, Bryant would never have been involved in the rape of Leslie Faber.

Chris Archer is a different story. In a photograph in *Our Guys*, he stands beside his brother, both of them in sweatshirts and varsity jackets. The caption reads:

Paul Archer (*left*) and his brother, Chris. Chris, a junior when this photo was taken, wrestled and played football. The brothers had known Leslie Faber since she was a child. State Exhibit: *State v. Christopher Archer et al.*

It's not difficult to see why prosecutors chose to admit this particular photograph into evidence. Paul's fair-haired cuteness could not have been a more effective foil for everything un-cute about the kid standing next to him with his game face on. In *Our Guys*, Chris emerges as a classic charismatic sociopath, and Lefkowitz, usually dry to a fault, waxes melodramatic: "People might describe Chris's appearance as 'arresting.'. . . it was the eyes, the freezing intensity, that could stop you dead. His eyes could read your soul." Our antihero never studies but makes excellent grades. He overflows with energy. A fellow Jock recalls, "There was something about Chris. . . . He was just fearless. He was the hardest hitter on the football team. And the way he carried himself on the mat."

Chris won "nicest eyes" the year after Bryant did. (He was free on bail at the time.) He must have had innumerable opportunities to hook up with girls, but it appears he had a thing for Leslie Faber. Soon after the rape, Leslie—whom Lefkowitz describes as "tall for her age, broad-shouldered, and somewhat overweight"—disclosed that Chris "had been bothering her" for the previous year and a half, calling her, wanting to talk about sex, trying to get her to meet him at night in a shed. "On the way to parties," Lefkowitz writes, "Chris would pound the dashboard of the car and chant lines from 'Paul Revere' about being hunted by the sheriff. Why was the sheriff after him? Because he 'did it' to the sheriff's daughter 'with a wiffleball bat.'"

The case took forever to adjudicate, but by 1993, Chris and the Scherzer twins had been found guilty of first-degree sexual assault, which in New Jersey is equivalent to rape, and Bryant had been found guilty of conspiracy to commit the same. Chris and the Scherzers appealed, but eventually, in 1997, all three began serving (short) prison terms. In the long interim between crime and punishment, life for the defendants went on at least somewhat normally. Chris, still free on bail, graduated from high school and matriculated at Boston College in 1990. Some months later, a Boston College security staffer contacted the Glen Ridge police to suggest they speak to a female student who had a story to tell about Archer. The young woman—who did not want to testify for fear of having her name "dragged through the mud"—told prosecutors that Chris had pulled her behind some bushes one night as they walked home from a bar. "Right here, right now," he said, and started attempting to remove her clothes. When she resisted, she stated, he "began punching her in her vagina" and "penetrated her vagina and her anus with his fingers." Then he jumped up and declared "I'm a rapist."

If you went to an American high school with an average parental tax bracket in the "comfortable" range, there's a good chance you know

Bryant Grober. Bry: cute and popular, on the teams it was cool to be on, kind of a dick around his friends but perfectly cordial when you were lab partners. Somewhere in your yearbook, there's a picture of him. It's a close-up reproduced large, because the yearbook editors wanted everyone to appreciate Bry's amazing eyes. Chris, with his equally amazing but soul-freezing eyes, might seem a more *unheimlich* figure. Both boys were rapists, not just the one who had the brio to announce it so insouciantly. Follower and leader, sheep and beastie boy, wound up in the same place. One was, by all accounts, miserable about it afterward; the other, not at all. But they both participated in sexually assaulting Leslie Faber and stripping her utterly of dignity. The father of a young woman who went to school with the guys said:

> If I think back about that period, I can see the group getting stronger, closer, every time they got together and humiliated a girl. What they enjoyed in common wasn't football. *This* was their *shared* experience. For them, this was what being a man among men was. My daughter would come home with stories—I'd just shake my head and wonder if they thought a girl was human.

ANECDOTES

W HEN I WAS GROWING UP, I never paid much attention to jocks. A robust mutual disinterest prevailed between my popular athletic male classmates and me. Lately, though, I've been trying to summon my memories of these boys. I remember the way they dressed: loose T-shirts obscuring their cultivated pecs; long, baggy, unflattering shorts; man-sandals that made them look like pensioners on a kibbutz. It was as if they were daring the world to find them unfoxy. The ensemble was both mufti and dishabille, conveying that the wearer was only *really* dressed when on the field, in full football or lacrosse regalia.

The way they sat—that too I recall quite vividly. They sprawled with weary abandon, feet on the rungs of their desks, knees apart, like women in birthing chairs. But there would be all this tension in their jaws—an *inordinate* amount, as if all their testosterone had bivouacked there to rest up for the next hallway dominance display. Lolling, practically supine, they'd chew gum, bearing down hard. Or they'd glare at the clock, masseters flexing. I can picture one of them punctuating a smart-ass remark with a sudden, teeth-gnashing smile—louche, twinkly, crocodilian.

Oh my God, you are so immature, their female friends would say, constantly. They were immature, but there was also something extremely precocious about them, something oddly adult. They acted just like cocky assholes twice their age, drawling their way through off-color anecdotes with the jaded amusement of i-bankers, and hailing one another in the halls with an air of grim camaraderie that said, *We few, we happy few.* How did they figure it all out so early—style, demeanor, a whole way of being a person—when the rest of us were still bumbling around? I didn't understand it then, but now I realize that, just like aristocrats, the jocks in my high school truly were the heirs of a venerable and highly prestigious tradition, one that has been handed down, older brother to younger, senior to freshman, ever since jocks became jocks, whenever that was.

I was always gleaning scattered bits of information about their sex lives—not on purpose. Once, one of them turned to me in homeroom and remarked, "So, last night this beautiful girl was lying on my bed, and I couldn't get it up. She's lying there naked, like, 'Hello?' and I'm just sitting there, looking down at my dick, like—" and here he shrugged puckishly. I found this cavalier disclosure striking, and enviable, suggesting as it did that his sexual confidence, like his parents' money, was an endlessly renewable resource. It was obvious that for him, sex was as ordinary as our suburb itself, a terrain he navigated absentmindedly in his black Wrangler, chanting words he knew by heart because he'd heard them so many times on the boom box in the weight room: *You ain't in between the sheets, I give it to you real raw in the back seat, What's my name, what's my name, what's my name, what's my name . . .*

When they talked in class about their conquests, it was always "this girl," as in "this girl was so fucking hot," or—less often, but just as boastfully—"this girl was so fucking fat/ugly." One girl they used to call Bloody Mary, much to her chagrin, because (I heard) one of the guys had gone down on her while she had her period. *She* then became a laughingstock. Another girl I worked with on the school paper dated a jock for a long time. It was said that he had secretly videotaped her giving him a blowjob while he was doing bong hits, and then duped this hilarious footage and given copies to his friends.

When I first read *Our Guys*, in my early twenties, it felt familiar to me. At certain moments—when Lefkowitz talks about voyeuring, or when he describes the cryptically coded jokes the boys included in their senior yearbook blurbs—I had that commonplace, unremarkable feeling you have when one piece of information fits smoothly into a broader constellation of things you already know. Granted, there were some real distinctions between my schoolmates and the Glen Ridge crew. A Glen Ridge Jock would have sooner shown up at school in a tennis dress than admit to performing oral sex, whereas the Bloody Mary story indicates that such reciprocity was not, in and of itself, stigmatized at my school. But it was the same culture. By early adulthood I had friends who had told me about the same kinds of behaviors in their own high schools and among frat guys in college. I knew without having to ask that the guys in these stories wore CO-ED NAKED LACROSSE T-shirts and Tevas, and that they were also part of the culture. It might look different in different places and at different times, and like any other culture, it had its internal critics and dissidents, but it was still substantially homogeneous. That rape was part of it—not something everyone did, maybe something only a small percentage did, but nevertheless a defining custom or tradition—that was so obvious it went without saying, even to myself.

PRIMARY RESEARCH

"THE EVENTS DESCRIBED below are *not* isolated or rare occurrences. These experiences—acquaintance gang rape—happen all too frequently at fraternity and/or other campus parties at colleges and universities across the country." So begins Julie K. Ehrhart and Bernice R. Sandler's 1985 report "Campus Gang Rape: Party Games?" Commissioned by the Association of American Colleges, the report marked the first effort to systematically examine the titular crime. The authors note that they began the project assuming that the few campus gang rapes they'd heard about were indeed isolated incidents. But after identifying more than fifty cases at schools across the United States, they came to believe the opposite: that these crimes were so frequent as to qualify as mundane. "On some campuses, [we] were told 'it happens almost every week.'"

The cases they looked at followed a consistent pattern from coast to coast, in schools small and large, public and private. There was remarkable consistency, for example, in the identity of the perpetrators. The authors did not find that campus gang rapes were committed by comp lit professors at some schools, at other schools by custodians, and at others by premed students. Rather, the crimes were overwhelmingly committed by athletes and fraternity brothers, and "the great majority of the reported incidents occurred at fraternity parties."

In every one of the frat-party rapes, "the scenario is basically the same": an intoxicated young woman becomes the target of "the 'friendly' persuasion of the brothers," unaware that their blandishments are "actually a planned pursuit of easy prey." Once the attack gets under way, "her confusion has turned to fear and panic, and escape seems impossible. She is unable to protest or her protests are ignored." While the victim is raped by multiple fraternity brothers, other men are probably watching. "Voyeurism is often a part of the acquaintance gang rape. At one campus, brothers not involved directly in the rape watched through a peephole; at another campus, pictures were taken."

The authors found a striking sameness in the fraternity brothers' terminology as well: *gang bang* and *pulling train* were the preferred designations. Fraternity members viewed pulling train as "'normal' party behavior. In fact, in almost all instances the men involved are *unaware* that their behavior is gang rape." Some frats even mentioned the activity on party invitations. If the woman was too intoxicated to resist, this was believed by the brothers to mean that she was "asking for it." Another thing that the fraternity gang rapists had in common was porn: they watched a great deal of it. As to what motivated them to commit rape, Ehrhart and Sandler arrived at exactly the same conclusion as the Glen Ridge dad: *This* was the frat guys' shared experience, their most intense form of bonding.

In 1987, the research psychologist Mary P. Koss and her colleagues Christine A. Gidycz and Nadine Wisniewski released the results of the first comprehensive study of sexual assault on campus. Having questioned thousands of students at dozens of American institutions of higher learning, Koss et al. found that one in four college women had been raped or had experienced attempted rape. They also found that thirty-eight per thousand female respondents had been raped in the preceding six months—a figure more than nine times higher than the federal government's estimate. And the study had serious implications beyond campus: "The findings support published assertions of high rates of rape and other forms of sexual aggression among large normal populations. Although the results are limited in generalizability to postsecondary students, this group represents 26% of all persons aged 18–24 in the United States."

NEWS

WHEN WORD GOT OUT that high school football heroes in affluent Glen Ridge had been charged with gang-raping an intellectually disabled young woman, hordes of journalists converged upon the town. None of them characterized the unfolding drama as a man-bites-dog story. There was disagreement about where, exactly, the wider problem lay: youth culture, the culture of masculinity, the culture of sports, or the culture of team sports. But from the beginning, the Glen Ridge rape was characterized by the media not as a shocking anomaly but as an abominable exemplar.

The Bergen County *Record*: "The Glen Ridge case raises troubling questions that should concern all of us. . . . What are we teaching our sons about the difference between acceptable sexual behavior and rape?"

The *Washington Post*: "Like so many men, [the Glen Ridge defendants] mistake hostility toward women for manly behavior. . . . For too long some of those acts have been seen as 'normal.'"

The *New York Times*: "The arc of the current mini-series begins in a suburban basement. High school football players are having their way with a retarded female classmate. . . . The real story [is] an anecdotal litany of sexual assaults by high school, college and professional athletes, singly and in groups. The evidence is mounting that athletes are disproportionately involved in exploitative, if not criminal, sexual acts."

NPR's *Morning Edition*: "There is then the awful conclusion [from Glen Ridge and similar cases] that there is a kind of esprit de corps, good old-fashioned team spirit, that encourages rape when young men on teams are together with women after hours."

Just a few years earlier, this understanding would have been conceptually impossible. As Koss put it in the *Times* in January 1989, "Ten years ago, there was no convincing evidence that acquaintance rape existed, although counselors suspected it. . . . Today the situation is dramatically different." At long last, Koss had proved the bizarrely controversial proposition that it is possible to be raped by an acquaintance. From there, it was but a small step to the idea that it is possible to be raped by more than one acquaintance at a time.

On February 17, 1986, the *New York Times* reporter Nadine Brozan cited Ehrhart and Sandler's research in a piece headlined "Gang Rape: A Rising Campus Concern." "Only now is the cloak of secrecy around group rape in collegiate settings beginning to lift," wrote Brozan. "Incidents of collegiate group rape seem to have many elements in common." An administrator told Brozan that the crime "can occur in a dormitory . . . but more often it happens in the fraternal or athletic setting because the members have that close relationship." The director of a university women's center added, "Many of the men seem to believe that having intercourse with a woman who is semiconscious, unconscious or severely intoxicated is sex rather than rape, because she is not fighting back."

Brozan noted that athletes and fraternity brothers at several large universities had recently been accused of felony rape. Less than two weeks after being acquitted of rape charges, University of Minnesota basketball player Mitch Lee had been arrested, with two of his teammates, on other rape charges. The Lee case caused "frustration and outrage . . . on the national level," wrote *Philadelphia Daily News* sports columnist Rich Hofmann in a four-part series on athletes and rape that ran in March 1986.

Then, in 1987, Koss and her colleagues published their study. This was hard data, not anecdote, and it was greeted with shock. It was at this point that the word *epidemic* began to crop up. A wave of rape awareness engulfed the nation, registering its magnitude via that enduring highwater mark, *Saturday Night Live* ("Let's take a look at our board. The categories are 'Halter Top,' 'She Was Drunk,' 'I Was Drunk' . . .").

Glen Ridge was one of a number of high-profile stories that broke against this backdrop of intensifying national concern. There was a gang rape involving Pi Kappa Alpha brothers at Florida State University in 1988, in which a female Florida State student was found passed out with her underwear pulled down and her skirt pulled up. She was bruised and scraped, and misogynistic epithets and fraternity symbols had been scrawled on her thighs. Her blood alcohol concentration was a near-lethal .349. Football players at Oklahoma; lacrosse players at St. John's . . . As the litany got longer, more opinion writers took up the matter. Perhaps the most thoughtful of these meditations was Robert Lipsyte's August 4, 1991, *New York Times* column, "The Manly Art of Self-Delusion." Among mainstream commentators, Lipsyte was unusual in asserting that phenomena often considered separately—gang rapes and single-perp rapes and domestic battery, misogyny and violence, behavior on the playing field and in the Pentagon—were in fact aspects of a single phenomenon: "Naked power. What you can get away with because you're a big boy, because too many people are afraid of you and dependent on you and hooked on a system of male entitlement." Lipsyte was also one of the only commentators to point out that despite all the attention that had been paid to these crimes, "the larger issue, of why a group of young men, particularly attractive, strong, privileged athletes, would engage in such activity, has yet to be fully discussed."

If Lipsyte hoped his essay would initiate such a discussion, he must have been disappointed. Not long after his column ran, the acquaintance-rape backlash began in earnest. The story of this disinformation campaign has been well told elsewhere (for example in Jody Raphael's 2013 book *Rape Is Rape*), but the upshot is that by 1993, rape deniers succeeded in shifting the debate to the question of whether sexual assault statistics were wildly inflated.

As to the general direction of coverage at that time, Koss, the lead researcher on the major 1987 study of sexual assault on campus, made the following comment in 1994: "I've actually had reporters tell me that they would love to write a story about the legitimate problem of rape but that their editors tell them that the only thing they're interested in hearing about is that rape is a bogus issue."

FORENSICS

ON SEPTEMBER 26, 2018, the attorney Michael Avenatti released an affidavit in which his client Julie Swetnick stated that when Judge Brett Kavanaugh was in high school, he and his friends regularly spiked the punch at parties with drugs or grain alcohol to incapacitate girls, who were then gang-raped "in a side room or bedroom by a 'train' of numerous boys." Swetnick said that she had been the victim of "one of these 'gang' or 'train' rapes where Mark Judge and Brett Kavanaugh were present."

The affidavit followed on the heels of Ronan Farrow and Jane Mayer's report in the *New Yorker* that Kavanaugh had dropped his pants during a dorm party in his first year at Yale and thrust his penis into the face of his fellow student Deborah Ramirez, causing her "to touch it without her consent." Christine Blasey Ford's allegations that Kavanaugh had assaulted her at a house party in 1982, when they were both teenagers, had preceded the Ramirez story.

Of the three allegations, only Swetnick's was widely dismissed as prima facie absurd. No one denied that a high school boy might hypothetically try to rape a peer at a house party, or that some notional young man might drop his pants in the course of collegiate carousing. But a number of Kavanaugh supporters let it be known that the idea that a bunch of prep school jocks would regularly gang-rape incapacitated young women was the craziest thing they'd ever heard. *National Review* stalwart David French—whose 2015 article "The Campus-Rape Lie" revisited the early-'90s rape-denial playbook so faithfully I could practically hear Wilson Phillips singing as I read—begged, "Please someone help me with this. Georgetown Prep boys frequently committed gang rape. Lots of people knew they were committing gang rape. And despite this common knowledge no one has talked publicly for three decades, until the day before a crucial Senate hearing. What?" Lindsey Graham (a Pi Kappa Phi man) weighed in with this: "I have a difficult time believing any person would continue to go to—according to the affidavit—ten parties over a two-year period where women were routinely gang raped and not report it."

Eventually, these hot takes congealed into the glob of craven fatuity that Susan Collins served up in her speech explaining why she would vote to confirm Kavanaugh to the Supreme Court. Before repeating the freewheelingly arbitrary GOP conclusion that Ford has the capacity to accurately perceive her own experience (in this case, the experience of someone trying to rape her) but not the capacity to distinguish between a person she knows (Brett Kavanaugh) and another person (the mystery teen who attacked her that long-ago night), Collins used the word *outlandish* to describe "the allegation that, when he was a teenager, Judge Kavanaugh drugged multiple girls and used their weakened state to facilitate gang rape."

And finally, Senate Democrats themselves took up the theme, arguing that the case against confirmation had been gaining traction until Avenatti jumped the shark. "We should have focused on the serious allegations that certainly appeared very credible to me," Gary Peters told CNN's Manu Raju.

"In almost all instances the men involved are *unaware* that their behavior is gang rape." "Many of the men seem to believe that having intercourse with a woman who is semiconscious, unconscious or severely intoxicated is sex rather than rape, because she is not fighting back." These aforementioned statements date from 1985 and 1986, respectively. Thirtysome years and two waves of rape awareness later, cluelessness continues to prevail. "Despite this common knowledge no one has talked publicly for three decades. . . ." The truly outlandish thing is not Swetnick's allegation, but how the utterly unexceptional and well-documented scenario she describes in fact refuses to become common knowledge. There is something genuinely uncanny about this learning curve that keeps swallowing its own tail.

I don't think French, Graham, et al. were pretending to be incredulous while really knowing full well that Justice Kavanaugh, to use his current honorific, has a history of abetting rape, attempting rape, and probably committing rape. When they hear *rape*, they likely think of stranger rape. They can't envision Brett and Squi and P. J. and Mark as gang rapists; if they did, they might have to reevaluate their own past behavior or wonder about their friends' past behavior.

In her 2007 book *Epistemic Injustice: Power & the Ethics of Knowing*, Miranda Fricker uses the term *credibility economy* to describe the social system that determines who is heard, who is believed, whose word carries weight. This is a useful concept, in part because it helps us to appreciate the fundamental dementedness of the system in question. Economists long ago abandoned their "rational actor" model, conceding that humans are, to put it mildly, not rational actors, and that human economies are therefore not rational, either. When bubbles collapse we see footage of frantic traders, but we don't see the meetings where finance professionals are like, "OK, so we're all in agreement, we're going to bet a billion dollars that housing prices will *literally never go down*." The same goes for the craziness of the credibility economy: it's usually hidden. But the Kavanaugh confirmation process made it blatantly, outrageously visible.

Kavanaugh, to the GOP, is sort of like a collateralized debt obliga-
tion: an instrument no one really understands and no one really *wants*
to understand. The more you think about a given CDO—the more
closely you scrutinize its trash assets, the longer you contemplate the
insane upside-down ziggurat of risk you're buying into . . . Well, when
you stare into the abyss it stares back into you. Kavanaugh's material
weaknesses, as an accountant might say, have always been apparent to
anyone who cared to look. But by virtue of his race and gender and the
education and upbringing his parents purchased for him, he entered
the credibility economy with considerable wealth. And that meant others would grant him credibility, the way having money means you can
borrow money. Informal transactions of belief, gentlemen's agreements
that aren't on the books, propelled him upward as they have propelled
so many of the mediocrities of the ruling class. "I never met him," said
Donald Trump on October 2, "but [I've] been hearing [about] this guy
named Brett Kavanaugh who is, who is like a perfect person, who is
destined for the Supreme Court. I've heard that for a long time."

And so it went, right up to the moment when this perfect person
was accused of attempted rape. Then, the fact that Kavanaugh was
merely one of many interchangeable Federalist Society orcs became
irrelevant. If a Republican Supreme Court nominee had been brought
down by a woman who said she had been sexually assaulted and was
believed, it would've triggered an unthinkable cascade of catastrophes.
And so, as the revelations and repudiations piled up—former clerks, former roommates, clergy, a retired Supreme Court justice, all saying that
this man was unfit for a lifetime appointment to a position of immense
power—Senate Republicans were forced to pick up the slack. They had
no choice but to take a big, big position on Brett.

Perhaps you had thought, as I had, that women were making progress, that our credibility, relative to men's, was rising. This is in fact
occurring. But if progress is radically provisional, it's not really progress.
Another useful thing about Fricker's "economy" formulation is that it
implies the existence of a credibility precariat, to which women belong.

P EOPLE IN PRECARIOUS positions have to move carefully. The witness
keeps everything rigorously well modulated. She says she went up a
very narrow set of stairs. She got to the top and suddenly someone was

pushing her from behind. She was shoved into the bedroom and the boys, two Prep guys, locked the door and turned up the music.

Christine Blasey, a 15-year-old girl who had spent every day all summer swimming and diving at the pool, had thrown on some clothes over her bathing suit and gone to this party. And then this guy Brett Kavanaugh, a senior, a Prep guy, was on top of her, clumsy, heavy, drunk, and gross, smelling of beer, groping stupidly, trying to get her bathing suit off. When she tried to yell, he put his hand over her mouth, and suddenly she couldn't breathe.

"I thought that Brett was accidentally going to kill me." But he didn't kill her. Mark jumped on top of them and they rolled off the bed. She ran into the bathroom. She heard the boys stumble down the stairs, and then she left the bathroom, walked downstairs, past Brett and Mark and the other people at the party, and out the front door. She doesn't say what that gauntlet felt like, but we can infer from her statement that it was terrifying: "I remember being on the street and feeling this enormous sense of relief that I had escaped that house and that Brett and Mark were not coming outside after me." It must have been surreal to escape and find herself back in the same world she'd left, on a quiet street in a nice suburban neighborhood, with everyone going about their business as if nothing had happened.

Too much scene setting is as dangerous as too much interiority: it could make a true story sound like fiction. What Ford provided in her testimony were the kinds of details that would be excluded from fiction because of their unsatisfying randomness (he jumped on top of them and they rolled off the bed?). She talked about the neurological signatures of trauma and PTSD. She used the word *sequelae*. She said, "Indelible in the hippocampus is the laughter." The statement, with its clinical detachment and the eerie absence of a possessive pronoun, conveys the numb dissociation of terror.

She knows that trauma smashes its own timeline into smithereens, a product of terror's disruptive effect on the normal imprinting of memory. She pieced together an event she probably remembers as a jumble of strobe flashes and told the tale seamlessly, chronologically, and calmly but not dispassionately. She knew she'd be penalized for too much emotion or too little. She walked the line flawlessly. It didn't do any good.

o   o   o

St. Joseph's was founded by the Jesuits in 1789, which means this year is its Bicentennial, so . . . *get ready to party! (Awkward beat.)* No, no, I'm kidding—Uh, the campus is one hundred and two acres (including, yes, a golf course, these . . . *pastoral* hills all around us).

THIS IS BRANDON HARDY, "handsome, wearing a navy blazer, khakis, and striped tie," leading a tour group around the hills and dales of his prep school campus. In addition to being handsome, Brandon is a senior and the captain of the St. Joseph's football team. He's basically the king of the school, and yet here he is, humbly playing docent, making a disarmingly lame joke, showing a pleasing hint of irony in the emphasis on *pastoral*. We're maybe thirty seconds into Roberto Aguirre-Sacasa's 2008 play *Good Boys and True*, and the protagonist has been deftly established as a likable kid. In addition to being a playwright, Aguirre-Sacasa has written for Marvel Comics and for television series including *Glee* and *Riverdale*. He knows how to write likable kids.

The plot centers on a sex tape that has been making the rounds at St. Joseph's. What exactly is going on in the video, which features a boy and a girl, is never made clear, but there is doubt as to whether the encounter is consensual. The boy can only be seen from the back. It looks like it could be Brandon. He insists that it's not.

As it turns out, we learn early in the play, Brandon is indeed the guy on the tape. From there, Aguirre-Sacasa just keeps revealing more and more awful things about Brandon. He is casually exploiting his best friend Justin, who is in love with him, for sexual favors. He brought the tape to school and engineered its "accidental" discovery. He's a homophobe who eventually denounces Justin as a "faggot." He targeted a vulnerable girl—one who goes to public school and is not pretty—because he wanted somebody he could pick up at the mall and manipulate into having sex with him that same afternoon, in an empty house where he'd already set up the camera.

In the final act, Brandon's mom, Elizabeth, confronts him, and he admits that he "used" the girl "and didn't care about her feelings." She demands to know how he could have behaved that way. "We all show each other . . . what we *do*," he explains. By "we" he means the football team. "It's like a *game*." Unsatisfied with this, she presses him until he confesses: "I wanted to do it! . . . I wanted to feel what it would feel like to—to—"

ELIZABETH. Tell me!

BRANDON. I DON'T KNOW! Something happened mom, inside me. Something happened, and I thought I could hurt her . . . Make her feel scared. . . . Because . . . she doesn't matter.

This outburst is the play's climactic revelation, but Elizabeth has already offered a startling confession of her own. It has to do with Brandon's father, Michael, who also attended St. Joseph's and was captain of the football team. Elizabeth grew up in the same area, and she and Michael began dating in their teens. One night at a party when the pair were in high school, in the late '50s, Michael disappeared with one of his friends. Elizabeth followed them to the back of the house, where she found a bunch of football players gathered. "And one of them was up on a ladder that had been set against the house, and he was . . . peering into a window. . . . Your father and his friends had organized a windowsill party."

Elizabeth explains that a girl from her school, Alice, was losing her virginity to a boy from St. Joe's, and "the boy's friends . . . were taking turns, watching them." Michael had specifically asked Elizabeth to bring Alice to the party. Elizabeth doesn't say Alice was raped, but she does say the boys targeted her because she was new in town and socially vulnerable.

Aguirre-Sacasa went to Georgetown Prep. He graduated in the late 1980s, when *Good Boys and True* is set. He has said in interviews that St. Joseph's is modeled on his alma mater, although the videotape scandal is fictional. I don't know if he made up the phrase *windowsill party*, but the incident itself doesn't feel like fiction to me.

Whether the windowsill party described in *Good Boys and True* is drawn from life or not, there's clearly more fact in Aguirre-Sacasa's fiction than there was in the Senate Judiciary Committee's own theatrical inquiry into the character of a Prep guy. While Christine Blasey Ford had to be temperate and measured, neither the nominee nor the Republican senators faced such constraints on their histrionics. They wound up staging a passive-aggressively gladiatorial spectacle as bizarre and decadent as anything imperial Rome produced.

One almost had to admire Lindsey Graham's deranged philippic. I have rarely felt as stunned as I did while watching the senator work himself to the brink of myocardial infarction, his disgustingly fake righteous fury visibly evolving into the even more disgusting real thing as he delivered himself of the opinion that a hearing in which a distinguished man is called to account for sexual misconduct is HELL, and then, without the slightest sign of awareness that rape and PTSD might also be hell, proceeded to a rhetorical anticlimax—*"He's the nicest person!!!"*—that surely ranks as one of the most ludicrous moments in the history of political oratory.

To the extent that any actual argument was put forward in Kavanaugh's defense, this was it: He's the nicest person. Affable, likable, a great dad, an *extremely* nice guy, which means he *could not* have done this, which proves he *did not* do this. Later, Renate Dolphin Schroeder, one of sixty-five women who signed a letter expressing this belief, learned that she was fodder for one of Brett and his friends' degrading jokes in *Cupola 1983*, their senior yearbook. But when the letter was signed, all the women presumably believed in the well-mannered and likable Brett who was organized and responsible, who primly recorded his Ivy League college interviews and his summery weekend plans on his calendar ("Go to St. Michael's," "Go to Connecticut"), who mugged goofily for the camera in *Cupola 1983*. The photo—Brett in a football shirt and shoulder pads, sticking out his tongue—appears in a collage of candid shots titled "Those Prep Guys Are the Biggest . . ."

The biggest what? It is left to the imagination of uninformed readers. The same phrase with the same dot-dot-dot crops up in a couple of the seniors' individual blurbs, including Kavanaugh's, confirming that it's an inside joke. As you turn each page, when you see a lengthy blurb, you know this is a popular guy. A paucity of private jokes indicates an uncool person, somebody who did not have enough friends, or whose friends did not have enough forbidden adventures, to build up that dense thicket of secret memories.

The other Brett, the perhaps not so likable Brett, is invisible in *Cupola 1983*, hidden in those coded references whose precise meaning is mostly irretrievable. And he is not in the calendars except as a cryptic trace, an ominous all-caps mantra among the cursive scrawls: LIFT. LIFT. LIFT.

"YOU'VE NEVER FORGOTTEN that laughter," Vermont senator Patrick Leahy said to Ford during the hearing. "You've never forgotten them laughing at you."

"They were laughing with each other," Ford corrected.

In her 1990 book *Fraternity Gang Rape*, the anthropologist Peggy Reeves Sanday notes, "I did not use the word 'fraternity' in the title to refer to fraternities generally as an institution. The phrase 'fraternity gang rape' refers to bonding through sex. . . . I use the word 'fraternity' . . . to mean a group of persons associated *by or as if by* ties of brotherhood." Mark and Brett strengthened the ties of brotherhood while assaulting Christine Blasey Ford. In their world—the world of Prep guys, and the Glen Ridge guys, and Brock Turner, and Owen Labrie, and the Steubenville football players, and the fraternity brothers Ehrhart and Sandler studied, and on and on—many guys hold the old-fashioned view that sex is something you do with someone you love. It's just that the people they love are their bros.

For them, sex is something you do *to* a woman, *with* your friends. Guys who organize their sex lives around these prepositional relationships engage in any or all of a specific array of behaviors, ranging from mild caddishness to heinous crime: talking about their partners in a degrading way; voyeuring; circulating photos or videos of sex; making adversarial efforts to seduce women they consciously disdain; hogging (slang for seeking out partners who are considered unattractive); conspiring to get prospective conquests drunk, slip them roofies, or otherwise diminish their capacity to consent; rape. The woman's responsiveness or lack thereof is irrelevant, because it is the responsiveness of the rapists' male friends that matters—whether the friends are standing right there during the act or are brought up to speed afterward.

And while what's happening is group bonding through sex, what's also happening is group bonding through shared risk, transgression, and secrets. The Glen Ridge numbers are worth reflecting upon. Thirteen boys were involved to varying degrees in a rape committed by four of them and conceived and set in motion by only one. Even the ones who wanted no part of the rape and left kept the crime secret, becoming, in effect, accessories after the fact. Chris Archer was at the center of a sprawling web of culpability and complicity. There is no data I know of indicating that jocks and frat guys rape at higher rates than other men in the general population.* But if rapists are not necessarily

---

* What *that* rate is—the percentage of all men who are rapists—is highly contested; a few years ago I frequently saw the figure 6 percent, but there is a school of thought that this is way too high. Six percent is certainly a staggeringly high number; it would mean, for instance, that should you find yourself in a New York City subway car that is crowded to capacity, you may estimate that there are two rapists with you in that car. Happily, if the 6 percent figure is wildly inflated to twice the real number, that would mean an average of only one rapist per car.

overrepresented in this milieu, *accomplices* to rape—helpers, watchers, or, to paraphrase Collins, facilitators—very likely are.

During the trial of Owen Labrie, the St. Paul's soccer captain who in 2014 assaulted a younger student as part of a contest in which male seniors vied to hook up with the most girls (the Senior Salute), it emerged that "Deny til you die" was an unofficial motto at the school. Texts and emails provided details about what Labrie and his friends were so intent on denying, revealing, for instance, that *slay* was the boys' word for sex. They used it in deliberately bad puns, referring to the last two months of the school year as Slaypril and Slay. This terminology is unusually vivid, but the predatory attitude it bespeaks is widespread. Whether crime is involved or not, sexual partners (excluding a privileged caste of girls, like Elizabeth in *Good Boys and True*) are viewed as quarry, something to catch via strength and/or cunning. Labrie said he "pulled every trick in the book" on the young woman he assaulted.

In a 1997 review of *Our Guys*, Russell Banks posed the following question: "If we are raising our male children to be feral, which is to say, if they are becoming incapable of empathy for others, especially their female counterparts, then what will their children be like?" Now we know the answer. Banks was talking about the generation of boys who graduated from high school in the late '80s, like the Glen Ridge rapists and like the Prep guys on whom Aguirre-Sacasa based Brandon, the nice, likable boy who decides to find a girl who doesn't matter and abuse and degrade her, just to see how it feels. This cohort had most of its children from the mid-'90s to the mid-2000s. Owen, Brock, the Steubenville defendants: all were born in that window. We're now trying to socialize this generation into our evolved ideas, but they've already been socialized, and in a few years they'll be socializing their sons.

Our privileged classes, elite and haute bourgeois alike, don't really need to produce men who are rapists, any more than they need to produce men who are good at soccer or football or lacrosse. What they need to produce are men who win contests, who modulate effortlessly between competing against their friends and allying with their friends to fend off the challenges of outsiders. Past their early twenties, men like Brett Kavanaugh are not supposed to live in big raucous groups and have drunken parties every weekend where they manipulate or force women to have sex with them. Men like Brett Kavanaugh are supposed to grow up and become basketball dads and leave their libertine ways behind.

And they mostly do. They learn to channel their aggression into socially sanctioned pursuits, such as expanding their professional, social, political, and financial power. They play by the rules, except when they don't. (What's a little cronyism among friends?) Webs of complicity—or as the men themselves would likely put it, brotherly bonds with one's oldest pals—become embedded in larger networks through which an intangible currency circulates.

Credibility *should* rest on reason, on a person's track record of truthfulness, on the presence or absence of corroboration. But like any other currency, it ultimately rests on a consensus about value, about what matters. This is the magical scaffolding of Brett Kavanaugh's good name. He's this perfect person, the nicest person. He just is. And now he is the law. +

BILL JENKINS, *PASS.* 2012, VENT COVER WITH ROCKS. 23.5 × 15.5 × 2". PHOTO BY CATHY CARVER. COURTESY OF THE ARTIST.

BASE CULTURE

Lyle Jeremy Rubin

M Y FIRST AND ONLY WAR TOUR took place in Afghanistan in 2010. I was a marine lieutenant then, a signals intelligence officer tasked with leading a platoon-size element of eighty to ninety men, spread across an area of operations the size of my home state of Connecticut, in the interception and exploitation of enemy communications. That was the official job description, anyway. The yearlong reality consisted of a tangle of rearguard management and frontline supervision. Years before Helmand Province, Afghanistan, however, there was Twentynine Palms, California. From the summer of 2006 to the summer of 2007, I was trained as a lance corporal in my military occupational specialty of tactical data systems administration (a specialty I would later jettison after earning my officer commission in Quantico, Virginia, in 2008). My schoolhouse was the Marine Corps Communication-Electronics School, which was abbreviated as MCCES, pronounced "mick-sess." For many, the wider location became "Twentynine Stumps" or "the Stumps." But for me it just became "the Palms."

Our time at the Palms was preceded by three weeks of marine combat training at Camp Geiger, North Carolina, and, before that, twelve weeks of marine basic training at Parris Island, South Carolina. The progression from Parris Island to Geiger to the Palms signaled, on the face of it, a slow return from barbaric intrigue to the tedium of civilization. Boot camp was everything you might have gathered from films you've seen or think you've seen. There were the recruits on the deck, scrubbing away with their scuzz brushes, like confused termites laboring about impenetrable wood. There were the recruits being called up to the quarterdeck, push-upping or crunching to untold woofs from the mad hats. There were the mad hats themselves, emptying footlockers as we stood at postshower attention, and there were their subsequent commands to have us dress up by the numbers. There were the orders for recruits to hit recruits, and there was the corralling or prodding of recruits into hard surfaces where the laws of physics finished the job. There was the rifle drill position that was called the "fag wrist" and the bayonet training that sounded off with "Kill kill kill haji!" (The last bayonet charge occurred during the Korean War.) There was the platoon sergeant who would abruptly emerge in the squad bay frothing, unhinged, and maybe drunk, flipping over everything within spitting distance, propelling recruits to vault off their racks before the whirlwind struck, all while he ranted about every person who had ever wronged him.

So not long after my boot camp graduation, there was also something appropriate about watching junior enlisted men assemble at a weapons expo to get the autograph of the actor R. Lee Ermey of *Full Metal Jacket* fame. He looked frail and friendly, not at all the drill instructor for whom he had become known. Apart from the obvious irony of active-duty personnel fetishizing Stanley Kubrick's antiwar film—at a weapons expo, no less—the way the marines lined up for his signature, like excited schoolboys amid the merchandise, struck me as at odds with the myth of the solemn warfighter set apart from the puerile hustle of American life. I hadn't abased myself, on my knees, scrubbing toilets at the level and in constant sight of my drill instructor's crotch just to join a club. That would have been, in the words of Ermey's Gunnery Sergeant Hartman, "Mickey Mouse shit."

I F BOOT CAMP HAD introduced in me a keen awareness of my country's violence and the overcompensating sentiment that went with it, my experience in school at Twentynine Palms took longer to register as a narrative. For a while, all I retained was unrelated impressions: a sulfuric stench that would come with the rain, something of which, years later, I would get a second whiff during the wet sand season in Afghanistan, or the sight of meth heads and tweakers (that's what we called them) on the public bus I'd take to pick up semi-niche items understocked on base, like cheap portable irons or rechargeable Bluetooth headphones. More trundled through the Walmart Supercenter of Yucca Valley, my final destination. They were alive with death, and their deathliness had an aggression to it, one that burned with a spirited rage. When I think back to their torn visages and beady eyes, I can't help but wonder how much of my paranoid apprehension of the locals was shaped by private insecurities. Professional-class rearing fused with entry-level military training had made me a nervous wreck. Whether I was outside the gate in the Mojave surrounded by what I imagined to be menacing junkies, or outside the wire in the Helmand surrounded by what I knew to be poppy farmers, my head was on a swivel, and the countenances of outsiders all took on the same cast. Writing this now, I'm embarrassed by the comparison. There is something ludicrous about relating foot patrols in a combat zone to Bluetooth shopping a few miles beyond a stateside base. But there was a way in which I had been conditioned, before and during my military years, to be suspicious of the outside, wherever that outside might be.

When I returned to the Palms for predeployment training in 2009, this time as an officer, I was briefed on how best to avoid killing scrappers during live fire exercises. These most dauntless of addicts, along with equally desperate immigrants, would trespass on small arms, artillery, and rocket or missile impact areas to scrounge for shell casings, unexploded ordnance, and other scrap metal they hoped to cash in at recycling centers or hawk on the black market. During the summer, some would expire from thirst. During the winter, some of their already frail bodies would freeze to death. Some would self-detonate with what they had found. I can't verify this online, but I remember one brief including incidents where some met their end amid the live fire itself. Some were chased down, cuffed, and sent to prison, sometimes for years. Some were deported.

I didn't think much of any of this at the time, during either my hurried excursion in 2009 or my extended stay in 2006 and 2007. This was how it was, this is how it had been for a while, and I had yet to allow myself to explore the haunting realities hiding behind such a thin layer of bureaucratic instruction. Others had taken on a superior posture toward the region's lumpenproletariat, much like they did toward most civilians. The lumpen were lazy and undisciplined, the sort that warranted whatever came their way. In a word made popular on Parris Island, they were *nasty*. That they had managed to find themselves in such a grotesquely helpless state made them all the nastier. I'd like to think the cause of my indifference lay elsewhere. In retrospect, I wasn't so much contemptuous as I was afraid, afraid of what their bare existence said about me and my place in the world. The thought that I had been living at the expense of others had crossed my mind more than once, but to see that cost in the flesh was too much to bear, and so I didn't think about it.

Occasionally I'd hear stories about marines who were assaulted by resentful townies or desperate transients. The "town," as a unified organism, was presented as hostile. I recall the station or unit commands issuing warnings and advisories of their own. Avoid X, Y, or Z bar. Do your Q, R, or S activities on base. W area is off-limits during T hours. Perhaps the superciliousness of some of my peers was related to this underlying fear. We were all eager to prove our toughness, yet anxious about having had it easier than the people we saw ourselves being superior to in strength, courage, and integrity. That is to say, we were soft, and those we considered losers were hard. This self-emasculating possibility, along with an unsurprising bias toward the status quo and propensity to follow orders, conspired to make us uninterested in their plight. At one level this was to be expected. We didn't sign up to help the stray or downtrodden. But according to the agitprop or many of our own self-rationalizations, this was precisely what we had volunteered for: We were supposed to be nation builders, culturally sensitive agents of humanitarian intervention, winners of hearts and minds. That we were nothing of the sort, even in relation to our compatriots, did not bode well.

Meanwhile, marines were being discharged dishonorably or on bad conduct for adultery. Marines were divorcing after walking in on partners committing adultery. Marines were being punished for pummeling the people they walked in on, or the people they walked in on were being punished for pummeling them. Marines were marrying locals either because they were young and in love or because they were milking the system through contract marriages. Marines were caught in threesomes or foursomes or some other nthsomes. Sometimes these tales were delivered with a lightheartedness they may have deserved. Sometimes they came loaded with hints of harassment, abuse, and rape. New arrivals each week contained a trickle of female marines, who promptly became the quarry of at least half the battalion, and their faces tended to undergo a jaded metamorphosis as the weeks progressed. In short, we (and by "we" I mostly mean the men) were acting like a privileged caste. Surrounded by a desert of suffering, we nourished our emotional lives by inflicting suffering on those we cherished or said we cherished.

If we weren't the ones doing the direct inflicting, we at least took our entertainment from the spectacle of other people's affliction.

Pain is weakness leaving the body. Most had internalized this boot camp mantra, and all had endured some form of arduous labor, torment, and sacrifice in the service. The marines I served with at the Palms hailed from a vast range of backgrounds, although few came from the upper reaches of society. In civilian life, many occupied lower rungs, and many found themselves in similarly oppressive situations on base (especially the women). But in relation to the area addicts and immigrants, we enjoyed our privilege and whatever semblance of narcissistic happiness or gratification it afforded. Often that enjoyment came at the expense of fellow marines and was frequently of a desperate, survivalist character, a kind of necessary Keynesian stimulus at the level of the individual. It was compulsive, cruel banter to keep the self-esteem sufficiently inflated, basically. But at least we weren't torturing ourselves for a fix, like those tweaking and scrapping on the outskirts. The political economy of the Palms was treating us better than it was treating them.

T HEN WE WENT to Afghanistan. On that front, I would prefer not to have to say anything at all. The commodification of America's wars tends to know no bounds. It also happens to be unavoidable for those of us who have taken part in them. I can't really speak about my past or my politics without risking the encouragement and benefits of America's cheap yet profitable obsession with war, an obsession that predates the now ancient-seeming date of my war's putative beginning, September 11, 2001. If the war involved any dignity, it is not deserving of an American audience that will make instantaneous patriotic sap from it. The mawkish standard requires pushback.

What I will say is that the explosions were regular and the combat was minimal. I was more a spectator than a participant. No matter how close I got, I was always at a remove. I never pulled the trigger, not even in the foot patrol that resulted in my Combat Action Ribbon (CAR). Everyone on that patrol was awarded the CAR. Rounds were fired by us and at us, and at one point we were forced to sprint and hit the prone behind some shrubbery. But after the initial fire had subsided and we had been ensconced long enough to feel comfortable, we took photographs of each other with someone's cell phone, waiting for the air strike that never came. I still have the photograph of me in the prone, which I later posted on Facebook for the likes. It's still on Facebook with the likes. A peasant walked toward us from the village we had been gunning down, and I was worried he might be strapped. I tried to be a good officer by ensuring the farmer was forced to lift up his shawl before approaching us any further. The man casually lifted, and I was ashamed the moment he did. He went about his day and we went back to base. We tried our best to follow in the steps of the men ahead of us, just as we had done on the way out, to minimize the chance of triggering a mine, but we were too thirsty and exhausted at that point to do it right. We were greeted by vehicles and cold bottled water not far beyond the base entrance, and we doused each other as we hopped on the truck beds and let ourselves be escorted back to the headquarter unit's guarded Shangri-la, where everyone boasted through the evening.

During my most frank interludes in Afghanistan, I'd refer to the grotesque mess as the amusement park ride. There was little amusement for the inhabitants of the villages we were leveling or the tenders of the opium fields we were burning. There wasn't much amusement for the marines being hit the hardest either, although they had a tendency to surprise when it came to their capacity to be amused. But for so many, myself included, the point, or one point anyway, was to be amused. This should come off as trite. Marines would be the first to concede it. So would the reporters, novelists, and filmmakers who narrate their exploits. But the observation must be closed off from the ethical debate in which it is embedded. The culture has deemed it kosher to note that marines have fun lighting shit on fire, blowing shit up, and dodging death. But when you, and especially as a current or former member of the armed services, move from this basic empirical observation to the question of whether the larger enterprise is just and necessary, you violate a taboo. That day we were shot at but ended up all right, we were amused. That day, months later, when a replacement for one of my marines stepped off on the same patrol, landed on an IED, and died, he was dead. Whether anyone was amused immediately before or after that death is a question we don't ask.

The list of questions never asked bends toward the infinite: What were the mercenaries I kept meeting truly there for? The ones who couldn't help letting me know how much they were making for a six-month stint? The ones who kept on bragging about raking in six figures, and how those numbers always paled in comparison to what their bosses were making back in Maryland or Virginia? What about those contractors, specifically in the intel world, who foisted a never-ending line of gadgetries on my men to be field-tested and then shipped off to the global marketplace? Why did the gear never work? Why was it so unwieldy? Why did it slow down ops, and why did no one seem to care that it usually had to be escorted by those with the appropriate clearance, which meant putting my guys at risk from point A to point B and back again? Why so much acceptance in the face of ambitious captains who wanted to be majors, ambitious majors who wanted to be lieutenant colonels, ambitious lieutenant colonels who wanted to be full birds, ambitious full birds who wanted to be generals, and ambitious generals who wanted an extra star, all putting other lives on the line to make it happen?

Then one time I watched a group of marines obliterate the corner of a remote hamlet with the totality of their arsenal, from the M4 carbine to the M249 light machine gun to the M240 machine gun to the Mk 19 grenade launcher to the AT4 recoilless smoothbore weapon to the FGM-148 Javelin missile to the BGM-71 TOW missile. They'd lost friends, they were bitter, and they had come to see their surroundings not only as hostile, as was already the case back in Twentynine Palms, but as damnable. They were heading home soon and had some underutilized weapon systems to play with. I took pictures along with everyone else. I told myself there was something I didn't know that justified the carnage I was consuming.

Then the time, while pissing on a small outpost before heading off to the next base on a convoy, I spotted a detainee crouched in a make-shift wooden box not much larger than his crouch. I found the sight wretched enough to jot it down in a notebook, but nothing more. Or the time I was asked to make sure another detainee sharing a back seat with me in an armored vehicle wasn't allowed to pull his shawl above his forearms, for fear he would find a way to remove the zip ties from his wrists. I watched the kid, a teenager really, shiver for fifteen minutes—it was wintertime in Helmand, and at an altitude of well over three thousand feet, the temperature was in the high twenties—before relenting and allowing him to cover up. He looked too much like my marines.

Fifteen minutes was a long time to discover the humanity of some-one sitting a couple feet to my left. Then again, I had spent over twenty-five years lapping up a political culture that had erased everything that made him human, so maybe it was more startling it took only fifteen.

That other provisional detainee cage would likely have failed detainee treatment regulations at a battalion or regimental base. The razing of that community was easier to accept because we were a good kilometer from the shells' impact. So many of the field and general officers at division-level headquarters were able to keep congratulating themselves for a job well done because they relied on secondary or tertiary reports from company officers looking to keep their jobs or advance their careers. And if their superiors ever bothered to visit the front, they did so under curated conditions.

The locals and vagabonds skirting around my schoolhouse in the Southern California desert were almost always, for me and my peers, over there. They were the immiserated background, and the only time we allowed them to come to the fore was when we skittishly passed them while going about our mundane chores. Either that or when they became a problem. When they scuffled with a member of our tribe at a bar or on the street out of resentment, or when they slinked through the perimeter of our impact zones in anguished search of some means of subsistence, they were liable to enter our sights. Some at that point were then chased, rounded up, and maybe even put away. That we never thought it was our responsibility to help them somehow, to serve and protect them, as it were, seems reasonable. It wasn't our job. However, according to the prognosticators of the postmodern military, working as trustworthy, socially responsible facilitators of a diverse and healthy civil society was exactly our job: David Petraeus had told me so in the *Counterinsurgency Field Manual*, David Kilcullen told me the same thing in *The Accidental Guerrilla*, as did David Galula in *Counterinsurgency Warfare*. And everyone serious agreed with the Davids.

I'll never forget the exhilaration in a battalion briefing room as forward-deployed Drug Enforcement Agency operatives crowed about their latest opium raid and burning of poppy fields. And it took a while for these memories to hark back to triumphant newspaper headlines or TV news segments of police swoops on Mojave meth labs. The juxtaposition of the Palms and the Helmand is not a perfect fit. Discerning the continuities at all is not something that came easily to me. Too many received wisdoms got in the way, especially the dichotomies among them: jargony distinctions like "schoolhouse" and "the fleet," predeployment and deployment, or stateside and "in country" (originally "Indian Country"). Also more widely recognized ideological divides between domestic and foreign, national and global that have always, in turn, been attended by the tacit distinctions between civilization and chaos, enlightenment and areas of darkness. I had been trained my entire life not to connect what, in the course of a slow and painful unlearning—an unlearning of which this essay is very much a part—I am now so insistent must connect. The gated perimeters, violent diversions, and rent faces in the background are not just over there, in the theater of war. They have come home, or were part of our home to begin with, exported and imported a thousand times over, across the earth. They are borderless, even ubiquitous.

LOOKING OVER MY old emails to family and friends from Afghanistan, I am struck by how little distance I've traveled in terms of what I understand. I am still inundated by a torrent of ghastly revelations I can neither fully contain nor channel. I still find available mediums of communication offensive to the task of honest speech. I still intuit something emancipatory about this paralysis, this failure I'm subject to. I still adore my marines just as much as I am beset by our shared past. So much of my daily routine I continue to think of as an act of moral quarantine: still stuck in the Afghan muck, I obsess over my bit in the killing and beseech others to join me in the obsession. Most of all, I still understand my misadventure, as I did in my most candid and tortured dispatches, more as a lesson about the meaning of the United States than a lesson about "war."

I now conceptualize the society I came from and the war to which I went as part of the same grotesque amusement park ride. If I have discovered anything since my homecoming, it is not that I never came home. It is not that my soul resides in Afghanistan. It is that my home has lost its peaceful veneer, stripped bare, like Twentynine Palms. An American who leaves for war never leaves America. The war that is America, rather, comes to the American. The war is the society and the society is the war, and one who sees that war sees America.

This is what becoming radicalized has meant for me, and it has been jolting. Not long after my discharge in 2011, while I was struggling with severe panic attacks and depression, close friends convinced me to try psychedelics. I found it healing at first, but the last trip landed me in an emergency room. Everyone had become a demon and I was the only human left in their company. From time to time, the psychosis reverberates. I have trouble with elevators and subways, especially when I'm intoxicated, it's off-hours, and I'm approaching absolute aloneness. Once I shared a metro car with only one other passenger, a man stretched out asleep across the seats, and I became convinced the car would never stop, the man would never wake up, and I would never escape. I would never die either. In *Four Quartets*, T. S. Eliot describes being on an "underground train" that stopped "too long between stations." He saw "behind every face the mental emptiness deepen / Leaving only the growing terror of nothing to think about." For me the terror runs deeper, where resonances of finality and emptiness are replaced by ones of eternity and hell. I originally attributed the contours of the bad trip to a gnawing sense of guilt. Another telling would have underlined the psychic costs of being shaken into seeing the killing fields behind the facade, even as everyone around you just kept seeing the facade. Such an isolating awakening can trigger, even without the self-reproach, an alienation akin to biblical doom.

I have tried my best to keep the treasured ones close, although I have lost a few along the way, and others have threatened to break with me. These have included fellow veterans. One fought in Israel's Lebanon war in 2006, around the same time I was making my way through the boot camp crucible. The other served as one of my most able linguists in Afghanistan. The latter is a Purple Heart recipient from a subsequent deployment, although he saw a great deal the first go-around, and we formed a bond in between the outbursts. I even got him and his wife to befriend my grandparents once he was out of active duty and attending graduate school in New York. My grandfather, who survived being shot in the head at Iwo Jima, has been doing therapy work with combat veterans at the VA for years. He still asks about my buddy.

I've had exchanges with each that imply recognition of the porousness of authorized propaganda. The linguist, for example, admits the war in Afghanistan has been a disaster and there is no hopeful path forward. But both, despite their time spent on the edge of the abyss, remain beholden to a colonial logic. For them the United States and Israel are flawed but necessary bulwarks against barbarism. For me the empire is rooted in the barbarism it pretends to oppose. It is exhausting having to declaim the same talking points over and over again: That the majority of the United States' official adversaries were once clients and allies. That almost every intervention comes with an ex post facto assessment from the government acknowledging the failure of the mission. That investigative reporters and historians almost always unearth internal documents betraying motives that not only run counter to public rationales but undermine all claims to humanitarian intent. That the United States supplies the world with a preponderance of its weapons and fuels a plurality of its animosities. That the United States is the only power to have ever dropped the bomb, that it did so twice, and that it did so not to end a world war (a war that was about to end anyway) but to launch what became a half-century-long cold war on superior footing. While not alone as a global malefactor, the United States is the world leader in conventional foreign invasions since 1945, with 12; has engineered at least 38 coups or regime changes since the Spanish American War of 1898; and has offered direct military support and training to dozens of governments with no regard for human rights. The United States incarcerates the most people today, both in absolute and relative terms. It has incarcerated the most people for at least thirty-some-odd years, and it either led the world in its incarceration rate or trailed closely behind the Soviet Union and South Africa for the preceding decades. As early as 1976, one study described America's rate as the "highest in the world and still rising." By any standard, the United States empire ranks among the world's most formidable producers of violence, and one would be hard-pressed to defend such all-consuming production on liberal democratic grounds.

I read Michael Walzer's *The Company of Critics* en route to Afghanistan. I was still a reluctant believer in the gospel of American righteousness then, and Walzer was the last, never mind the most refined, preacher I could believe. When he wrote in *Arguing About War* that the global fight against terrorism was "not backward looking and retributive, but forward looking and preventive," that was enough to keep me faithful. Walzer had come after a more vulgar procession of neoconservative evangelists like Bill Kristol and Robert Kagan. These were the men who had ushered me to the right as an idealistic high school student, and I became quite the campus missionary when, weeks into my freshman year of college, the two towers fell. I became an opinion columnist and an op-ed editor for the school newspaper, where I penned romantic paeans to the democratizing missions in Iraq and Afghanistan. One of my final contributions was a somber explanation for why I felt obligated to follow in my grandfather's footsteps and don the uniform. But by the third month of my deployment, even the subtle apologetics of Walzer struck me as dangerously absurd. If only Walzer and others could see what I saw. If only those who saw it with me could really see it. +

MINA CHEON, *UMMA RISES: TOWARDS GLOBAL PEACE*. 2017, YVES KLEIN BLUE DIP PAINTING, ARCHIVAL DIGITAL PRINT ON CANVAS. 30 × 40". COURTESY OF THE ARTIST AND ETHAN COHEN GALLERY.

CONVERSATIONS WITH BONGJUN

Christina Nichol

I N THE MID-'90S, when I taught English at a foreign-language high school in Pusan, South Korea, I asked my students to keep English-language journals throughout the semester. When they weren't writing about the mental agony of being "study machines," they mourned the conflict between North and South Korea. Korea, they wrote, was a divided heart, and reunification their greatest hope.

At the time I wasn't particularly interested in Korean politics. Whenever I didn't have to be at the high school, I was hiking to the top of sun-dappled, bouldery cliffs, reading Korean Zen poetry, or teaching English to two extremely unorthodox Buddhist monks. These monks lived in a temple at the edge of the city located directly behind an *Indiana Jones and the Temple of Doom*–themed amusement park. They meditated while the *chunga chunga whee zee hee* carnival sounds blared around them.

For some reason, the English words the monks most wanted to learn were the sounds animals make in America. When I explained that American cows say *moo*, one of the monks sagely replied, "Korean cows say *eum mae*. American cows are much more polite!" In exchange for English animal noises, they would teach me the Korean onomatopoeia for different types of rain: *churook churook*, or *dduk dduk dduk*.

After our lessons, we would usually sit on the veranda watching the rain or the moon. Looking back, I spent a lot of my time in Korea looking at the moon. The moon reflected in the water fountains and the little droplets of rainwater, the moon shining on the baby Buddha statues in the treetops—it felt like an all-consuming reality, or one mind pervading all events. I felt lonely most of the time I was in Korea, but it didn't bother me. The moon endowed everything with a strange, artistic feeling.

Other times, we would go inside and watch Hollywood movies like *Forrest Gump* and *Easy Rider* while eating the choco pies and drinking the bottles of Chivas Regal that businessmen had left for Buddha. Sometimes the monks would watch court cases on the Buddhist cable station, but whenever I asked what was happening they would slap the floor and say, "No problem!" They seemed to want to protect me from knowing anything about the country's political scandals. "You have no attachment to Korea," one monk always said, "so we are the same!"

But sometimes, late at night, the monks would turn off the TV, dim their lava lamps, and turn on the stereo. (They had the best speaker setup in all of Pusan.) We would lie on the heated floor, all of us listening to some kind of underground music with words I couldn't understand, but through which I could feel a profound, spiritual pathos. My Korean and their English weren't good enough to explain what those underneath stories were really about. Instead, the monks just took care of me: fed me choco pies, scared away the ghosts that lurked around the carnival, drove me to the airport, the bus stop, and the train station. They continued to let me in even after I accidentally poked a hole in their paper doors with my finger, gave me endless cups of tea and pillows to nap on, told me jokes. Above all, they gave me space to be a confused twentysomething who liked to look at the moon. They didn't think that was weird; instead, they also came out to look at the moon. When I left Korea, I vowed that whenever I met a Korean who had come to the US, I would try to take care of that person the way the monks had taken care of me. I didn't anticipate that this would take fifteen years.

B ONGJUN FIRST contacted me because he had read a novel I'd written and, as a South Korean, said he could identify with the novel's protagonist, a foreigner who comes to America. Also, like my protagonist, his favorite movie was *Jesus Christ Superstar*. He wrote that even though he was a physicist, after listening to Garrison Keillor on NPR, he had developed a respect for both Lutherans and English majors. He told me that he wanted to write his own book.

"What kind of book do you want to write?" I typed back unenthusiastically, assuming it would be something boring about physics formulas.

"A book about how jokes work," he wrote back.

Oh! I thought. This sounds like the kind of man for me!

I didn't know at the time that he was interested in how jokes work because he wanted to figure out how humor could topple dictators and children of former dictators, specifically South Korea's president at the time, Park Geun-hye, the daughter of Korea's old strongman dictator, Park Chung-hee.

O NE VALENTINE'S DAY several years ago, a few months after we had met, Bongjun told me he was thinking of getting American citizenship. We were driving back from a hike along the Northern California coast, where the silhouetted pine tree cliffs resemble those on the east coast of Korea.

"Really?" I asked, staring at him in the driver's seat. "Why?"

"With an American passport I can go to North Korea," he said. "I want to teach them science and how to build lasers. Will you come with me?"

"Are you serious?" I asked. "Don't they kidnap people? Or force them to work in labor camps? Haven't you read that Barbara Demick book?"

"No. But we grew up with all those stories from North Korean defectors who always had some agenda. You never hear about the defectors who came to South Korea and were so shocked by all the homeless people that they went back home again. The only thing we know for sure about North Korea is that all the children there learn musical instruments. I hear the land is very beautiful. Our most beautiful mountains are there. In North Korea you can still see what the Asian mind was like in the old times, uncorrupted by capitalism. The people are very sincere and simple. They get happy at happy things and sad at sad things. I think you would like the people so much. They don't know how to . . . what is the word? Prevaricate?"

"When I was living in Pusan everyone in North Korea was starving," I said. "There were recipes in the newspaper for how to cook with weeds. They don't even produce anything."

"Their currency is choco pies," he said with a cautious optimism. "And they export some furs to Russia. Otter, badger, and rabbit. And some unregulated pills. I think they also have high-quality plastic pipes and some kind of jewelry that purifies the blood."

We stopped at a Shell station and Bongjun got out to pump gas. I watched him as he cleaned the windshield. He wore thick glasses and had his hair up in the spiked South Korean style that had last been fashionable in 1997. He carried pens in his front pocket inside an actual pocket protector. We hadn't been together that long and I was still dubious about the relationship. I come from a family of artists, teachers, and other impractical people who lean toward the spiritual nature of things, and I felt like my family was pushing him on me a little, as if everyone had agreed that we all needed some science to ground us. My mother's partner had tacked up an enormous poster of the periodic table in his bathroom. My mother had acquired a pocket-size periodic table and now studied it while blow-drying her hair. She had become enamored with the story of gases, how most elements in the world are reactive, but how a few noble gases—helium, neon, argon, krypton, xenon, and radon—are basically unreactive.

After meeting Bongjun, my aunt had said, "He notices all the details, hummingbirds in their little nests. He brings blessings." Then she looked up the word *science* in the dictionary. "It means 'to shed, to discard ignorance,'" she read. "We need this type of influence in our family."

When I told Bongjun that my aunt had looked up the word *science* and how it meant to discard ignorance, he said, "Hmm, that's interesting. I thought it meant cause and effect in Korean."

Ha ha, I now thought. Wait until they hear that Bongjun wants to move to North Korea.

When he got back in the car I asked, "What about their crazy leader?"

"Americans don't understand the North Koreans," he said, and then proceeded to tell me the following story: If a mother leaves her child and the child feels abandoned, and then the mother returns home, the child has three possible reactions. One is that the child runs as fast as he can and hugs the mother. The second is that the child gets angry and throws a tantrum, but he still wants the attention of the mother. And the third is that the child doesn't care anymore and ignores the mother. The third child's reaction is the most dangerous because he has stopped caring and has shut down his heart. "But the second reaction is North Korea," Bongjun said. "He is angry but only because he feels abandoned. He still cares."

"Hmm," I said, noncommittally.

"Imagine what it's like there. During the Korean War the US carpet-bombed them. There was nothing left standing. But the US still refuses to sign a peace treaty. As our good president Kim Dae-jung recognized, in the Asian mentality we just need to save face. If a Korean face is saved he will give two for one. So much can be accomplished. The United States doesn't understand this."

I HADN'T BEEN BACK to South Korea in a decade and a half, but according to the Western news media it looked like all my students' suffering had been worth it: the country was thriving. South Korea had made shrewd financial investments in science, IT, manufacturing, K-pop, and skin-care products, and now it was the future. It was the new, hip, aspirant Asian country, catapulted onto the world stage by K-dramas. It was a B-boy and K-pop heartthrob soap-opera nation: laser shows in the streets, superfast internet, Samsung, Hyundai, LG, Gangnam style; Koreans now even poured melted cheddar cheese onto their barbecues. Their vanity factor had surpassed our own: 20 percent of the country was getting eye and jaw operations.

In Seoul you could spend the day seeing and being seen in experiential themed cafés with dogs, cats, raccoons, or even two sheep wandering around. It was a land of kitsch, where you could order a cotton-candy latte, or an iceberg macchiato. You could spoon cake out of a flowerpot or sip coffee out of tiny toilet bowls. You could even order juice the color of your favorite chakra and drink it while getting your tarot cards read. South Korea had industrialized and grown their economy, trendiness, and café-motif power so rapidly that, as far as I understood, reuniting with the North would dilute all their progress. I imagined they no longer wanted to do this.

One afternoon as we were walking through Armstrong grove, an old-growth redwood forest close to where I live, Bongjun told me he didn't think he could move back to South Korea. When he had visited recently, the spirit of unity he had grown up with was gone. "Now people only worry about their paychecks, what kind of car they drive, or which elite schools to send their children to. Few people can even afford to get married anymore. A lot of Korean men go to Russia or Vietnam to find wives because Korean women will only marry a man with strong economic power. Most people can't afford to buy a house. As we say in Korea, 'The landlord is more powerful than the Lord.'"

The stillness of the redwood-rinsed air slowed our conversation and for a while we walked in silence. The Korea I remembered wasn't anything like the one Bongjun described.

Bongjun explained further: "In the 1990s, when you were there, the country was improving. People were working hard to build a better society together. They were optimistic. There was an emotional momentum that things would be OK. But after the economic crisis in 1997, Western investors ordered the Korean government to lift all the restrictions and regulations and branded it a 'probusiness environment.' This created some billionaires, but the poor people fell into an endless hole. People's mind-sets changed. And then they got nostalgic, so we elected the stupid president we have now, the daughter of the second dictator, and the dictatorship returned. These days Hyundai and Samsung are our only employers. Korea is kind of like George Bush's dream country. We've started calling it Hell Korea. Even North Korea doesn't suffer like the South Koreans do now."

"What do you mean, they don't suffer?" I asked. I reminded him of the starvation.

"They don't suffer morally like South Korea. Kim Il-sung fought against the Japanese traitors. He was a kind of war hero at first. All those idealists had a project to believe in. It didn't work out, but imagine what it's like for South Koreans, for those who have to work for the elite, for those who collaborated with Japan and got rich when Japan colonized Korea. We have a popular saying in Korea now: 'People who sold the nation live well for three generations. People who fought for the nation suffer for three generations.'"

I didn't know how to respond to this.

"Would you write about this in a book?" Bongjun asked.

"But I write fiction."

"I know. I just mean put in a little hint, like Victor Hugo. Korea has reached the point where they understand the concept of the 99 percent. Maybe if the US succeeds, Korea may follow because we follow everything you do."

SOON AFTER THIS, Bongjun started reading *How to Topple Dictators with Humor* by the Serbian writer Srđa Popović, one of the founders of the Otpor! movement, which helped topple Slobodan Milošević. Actually, that was the title of the Korean version. I started reading the English version, called *Blueprint for Revolution: How to Use Rice Pudding, Lego Men, and Other Nonviolent Techniques to Galvanize Communities, Overthrow Dictators, or Simply Change the World.*

Popović describes various maneuvers people can perform to make their oppressors look ridiculous, like letting loose a bunch of ping-pong balls with political messages, so the police have to chase ping-pong balls down the street. Or the way Polish citizens living under Communism protested state television by taking their TVs for a walk every evening in a wheelbarrow. When Bongjun read that section he said, "You couldn't do that in Korea. The TVs are too big."

We were at Bongjun's apartment, sitting on the floor because he has so many bookshelves that there's no room left for a couch. "I don't think Popović's book is that funny," Bongjun said. "Can I tell you a story about our president's father, our second dictator? All the men in my generation know this story and think it's so funny.

"OK."

"Park Chung-hee, our president's father, was a guy who just wanted to go up the ladder in society. He was a schoolteacher, but that didn't really satisfy him, so during the Japanese occupation, before World War II, he decided he wanted to join the Japanese Imperial Guard. The Japanese were policing Korea and they wore this uniform he loved. Because he was so short, he thought if he had a long sword he would look taller.

"There was a Japanese military school in Manchuria, like West Point, but he was too old to be admitted. So he wrote a letter to the head of the school with his own blood. Writing with your blood was a form of strong resolution. Basically he was saying, 'I will be a loyal servant to the Japanese emperor.' That kind of bullshit. This letter even got printed in the newspaper in 1939. After he graduated from military school, he served in Manchuria and fought against the Korean resistance, though he only ended up serving a couple of years. After Japan got defeated, he came back and eventually joined the communist Worker's Party. But South Korea didn't like the Communists, so he got arrested and was sentenced to death. And do you know how he saved his life? By selling out his comrades. He was the only one who survived among them all. So it's funny!"

"How is that funny? That's horrible!"

"Because he lost his dignity. He was so weak and pathetic, kissing the boots of his captors, that he betrayed his friends. Heh heh!"

"But that's still not funny. In order for this guy to be funny, you would have to do something like *Springtime for Hitler*, where you find the most ridiculous aspect of the tyrant and play that up. Maybe you'd have to portray his wife as really naggy or something."

"But that actually happened! He had such funny women problems! His personal philosophy was that what happens below the belly button is no one else's business. Park Chung-hee had so many mistresses. In public his wife kind of portrayed herself as Eva Perón, but she was so jealous that we privately nicknamed her the jealous queen of the nation. The inside story is that she was so jealous that she killed her husband's mistress."

"Wait. The wife killed her husband's mistress?"

"It's a rumor, but there's lots of evidence. The mistress was found dead in a car, shot with a handgun. Her own brother confessed to shooting her. But, first of all, at that time in Korea, in the 1970s, regular people didn't own cars, and they definitely didn't own handguns. Also, her brother had a gun wound in his own leg. Why would he shoot himself in the leg? It was really scandalous. Also, no weapon was found. But then Park got so angry that he killed his wife."

"The dictator killed his own wife?"

"Yes. It's a rumor, but there is lots of evidence. And then a few years later, Kim Jae-gyu, Park Chung-hee's henchman, his right-hand man, killed him."

The low-key way Bongjun narrated all this history was almost as strange as the history itself.

"Park Chung-hee had already been in power for eighteen years, and people were getting tired of him. In the beginning, the economy was growing fast, but then there were some failures, and people started complaining and demanding democracy. But he changed the constitution and was able to dismember the National Assembly and do whatever he wanted to do. After that it was like martial law: we had a curfew, and if anyone was on the street after midnight we had to rush home like Cinderella. So in 1979, one of his right-hand men killed him at a party. The funny thing is they believe everyone at the party was naked."

At this point I really didn't know what to say. Bongjun kept going.

"Our president, Park Geun-hye, is the daughter of Park Chung-hee. So look. Her mom got killed, maybe by her dad. Her dad got killed by his friend. Not long ago the steward of Park Chung-hee's birth home got killed. They found his naked body in the front yard of her father's house. And her two second cousins died in a murder-suicide. I'm telling you, this is one fucked-up family! One of her father's henchmen escaped to America and testified against him. Park Chung-hee hated him so much that many people think this henchman was put in a wood chipper and fed to a nearby chicken farm. So . . . our current president grew up watching all these stories. Imagine what kind of person she is."

I didn't have to ask if he had any funny stories about the current president.

"I didn't tell you about our president. She loves to wear dresses. You can buy a paper-doll kit in Korea and put six hundred different dresses on her," he joked. "She really enjoys going to other countries; she goes to meet the kings and queens in her beautiful dresses, but she is not smart enough to do any business. And she pays so much money to get her hair done, like Marge Simpson. When that ferryboat accident happened and the three hundred schoolchildren died, she was missing for eight hours. Do you know what she was doing? She was getting her hair done. Let me show you the video . . . just a sec."

I STARTED COMPLAINING to Bongjun that all he did was talk about how terrible the South Korean government was. Whenever he emailed me some new depressing fact about South Korea, like a picture of a mayor crying because a hospital facility in his town was shutting down, I would try to remind him of old Korean Zen poems about nature, or the names of fancy Korean teas from Cheju Island: Song of the Wind, Sun-Soaked Hillside, Rainy Day Meditation, Cherry Blossom Explosion. I tried to describe to Bongjun the music that the Korean monks used to listen to.

"Was it like a marching song?" he asked.

"No," I said. "I never heard anyone else listen to this type of music in Korea." I described to Bongjun everything I knew about the monk I was closer to. He had been studying to be a lawyer and had passed his first judicial exams, but then the military fired into a crowd of students and killed many of his friends. I couldn't understand a lot of what he told me because most of his words were in onomatopoeia, like *tang tang* for bullets and *bbibbo-bbibbo* for the sound of a siren. "So then he failed his last exam and became a monk," I said. "He was from Kwangju."

Bongjun had lived in Kwangju. "The people there are very politically progressive," he said. "Kwangju is kind of like the rebellious area of Korea. That is why Park Chung-hee hated them so much. That monk must have been listening to political protest songs. These were prohibited in public during the time you lived there. Those songs were like hidden treasures. Was it this song?"

Bongjun opened his computer and pulled up a song on YouTube with a military marching beat.

"No, that sounds too patriotic," I said.

"OK, wait. There are all kinds of songs," he said.

"It sounded like some kind of techno fugue music for ghosts."

"Techno ghost music? OK, how about this one?"

"Yes, it sounded like that!"

"This song is about Cheju Island, the massacre on Cheju Island under our first dictator, Syngman Rhee, the one the US installed after World War II. It's very dreary.

"This one is a little bit more upbeat. It came out after the massacre at Kwangju. The words go, 'Time passes but the mountains and rivers will remember our loud shouting. So I'm going forward. Anyone who is still alive come join me.' This song has a very cute story behind it."

"Cute story? What are you talking about? In the video everyone is dead!"

"The final day of the Kwangju massacre, everyone gathered at city hall. They had barricaded the building and they were waiting for the government military tanks to come kill them. There were twenty or thirty people still left, and one of them was the spokesperson for the rebel force. He got killed there, and his friends, when they had the funeral, thought he shouldn't die as a bachelor, or his ghost would hold a grudge. There was also another activist who had died, who had mentored the spokesperson, so they decided they should get those two dead people married. They gave them a spirit marriage, and a poet made a song out of it, and then they used this song for the wedding ceremony, so that is why the title is 'March for the Beloved.' And since this was made in such a nice way we started to sing this song at every protest."

O N WALKS, BONGJUN would pick up bits of wood or acorns or point at a crocus flower and declare how *cute* American nature is. Standing in the driveway, when we were getting ready to go somewhere, Bongjun pointed at a black thing that looked like a squashed cockroach. A whole army of them had left purple stains on the concrete. "What is this?" he asked.

"I have no idea," I said. "But hurry! We're late!"

Instead of getting in the car, he stopped someone walking toward him on the sidewalk. "What is this?" he asked, pointing at the squished cockroach.

"That's an olive," the man said.

"Christina, did you know you have an olive tree?"

"Oh. No. Actually I didn't know that," I said.

THERE IS A PART OF ME that loves how much time it takes to attain real insight into anything. Whenever I talked with Bongjun on the phone, the classical, physical world started vibrating a little. But sometimes the minutiae of the quantum world got to be too much and I had to hang up.

When I was at a writing retreat in eastern Oregon, Bongjun called to tell me that he wanted to collaborate on a story that expressed the quantum physics point of view. "Do you mean that you want me to translate physics formulas?" I asked. "I'm not interested in doing that."

"Open your mind, Christina. I'm talking about breaking the norm."

"But people are already breaking the norm in experimental writing. In grammar. In poetry."

"I'm not talking about grammar! I'm talking about breaking the *norm*!"

The wind had started blowing hard and it was difficult to hear. "Which norm?" I asked.

"Norm. N-O-R-M! Open your mind more. You are like some of my students who think that if they study too much science it will kill their souls. Can't you just open your mind? I am talking about making a story where sometimes instead of falling from the tree, the apple goes up."

"Have you ever seen that happen?" I asked. I glanced at a tree and imagined the leaves floating up.

"No. But quantum physics says it's possible."

"THIS RELATIONSHIP makes me feel insane sometimes," I said a few weeks later to my mother over coffee. "I'm tired of being the bossy one, while he gets to be the dreamy one picking up acorns and squashed olives. Do you know Bongjun's idea of paradise? He wants to drink rice wine in a peach orchard while playing political protest songs on his guitar and riding a donkey."

"A donkey? Is that part of his culture?"

"During the Joseon dynasty all the Korean aristocrats rode donkeys. But he had never heard the sound of a donkey before, so he found a YouTube video of ten hours of donkey sounds."

My mother started laughing. I glared at her.

"I'm sorry. I'm sorry," she said, still laughing. "I was just thinking about how on the ukulele, the same two chords play two different songs." She took her ukulele off the coffee table and started strumming, "'Tea for two, and two for tea. Me for you, and you for me.' That's the song Bongjun has been singing. But the same chords play this Santana song. 'You've got to change your evil ways, baby!' That's what *you* keep singing." She was right. Which song was correct for the situation?

M Y RELATIONSHIP with Bongjun improved the morning Donald Trump was elected. That day Bongjun finally admitted that American politicians might be as insane as their North Korean counterparts. There was a joke circulating throughout South Korea that Kim Jong-un was relieved that he wasn't the only crazy world leader anymore. Watching the black limousines in front of Trump Tower, it felt as though we had just voluntarily elected a dictator, a third-world thug. But Bongjun, who had lived under the South Korean military dictatorships of the '80s and early '90s, had a wide-angle lens on the whole situation. "Bad things will happen," he said. "A lot of people will get hurt. Families will get separated. The environment will suffer. And then things will correct themselves."

"But what can we do in the meantime?" I asked.

"What can we do? That is the question! That's why I love that book by Chernyshevsky: *What to Do About Things.*"

"I think it was called *What Is to Be Done?* The Russians have a thing for the passive voice."

A WEEK BEFORE THE ELECTION, we had signed up to attend a political event in Berkeley sponsored by a progressive rabbi. The original title of the event was "How to Keep Hillary Clinton Staying the Course After She Is Elected." Now, standing outside the church to pay our $10 entrance fee with others dressed in mourning clothes, the tenor of the event was funereal.

The rabbi must have mentioned a speech Gandhi made in the 1930s, because I made a note to look up Gandhi's speech from that time. He said something about how benevolence exists outside our sentences and that the meaning of God was "that which is transformed into what ought to be." "We need a new culture," he said. "We need to connect to the new story. The new story is found in the sciences, in quantum physics." I glanced over at Bongjun to see how he was taking this in but couldn't read his expression. Then I went back to taking notes. "The underlying narrative that we live under is that discrete inner particles are made of matter. But the new story that science proves, the *new* story we need to propose to our friends and colleagues—and we'll have a sign-up sheet afterward for our leadership program on how to do that—is that the universe consists of consciousness first, which *then* creates matter. Consciousness comes first. We must respond to the universe with radical amazement." He repeated the phrase *radical amazement* a number of times. "Do not let in the reality police. The reality police are not allowed."

Bongjun wasn't convinced by the talk.

"Why do you Americans always need a new story? Just look at the old story and correct it. You already have titanium. You have nuclear bombs. Why do you need any more powerful tools? Why does there need to be some theory that consciousness comes from matter versus matter comes from consciousness? The religious figures these days are always looking for scientists to prove their theories, but why do they need science? Physicists aren't looking for that kind of power or magic. The US needs to realize they are not the bosses of the world. Is humility *so* hard for Americans that they need to substitute magic instead? Is magic easier than just facing the truth?"

"I suppose . . . yes."

CONFUCIUS SAID THAT by the time he was 50, he understood the will of heaven. By the time he was 60, he had developed the ability to understand another person's perspective. Presumably, according to Confucius, understanding another person's viewpoint requires a higher skill set than knowing the will of heaven.

I imagine Confucius holding the US and Korea in his right and left palms, trying to understand both sides. Since 1993, anytime South Korea has had a conservative president, we've had a liberal one, and vice versa. When they elected the conservative Kim Young-sam, we had Bill Clinton. When they elected the liberal Kim Dae-jung, we had George Bush. When they elected a human rights lawyer, Roh Moo-hyun, we still had

George Bush. But then when they got Lee Myung-bak (whom Bongjun calls Two Megabyte, referring to the size of his brain), we got Obama. When we reelected Obama, they elected Park Geun-hye. A few days before Trump was elected, a million South Koreans took to the streets to protest their president.

I asked Bongjun what was going on. "Remember how our president's mom got killed when she was young? Our president was in her twenties, hidden away and very depressed. So this guy, we call him a Korean Rasputin—he was a monk, then he became a pastor or something and had six wives—it's an interesting story, like your Rajneesh. Anyway, this Korean Rasputin wrote a letter to our president saying, 'I am a messenger of your late mom. Your mom shows up in my dreams. She speaks through me. Your mother has paved the way for you to become a leader, but you are so stupid that you don't know, so you have succumbed to sorrow.' So our president got hooked on this guy. Rasputin also had a daughter, and this lady followed Park Geun-hye around like a little sister. But our president—probably because she has a weak mind—was manipulated by this woman. It's all so fucked up, I can't believe I remember all this shit! Anyway, it just came out in the news that Choi Soon-sil—that's Rasputin's daughter—has been controlling the president and stealing millions of dollars from the nation.

"Oh, but now I remember the funny part. So, until now, North Korea has been really good at playing chicken. They usually say, 'If you don't do this, there will be a war and Seoul will be on fire.' But when they learned that the South Korean president was a puppet of Rasputin, they realized that South Korea is crazier than they thought and started panicking. They're saying, 'Wow. We've really been playing with fire. Those South Korean leaders are real maniacs!'"

B Y THANKSGIVING, protesting in South Korea had become the primary weekend social activity. People cooked bulgogi and sang protest songs on the street. Kids sat on their parents' shoulders and waved little Korean flags, while their parents shook lit torches. "Look," Bongjun said, pointing to a newsclip. "They are playing a song from Kwangju. They are really partying now. Grannies dancing, punching their fists, wearing their sunglasses. But they keep only playing the first verse! Oh, ha ha! A guy just yelled out, 'Don't stop. Play us the second verse! We have to listen to the second verse!'"

In the history of nonviolent revolutions, the critical mass required for regime change is 3.5 percent of the population. At the Thanksgiving table, while the rest of my family bemoaned the state of America, the South Korean protesters had hit 3 percent. Bongjun could barely contain his optimism about the direction South Korea was heading in.

"Are they protesting Trump?" my cousin asked.

"Our president is crazier than Trump," Bongjun said.

A week later, South Korea reached critical mass; 3.5 percent of the South Korean population, almost two million people, chucked their torches and held up the candle app on their phones. At that point a vote was passed to impeach Park Geun-hye.

IN MAY 2017, South Korea elected Moon Jae-in, a progressive human rights lawyer, to the presidency. I was away in Michigan teaching at a boarding school, but Bongjun sent me daily updates about South Korea's progress. Moon's parents had been refugees from North Korea and had settled in Pusan, where Moon's father sold socks. The family was so poor they sustained themselves on dried milk from the Catholic Church. Moon Jae-in and his wife, Kim Jung-sook, met as students when they were protesting Park Chung-hee. Moon Jae-in had been blinded by tear gas, and when he opened his eyes, the first person he saw was Kim Jung-sook, the woman who was holding his head.

After Moon was elected, his wife continued to wear sweat suits and invited a protester to eat noodles with her. The new president worked quickly. "There are a lot of things Moon can do without changing the law," Bongjun said. "He's doing most of it as fast as he can, *bum bum bum*. He ordered the investigation of the Kwangju massacre and the ferryboat accident. And he's trying to go back to the sunshine policy with North Korea."

"What's the sunshine policy?" I asked.

"It's a story about the wind and sun and a traveler. The wind and the sun have a competition to see who can take off the traveler's jacket. The wind blows and the traveler hangs on to the jacket harder and harder. Now it's the sun's turn, and the sun just shines on warmly and the traveler takes off his jacket. So that's the policy our good president Kim Dae-jung first used on North Korea. Instead of going harsh on North Korea, he applied the sunshine story. And it worked. North Korea was starting to open up. But then when Two Megabyte got into power, it went back to the old way, we lost communication, and North Korea developed all the nuclear weapons. North Korea hasn't responded yet, but I think it will happen."

Soon after, Trump tweeted about Little Rocket Man and it looked—briefly—as if we were on the verge of a nuclear war. "I too have a Nuclear Button," he wrote, "but it is a much bigger & more powerful one than his, and my Button works!"

A FEW MONTHS LATER Bongjun called at five in the morning. He was ecstatic, as much as a scientist can be. "Kim Jong-un says he is willing to denuclearize," he said. It was the best thing that had happened to Korea in Bongjun's lifetime. "President Moon is so smart," Bongjun said. "He really psyched out Trump. He told him, 'Because you are so *great* and as *powerful* as the largest star in the Milky Way, Kim Jong-un is now willing to negotiate.' Moon Jae-in is a genius!"

In April, for the first time in thirteen years, a South Korean delegation of artists, K-pop stars, and folk singers traveled to Pyongyang to perform in a concert called "Spring Is Coming." A musician named Kang San-ae, who lives in New York but whose parents were North Korean, also flew to Pyongyang. "He sang a song called 'Raguyo,'" Bongjun said. "I don't know how to translate the title. It's a song about another song that Kang San-ae's father used to sing called 'The Sailor in the Blue Water of Tumen River.' The Tumen River is part of the border between North Korea and China. The song goes like this:

> I've never seen "the sailor in the blue water of Tumen River"
> However, I know that song very well
> Because it was my dad's eighteenth repertoire

"'Eighteenth repertoire' means their favorite song, like their encore song. Have some more soju." Bongjun put his hand on his heart and poured me another glassful. He continued his translation with tears in his eyes:

> I've never been to "snowstorm Hungnam Harbor"
> But I know this song so well because that was my mom's eighteenth repertoire
> I don't have much life left, she would say,
> And that she wanted to visit there before she died

"So this guy, his son, went to Pyongyang a couple weeks ago and sang it, and it resonated. The ice is melting."

I N MAY, DURING the surprise summit meeting between Kim Jong-un and President Moon, we watched the unedited footage that was broadcast live throughout South Korea: President Moon helping Kim Jong-un step across the border into South Korea. Kim Jong-un doing the same, into North Korea. I was riveted—the two Korean leaders talking for half an hour in the forest, on a bridge in the demilitarized zone. One talking, one listening, and then the other talking and the other listening, both of them looking like they had a real connection with each other. They spoke the same language with a politeness I hadn't witnessed in any American politicians in a long time. We watched the unstaged evening scenes with Kim Jong-un's sister and his wife all eating together, Kim Jong-un starting to look bleary-eyed at all the endless traditional singing performances.

"The funny thing is, this summit meeting is influencing other leaders," Bongjun said afterward. "The Kashmir news service says that the politicians in Kashmir referred to the South Korean summit meeting and suggested that India and Kashmir should have a similar summit as well. Even the Taiwanese leader contacted China. She actually proposed to Xi Jinping that they talk."

"I never heard anything about that."

"It's in the Korean news."

A FTER THE SUMMIT, South Koreans began to remark how much more polite the North Korean elite was than their own. They didn't hit airline stewardesses on the head with rolled-up newspapers if their noodles weren't cooked properly, or have tantrums because their macadamia nuts weren't served on a plate, both of which happened with Cho Hyun-ah, otherwise known as the macadamia nut queen. *Naengmyun*, North Korea's traditional cold noodle dish, was suddenly fashionable in South Korea.

" C AN I SHOW YOU this picture of Pyongyang from Ddanzi News?" Bongjun asked one morning, putting his computer in front of my face.

"So here are three people. This guy used to be a judge but during Two Megabyte's time he got fired. This woman is a North Korean defector. This guy's a reporter who has been traveling to North Korea for the last ten years. They are all talking about how most people think of North Korea as very poor. So this reporter is showing this picture of Pyongyang. All these people are using cell phones and wearing skinny jeans. Here's an iPad with a menu on it. This department store is filled with suitcases, electric bikes, all those things. Here's an Italian restaurant with spaghetti and pizza. Actually, their pizza doesn't look that exciting."

"But can the average North Korean go there?" I asked.

"The reporter says that's what everyone asks. He says yes."

I agreed that this was amazing but asked if we could talk about something besides North Korea. This did not register. "Christina, have you seen how beautiful these pictures of North Korea are? These mountains look like the Alps. For so long we believed these people were our enemies." Now he had tears in his eyes again.

"The Marin Art and Garden Center is also really beautiful," I said. I wanted to explain to Bongjun how at the Marin Art and Garden Center, which I'd visited the day before with my nephew, no one was thinking about North Korea. My nephew and I wandered through the rose garden reading all the weird rose names, like Anemone and Aloha and White Pet. "Sometimes I just want to be a simple American person," I told Bongjun. "We should go to this new beer pub in Alameda my brother was telling me about."

"But first can I read you what this one Korean guy in the comments section says? He says, 'When we're united with North Korea, I want to go to that beautiful mountain and build a kiosk and sell ramen to tourists.'"

I gave up. We weren't going to talk about roses or breweries. "OK, just tell me. What else are they saying?"

"It's so funny. This guy says, 'I want to go there when we become reunited, but we should put restrictions so we don't just build cheap love motels.' Someone else says, 'Soon there will be these telephone poles and wooden decks.' This guy says, 'Rainbow-colored signs will cover the sky: Pusan Restaurant, Taejon Restaurant, Cheongju Restaurant.' This guy says, 'When it's hot it will be killer to go there and eat *naemyun*. The North will come here and eat fermented stingray.' Another guy says, 'I want to go backpacking there. Now we will have our very own Switzerland.' The RV business is doing really well. Before, South Korea wasn't really big enough for anyone to own an RV because you can drive from top to bottom in one day. But now they are talking about making a train that starts in South Korea and goes through North Korea and connects to Europe. Koreans are so used to the notion of living on an island. And then all of a sudden we realize that we are not an island anymore, and that gives you a very positive sensation!"

I made the mistake of showing my mom and her partner the videos of Kim Jong-un and Moon Jae-in talking together and of the laser dance the Korean artists performed for Kim Jong-un the evening of the summit meeting. There were barbed-wire fences morphing into butterflies, and a tagline that read "Peace. New Beginning."

When the video finished I felt choked up. My mother's partner was unmoved. "How can you trust a mass murderer?" he asked, predictably. I then reacted predictably. The two of them accused me of being a reactive gas on the periodic table. "Be more like a noble gas," my mother advised.

"You've turned me into some sort of North Korean sympathizer," I said to Bongjun.

"Do Americans think they have better judgment than fifty million Koreans? That's a little insulting. Fifty million Koreans are thinking that either Kim Jong-un is the most perfect actor, or we have been led to believe the wrong thing about him. That's why they showed that unedited live footage of Kim Jong-un talking with President Moon, so everyone could see for themselves and form their own opinion. Let me show you this. This is my favorite Korean show. Kim O-jun's *Black House.* In this show, Kim O-jun went over the summit meeting frame by frame. He invited a psychologist who specializes in reading people's nonverbal communication. Here she is talking about mirroring. When two people are connected, they mirror each other. When someone blinks his eyes, the other person subconsciously blinks his eyes. Here President Moon adjusts his glasses, and then, a few seconds later, Kim Jong-un adjusts his glasses. Here Moon shifts his leg, and then Kim Jong-un shifts his leg. If Kim Jong-un is really doing this in some sort of manipulative way, that would be superpower behavior."

I TOLD BONGJUN that every single person I was talking to—other than him—always said, "Aren't they all starving there?" whenever I defended Kim Jong-un. "You're asking me to believe a mass murderer," I said.

"I'm not asking you to do anything. But who did he murder?"

"His uncle and his brother."

"That's not mass murder. China was conspiring with them to over-throw North Korea. He was defending his regime. Besides, it's still a rumor. Just like the rumor that Park Geun-hye sacrificed those three hundred school children who died in the ferryboat accident for her cult. Why aren't Americans talking about that?"

"All I'm saying is, anyone who sends his people to labor camps is not a trustworthy person."

"And is the US trustworthy? I really don't understand why Americans think Kim Jong-un is any worse than any of the dictators they installed in South Korea like Lee Seung Man. He killed his political enemies, too. He killed Kim Koo—the leader of the government in exile. He massacred so many South Korean farmers. And under Park Chung-hee's rule, if someone was caught singing "Bridge over Troubled Water," the policeman came up to him and said, 'You think there are troubled waters in our country?' And then that person would disappear forever."

A LETHARGY WAS PRESSING down on me. I felt like a squished olive. I had been trying to take Confucius's advice and understand the other viewpoint, but the psychic toll was depleting me. Everything felt upside down. I didn't want to hear anything more about North Korea. I just wanted to do American things. Play Marco Polo in a swimming pool. Bet on a horse race. Jump on one of those jumpy castles. Maybe I just needed some vitamin B. I made popcorn and added brewer's yeast and sat down to watch Agnès Varda's *The Gleaners and I*. Halfway through, a French grape grower who moonlights as a psychotherapist described his philosophy of therapy. "What distinguishes me," he says, "is that I have tried to integrate into man's psyche the Other above the Ego. In other words, I developed an anti-ego philosophy, a philosophy that shows how man first originates in the Other."

The self "originating in the other" was my philosophy, too, but now it was clamping down on me from all sides. I thought of one of my students, who described how the minister at her church had told his congregation that our lives are a playlist. You never knew which song was going to come on next. I lay on the floor and stared at the ceiling, waiting for the next song. I hoped it would be more upbeat than the current dirge.

My old roommate from Florida called. I told him how all I could think and write about was North Korea, and that I was writing a book about Buddhism, quantum physics, and North Korea, partly in ono-matopoeia. "And climate change. It's not really a very good conversation starter. Did I tell you about the last time Bongjun and I went to Korea, and a guy gave us directions in onomatopoeia?" I asked.

"What? What does that even sound like? *Rumm rumm. Bbrbrbrbr. RRRRRT! Walk walk walk. Ding dong.* People are walking around like that?"

An hour later he emailed a link to a YouTube video. "No wonder Trump is the perfect person to negotiate with the Koreans," he wrote. "Have you seen this video where he speaks in Bing Bing Language?!"

The genius who edited the video compiled all the instances of Trump using the words *bing bing* to refer to the following: using Twit-ter, pressing buttons, distributing checks, a marine's shooting, shooting in the old days, maps, mouths, cleaning repairs, a fourteen-point plan, Anthony Weiner, Trump's opponents, playing football, playing cards, tunnels, a rocket ship going backward, a human dropped from a plane, pumps, puppets, hanging up the phone.

Perhaps the summit in Singapore would go well after all.

A FEW DAYS LATER, Bongjun and I watched a forty-two-minute-long film from KCTV (Korean Central Television, a North Korean state-owned broadcaster) documenting the summit. The film featured close-ups of Kim boarding an Air China plane, Kim in his hotel room, and Kim walking in the gardens (Bongjun sighing, "Why can't he just go on a diet?") while North Korea's most recognized announcer, Ri Chun-hee, notorious for her ardent, gustatory exclamations, told us what was going on. I turned on YouTube's autogenerated English subtitles so that Bongjun wouldn't have to translate and encountered one of the most surreal translations of the 21st century. I could understand why Kim Jong-un would be autotranslated as "Our Great Leader Chairman Sea-weed," since the name Kim does, in fact, mean "seaweed" in Korean, but why North Korea, more than once, was called "the People's Republic of Pretzel Insurance" was bewildering. As Chairman Seaweed walked up the red-carpeted steps to board his version of Air Force One, the subtitles read, "I have climbed the Chinese castle." While his military leaders waved goodbye to him from the tarmac, the subtitles read, "It is our hope that you will find a strong pine tree." Perhaps that was a reference to what was next translated as the "contemporary needs of pine needle crocodile cotton."

Only half a million people had watched this video, the same number as had watched Trump's Bing Bing video. But it was so surprisingly fresh that the usual vitriol of toxic commentary was toned down. In the YouTube comments I'd finally found bipartisan camaraderie. My favorite ones:

> Damn. Trump needs to hire NK propaganda guys. they make him appear somewhat less of a moron . . .

> I am surprised this NK production provided more video footage, more comprehensive coverage, much more interesting angles than any one else

> This is how the news should be, very informative.

> Best coverage yet . . . . CNN should go to NK and learn a thing or two . . . .

> no wonder Korean people cry when they watch their president. because the music and narration make me cry also even though I don't understand the language. so emotional. just like watching twilight

> Good and honest documentary

> Finally, there seems to be a ray of hope for mankind.

"BONGJUN?" I ASKED one evening. "Tomorrow, can we not talk about North Korea? I just want to be a simple, happy American for a day."

"Garrison Keillor says to be happy you just need to eat more ketchup," Bongjun said.

"OK, tomorrow we'll make french fries for breakfast and eat them with ketchup."

"And make egg fries too."

"You mean a fried egg?"

"Egg fries. Fried egg. Whatever! You Americans treat words like they're Clark Kent. When he wears glasses, you can't even recognize that he is Superman!"

For the first time in weeks, I felt calm, like I was lying on a heated temple floor in South Korea. +

SHOP.NPLUSONEMAG.COM

KIM FISHER, *HEDGE #1*. 2018, ALUMINIUM COLLAGED HAND PRINTED SCREEN PRINTS. 52 × 40 × 1.3". PHOTO BY PATRICK JAMESON. COURTESY OF THE ARTIST AND THE MODERN INSTITUTE/TOBY WEBSTER LTD, GLASGOW.

HOMESCHOOL

Meghan O'Gieblyn

FOR MOST OF MY CHILDHOOD—from kindergarten until tenth grade—I did not attend school. *Homeschooled* is the term I used as a kid, the term I still use today for expediency, though it has always seemed misleading, since schooling is what my mother meant to spare us from by keeping us at home. We lived during those years on a farm in Vermont that sat thirty miles outside the nearest functional town and was, in a lot of ways, autonomous. We ate eggs from our own chickens, heated the house with a wood-burning stove, and got our water from a local spring, which was just a PVC pipe extending from the side of a mountain next to a sign warning that the county could not guarantee the quality of the water. I spent most mornings doing the chores I shared with my brothers: feeding the chickens, stocking the woodbin, hauling hay bales out to the sheep pasture. After that, the day was my own. Sometimes I read alone in my room, or sat at the kitchen table drawing comics in my sketchbook. As the oldest, I was often responsible for the younger kids, but like most children in large families they were easy—hungry for attention, game for whatever task I invented. We made baroque concoctions of flour and spices in the mixer and played with the bottle-fed lambs that slept in the kitchen in a baby hamper and wobbled freely around the house all day. We were always trying to teach them to sit or roll over, as if they were dogs.

My mom was usually outdoors, tinkering with something in the barn or traipsing around the pasture, examining the sheep for hoof rot. It was just her and us. Our dad left when I was 8—first for inpatient treatment for what in those days was called "manic depression," then the following year for good, when he returned to the small Oregon town where he'd grown up. At the time my mom was pregnant with her fourth child. Even though we lived in a remote area, with no other adult in the house, she insisted on giving birth naturally, at home. The night her labor started, I was the one who called the midwife, who instructed me to fetch a heating pad and rubbing alcohol; she'd be there in forty minutes. When she arrived, I helped ferry towels back and forth from the bathroom, and was allowed to stay in the room for the birth.

This was, according to my mom, "an experience"—one of many things I would never have learned at school. The sole purpose of schools, she often said, was to teach children to stand in lines. They were places people sent their children to do "busy work"—one of her favorite phrases, a catchall for all manner of scholastic activity, from the pointless tasks contrived to habituate children to following rules (worksheets, self-assessments) to the required subjects she considered vehicles for the state's ideological agenda (sex education, evolutionary biology). My mom had been sent as a teenager to a boarding school in the South, a missionary reform academy that liberally practiced corporal punishment and from which she fled, sneaking out at night and hitchhiking back home to Michigan. Her animosity toward institutions must have stemmed from that experience, but she rarely mentioned it—and anyway, she rejected all forms of schooling: public and private, religious and secular.

Learning was something else. It was happening all the time, whether we were conscious of it or not, like breathing. In a letter to the state department of education, she referred to her pedagogy as "delight-directed integrated study," a term I believe she made up. She was required to write these letters every year, one for each child, detailing how she would teach the core subjects. I read them for the first time a couple years ago and was awed by their expansive, often creative notion of what qualifies as education. On the topic of Comprehensive Health, she wrote: "Meghan had a great introduction to the health care system this past spring when she spent four days in the hospital having her appendix out." On Citizenship, History, and Government: "We hope to have contact with a family of Russian immigrants through friends of ours who will be sponsoring them. This should help make real to Meghan some of the freedoms we enjoy in this country." All the letters were written in the same shrugging, breezy tone that was her primary mode of defense, and barely concealed her hostility toward state intervention. On sex education: "Presently she is gaining a good base of information by being involved with the life cycles in our barn, and some sheep we will breed this fall."

My mom considered music the most important part of our education. Each of us kids played at least one instrument, and the only time she interfered with our day was when the house was quiet for more than an hour. "I don't hear any practicing!" she'd call out. She also placed a disproportionate emphasis on memorization. By the age of 10 I could, if prompted, recite entire chapters of the King James Bible. My mom would turn to me while we were weeding the garden or waiting in line at the supermarket and say, "Let's hear Luke 2." We did, technically, have textbooks; they came in the mail each August from a Christian education wholesaler in Texas. Occasionally, my mom would flip through one and comment on something, but they remained for the most part untouched, stacked on the kitchen sideboard. Subjects that didn't interest her were more or less neglected. I went for years without doing formal arithmetic. Until tenth grade, my knowledge of earth sciences began and ended with Genesis. Every few months my mom would recognize the lapse and try to remedy it with an outsize gesture. Once, she returned from a walk with a dead painted turtle she'd found on the side of the road, placed it on our backyard picnic table, pulled out a makeshift assortment of surgical tools—a screwdriver, dinner forks, a butcher knife—and announced we were having "science class."

But the vast majority of our day was spent doing nothing. My mom talked about the importance of "hayloft time," her term for idle reflection. Children needed to think, she was always saying. They needed to spend a lot of time alone. She believed that extended bouts of solitude would cultivate autonomy and independence of thought. I did hole up many afternoons atop the ziggurat of hay bales, reading, or sometimes just lying there in silence, watching the chaff fall from the rafters. I also spent a lot of time in the woods, which I called "exploring." Behind the sheep pasture was a dirt road that led up the mountain to a network of abandoned logging trails that were, for all I could tell, limitless. I walked them every day and never saw another person. It wasn't uncommon to stumble on a hidden wonder: a meadow, an overgrown pasture, tiered waterfalls that ran green over carpets of algae. In those moments I experienced life as early humans might have, in a condition not unlike the one idealized by the Romantics, my mind as empty and stark as the bars of sunlight crossing the forest floor. I walked until I was tired, or until the shadows grew long and the sun dipped below the mountains, and then I headed home.

To RAISE A CHILD OF NATURE—a child who is truly free—you must first remove him from society. Take him out of the city, with its vanities, its hierarchies, its parades of status, and away from the village, where he might learn the vices of peasants. Give him a wide stretch of land where he can wander wherever he wishes. Give him a tutor who does not teach but simply serves as a model. The overprotected child will grow up to be weak. Let him discover the limits of his freedom, learning from his own mistakes. Exercise his body, but keep his mind idle for as long as possible. When he grows older, he will read what he chooses to read, and will teach himself whatever he finds useful. By then, he will be a true freethinker, and approach every idea as a skeptic.

This is more or less the pedagogy laid out by Jean-Jacques Rousseau in *Émile, or On Education*, the vade mecum of modern homeschooling. Perhaps that's going too far. No homeschooler I've known has acknowledged its influence, but the book was the first to present a systematic argument that supports parents pulling their children out of schools and rearing them at home. If you were to trace the basic philosophical precepts of the American homeschooling movement back through the tributaries of history in search of their source, you would find them all in Rousseau: society and its institutions degrade the natural inclinations; spontaneous action is superior to habit; children are malleable and must be cultivated carefully and deliberately, like plants.

In the beginning, modern American homeschoolers called themselves "unschoolers," a nod to the Rousseauian idea that true education is naturalistic and self-directed. The term was coined by John Holt, a school reformer who'd gradually lost faith in reform. Holt believed that America was "a sick society" obsessed with violence, luxury, and power, and that public life rewarded groupthink and totalitarian consensus. During the free school movement of the 1960s, he wrote books outlining how schools could give children more freedom and autonomy, but he eventually became disillusioned with the charade of formal education. Schools could never be changed because they were inextricably linked to the corporate workforce; their sole task was to prepare children to be docile employees. "It was becoming clear to me that the great majority of boring, regimented schools were doing exactly what they had always done and what most people wanted them to do," he writes in his book *Teach Your Own*: "Teach children about Reality. Teach them that Life Is No Picnic. Teach them to Shut Up And Do What You're Told."

In the late 1970s, Holt began arguing that parents were perfectly capable of educating their own children. He started a newsletter, *Growing Without Schooling*, to connect his growing band of disciples, most of whom were hippies—back-to-the-landers, people living on communal farms—who believed unschooling was an ancient, intuitive way of raising children. Parents wrote in to share that their kids were "flowering" at home: a child of barely 2 had learned to cook meals for himself, using knives and a stove; a child of 3 had taught himself to read without instruction, and was so immersed in nature he could recognize and name every kind of tree. "By the time he was 5," the father wrote, "he was so used to getting up in the morning with the ecstatic prospect of learning all day long that I hated to disabuse him of the notion that learning was natural by sending him to school."

But if you read the newsletter carefully, it's clear that not everyone maintained this laissez-faire approach. One father claims he has "eminent domain" over his children, which gives him the right "to rear and to train them according to the dictates of my own conscience before God." A mother, who describes her family as "church-going Catholics," writes that with her children at home, she and her husband can better oversee their socialization, their television viewing, and their sugar consumption. It turns out the hippies were not the only ones reading Holt's newsletter. His subscribers included a number of religious conservatives—evangelicals, Catholics, Seventh Day Adventists—who shared his belief that state education was a form of mind control, though for quite different reasons. For them, schools were not brainwashing children with capitalist values, but with the agenda of the radical left, which, according to the rhetoric, included evolutionary biology, sex education, and secular humanism.

In the second issue of *Growing Without Schooling*, Holt acknowledged that his disciples were "mixed allies" whose grievances about schools varied dramatically. He saw this diversity as a strength, proof of the movement's potential to transcend political and religious lines. It's hard not to wince at his naivete. In the coming decades, homeschooling would become almost entirely dominated by fundamentalist Christians, who had a more ambitious social agenda, massive organizational wealth, and—perhaps most crucially—a large contingent of mothers who were willing to forego careers and stay home with their children. In those early, heady days of utopianism, it was perhaps difficult to grasp a truth that is all too plain now: that countercultural ideals like freedom, individualism, and antiauthoritarianism can be commandeered by the very institutional powers they were contrived to fight.

But perhaps the problem lies closer to the source, with the Enlightenment notion of absolute freedom. Rousseau speaks passionately of liberating children, and yet his pedagogy involves highly specific prescriptions for how a child should be bathed (in ice-cold water), where he should be raised (in a temperate climate, like France), how he should be fed (sparsely; too much food will disrupt his digestion). Émile cannot have contact with other children, or see doctors or priests during his early years. "You will not be master of the child if you cannot control every one about him," the author warns. It is this contradiction in Rousseau—what Jacob Talmon called the "transition from absolute freedom to absolute necessity"—that led cold-war critics like Talmon and Isaiah Berlin to argue that his philosophy led, logically, to totalitarianism and other forms of social control. Like Rousseau, Holt believed true liberty was not merely the absence of unjust restraint, but the absence of all possible restraint. And from there it is only a short leap to the insistence that one must vigilantly maintain this freedom at any cost—and, finally, to the gnawing paranoia that there are subtle forces, everywhere and invisible, conspiring to constrict it.

M Y CHILDHOOD WAS, in many ways, a walled garden constructed in accordance with 19th-century notions of innocence and autonomy. I was aware on some level that there was a broader culture from which we had deliberately exempted ourselves. My mother called it the World, which was neither the planet nor the cosmos, but a system of interlocking ideologies that were everywhere and in everything. Sometimes the World was capitalism, as when she complained that Christmas had been co-opted by the World's consumerism. Other times it was socialism, which was synonymous with the State, a vast and elusive force that had the power to take children from their parents. The World was feminism, environmentalism, secular humanism—ideologies that sprang from a single source and reinforced one another. We were to be in the World but not of it, existing within its physical coordinates but uncontaminated by its values. "Schoolkids," according to her, were hopeless products of the World. They could not think for themselves, but simply mimicked behavior they'd seen on television. ("Stop popping your gum," she would say. "You look like a schoolkid.") Media made for children was naturally suspect. My mom once pronounced an animated film about dinosaurs Darwinian propaganda, and marched us out of a community sing-along because a folk song espoused new age pantheism. I have more than once considered the brilliance she would have achieved as a critic, so relentless she was in deconstructing any artifact and reducing it to its essential message. Of all the things she taught me, this was the most formative: that life concealed vast power structures warring for control of my mind; that my only hope for freedom was to be vigilant in recognizing them and calling them by name.

Everyone we knew was like us. In those dark ages before chat rooms and social networks, my mom maintained some mysterious sonar for locating like-minded people: fundamentalists who shopped at cooperative groceries, strained their own yogurt, and spoke in tongues at the dinner table. For several years, our social life orbited around a weekly Bible study we attended at the house of a large extended homeschool family who took us into their fold. While the adults met upstairs, my siblings and I were abandoned to the other children, all cousins, who were less a peer group than a kind of child gang. The leaders were the two oldest boys, who wore matching fox-tooth necklaces and led us on long treks through the acres of swampland behind their house. Sometimes we were supposed to be looking for something—candle quartz, which they called crystals, or a fisher-cat that had been spotted in the area—but the expeditions were more often a hazing ritual, a test to see how far we would follow them into the darkened woods, crossing thin ice, crawling through the live wires of electrical fencing, climbing into abandoned deer blinds. I lagged at the back of the group, making sure my brothers, who were among the youngest, didn't get lost.

The girls all wore their hair long, grazing the backs of their knees. They were slightly older than me, and though they were kind—teaching me crochet stitches and braiding my hair—I was never sure whether I was their equal or their charge. During the coldest months, the boys gave up on their treks and we all hung out in the basement, occupying

ourselves with a variety of homemade distractions that I am embarrassed to reproduce here. For a year or so, we were very into puppetry.
We were once disciplined for "playing" Communion, passing around
plates of broken saltines and Welch's grape juice. (Apparently this was
sacrilege.) When I think back on those evenings, all I can think of is
all that blood in close quarters, edging up on puberty. Most of the girls
were in love with their cousins, and spoke of it wistfully, as a kind of
romantic tragedy. "I'm sure Sean likes you," one of them confessed to
me, sighing. "He'll never love me, because I'm his cousin."

We did occasionally have contact with larger groups. We went to
church on Sundays, and in summer attended a missionary camp on Lake
Michigan. In September, we sometimes went to Six Flags, which had a
"homeschool day" discount to capitalize on the back-to-school lull. It
was there, more than anywhere, that one could glimpse the movement
in its entirety. The Christian Reconstructionists were easiest to spot
(patriotic T-shirts), as were the macrobiotic hippies, who overlapped
somewhat with the anti-vaxxers, the anarchists, and the preppers. There
were the rich suburban kids whose parents had pulled them from school
to better facilitate backpacking trips to Mongolia, and Mennonite girls
in long denim skirts, plus the occasional Quiverfull family number-
ing twelve, fifteen, twenty-five. The full spectrum, in other words, of
American private dissent. But even then, it didn't feel like a community
so much as a summit of isolated tribes. Families came and left together,
and remained as units throughout the day. The kids didn't talk. Concessions were a graveyard; everyone brought packed lunches.

Earlier this year, while going through some files my mom gave
me, I came across a homeschool newsletter on the topic of socialization. I expected the authors would rehearse the arguments I'd heard
as a child—that schools did not have a monopoly on social life; that
there were plenty of other ways to meet people—and was surprised
to find something else. The first article was by Sue Welch, a Christian
homeschooling advocate. "The world says that our children need to
spend large amounts of time with many of their own age-mates," she
wrote. "This produces the desired effect of conformity." She went on
to argue that socialization was a myth, devised by the state and their
coterie of child psychologists to woo children away from the ideology of
their parents. (The first definition of *socialize*, she pointed out, was "to
place under government or group ownership or control.") Parents who

accepted this wisdom were themselves victims of false consciousness: "Our own socialization has conditioned us to accept current opinion or psychological studies over God's revealed truth." The other authors more or less reiterated her argument: socialization was not only over-blown, it was actively detrimental to children.

Poring over these documents, my first instinct was to dismiss these ideas as the fringe of the fringe. Like many adults who have left extremist religious backgrounds, I long ago came to terms with the fact that I was raised in a culture whose defining ethos was fear. But I always believed that fear was subliminal, and that the restrictions it spawned were carried out in a kind of dream-state by parents who had fallen under the sway of talk radio and the ambient alarm of the culture wars. I had a difficult time believing that isolation was systematically prescribed by homeschooling leaders, and that my own cloistered childhood was the result of my mother heeding their advice. Some additional research proved the breadth of my ignorance. This view of socialization appears in all the landmark homeschooling literature, including the work of Holt, who claimed that kids benefited from a limited number of friends and recommended that children spend substantial time alone. It reaches poetic heights in the books of Raymond Moore, a frequent guest on James Dobson's radio program *Family Talk* who popularized homeschooling among religious conservatives. In his 1981 book *Home Grown Kids*, "peer dependency" among children is referred to as "a social cancer" again and again.

Then there's this, from one of the most famous homeschooling advocates: "Thus the oversocialized person is kept on a psychological leash and spends his life running on rails that society has laid down for him. In many oversocialized people this results in a sense of constraint and powerlessness that can be a severe hardship. We suggest that oversocialization is among the more serious cruelties that human beings inflict on one another." OK, I lied. That one's Ted Kaczynski.

THE ENLIGHTENMENT IDEA that humans are infinitely malleable naturally has a dark side. If children can, as Rousseau claimed, be perfected through careful observance and social control, they can also be ruined if these methods are faulty or perverted. An entire strain of counter-Enlightenment thought stemmed from this idea, the most well-known example being Mary Shelley's *Frankenstein*. Although the novel is often read as a parable about technological hubris, Shelley herself envisioned it as a drama about child-rearing, and wrote it, in part, as a critique of Rousseau's pedagogy. Victor's monster is born good and begins his life, like Émile, in the state of nature: he roams the countryside and educates himself by reading in isolation. But because his "parent" abandons him without completing his education, the child is unable to fully integrate himself into human society. When he finally emerges from nature and enters a village, people find him hideous and regard him as a monster. He is forced to retreat back into isolation, and eventually his alienation transforms him into a murderer.

In March 2018, Mark Conditt, a 23-year-old man better known as the Austin package bomber, blew himself up in a Ford Ranger on the side of Interstate 35 outside Austin, Texas. Over the previous three weeks, Conditt had shipped homemade bombs in FedEx packages to various homes in the Austin area, all of them sent from the cryptic alias Kelly Killmore. While the attacks were initially believed to be racially motivated—the first two victims were people of color—later targets were white and lived in an upper-middle-class suburb. Conditt's motivations became even more puzzling after police recovered a twenty-five-minute confession video that did not mention anything about terrorism or hate. The interim police chief described the video as "the outcry of a very challenged young man talking about challenges in his personal life."

The lone eccentricity of Conditt's background was that he had been homeschooled. A local newspaper managed to reach Jeremiah Jensen, a friend of Conditt's, who alluded to the social struggles his friend faced as a homeschooler. "It's just very difficult for a lot of [homeschooled] kids to find a way to fit in once they are out in the real world," he told the paper. "I have a feeling that is what happened with Mark. I don't remember him ever being sure of what he wanted to do." Perhaps because there was no clear motive, Conditt's homeschooling seemed increasingly suspicious. BuzzFeed reported that in high school, Conditt had belonged to a Christian homeschool group called RIOT. The article cited a former group member who said that in addition to studying the Bible, RIOT members shot guns at a range and carried knives. She also noted that the kids were "very into science" and did experiments with chemicals.

A friend of mine who knew I was homeschooled sent me a link to the story the day it was published: "Ever heard of this homeschool Riot group?" He was under the impression—one that the article did not discourage—that the group was a radical nationwide cell network of Christian terrorists. I pointed out that RIOT was actually an acronym—Righteous Invasion of Truth—and the title of a 1995 album by Carman, who is basically the Barry Manilow of Christian contemporary music. Not exactly a figurehead of violent dissent. I linked a response article from HuffPost that excerpted a RIOT brochure, which was written in sunny, sociable language and interviewed one of the RIOT mothers, who spoke of the group in similarly benign terms. "Water balloons, cream pies, frisbee, etc.," she said. "That's what it is." By then, it was a moot point. People on Twitter were already proclaiming RIOT a neo-Nazi group and comparing it to ISIS.

I didn't rule out the possibility that homeschooling had contributed in some way to Conditt's sense of alienation. But the notion that he had been "radicalized" struck me as hysterical. It attributed to homeschooling the same vaguely conspiratorial powers of mind control that my mom ascribed to the World, and fell in line with some of the more outrageous assumptions people harbored about homeschoolers (how many times have I been asked if my parents kept us in cages or forbade us to leave the house?). My mother once pointed out that these stereotypes revealed how much people feared homeschoolers, which in turn revealed their own fear that they themselves were not free.

But after a while, I regretted defending the group to my friend. Why, after all, do I find it necessary to make these distinctions? Why, when I hear stories like these, do I immediately think of what my mother would say? It's difficult to account for why I still occasionally find myself defending homeschooling, despite everything I know about its detrimental effects and my own enduring alienation.

WHEN I WAS 11, my mom sold the farm, which had become untenable, and moved our family back to the Midwest. Her family lived in Michigan, and we moved, in part, to be closer to them, but our life there was, in some sense, as itinerant and isolated as it had been in Vermont. For several years we moved between seemingly identical towns in Illinois and Michigan, where we ate at the same chain restaurants, shopped at the same big-box stores, and attended nondenominational churches that were so similar to one another in their worship style and theology that they, too, seemed like franchises. We were closer to civilization but still resisting its pull, circling the outskirts of communities,

protected by the dull scrim of suburban anonymity. Everything changed
when my mother got remarried, to a man she'd met at church. He had
a daughter, which brought another child into our family, and soon after
the wedding we all moved to a lakeside town in Wisconsin, a place that
was, unavoidably, a community. Neighbors came by to introduce themselves and invited us to picnics and block parties. My parents began
hosting dinners at our house. That fall, my mom suggested that if we
ever wanted to try school, this would be a good time.

After all her years of embattled opposition to schooling, I'm still
unsure what led to her change of mind. It's possible she was simply
exhausted by the stress of raising five children and wanted us out of the
house, but it might have had something to do with the cultural shift taking place in those years. By the late 1990s, the countercultural Jesus People fundamentalism to which my mother subscribed had been absorbed
by the megachurch movement—a brand of evangelicalism that was
more suburban and upbeat, concerned with engaging the culture rather
than resisting it. I was then 15 years old, approaching what would have
been the tenth grade. Although I maintained some misgivings about
attending school, I suspected this was my one shot, and my siblings had
agreed to go without hesitation. I said yes.

The school itself was a kind of nightmare: a large public institution with two campuses and a multimillion-dollar hockey rink that
had been endowed by one of the parents. The football team was the
Division 1 state champion, and on Fridays all the popular girls wore
red tartan kilts to class to announce the weekend's field hockey match.
The whole place smelled like an Abercrombie. My academic performance that first year was predictably uneven. I failed chemistry and
barely scraped by in algebra. In music theory, I found the curriculum
so elementary that the teacher eventually gave me a private desk in the
corner and said I could use the hour to study for other classes. Things
should have evened out over time, but my problem was not a dearth
of knowledge but of discipline. I could not bring myself to concentrate
on subjects that bored me. The one time I was formally reprimanded,
it was for forging a note to get out of sociology so that I could work in
the studio on a video production assignment. The principal, once the
situation was sorted out, was baffled. "This is the first time I've sent
someone to detention for doing homework," he said. I didn't understand what I'd done wrong. Why should I have to sit in a classroom

where I was learning nothing useful, when there were things I wanted to do just down the hall?

I wish I could say I maintained the same aristocratic indifference in my social life, but I wanted desperately to be liked, and this made me painfully self-conscious. At lunch, I had a difficult time following conversations. Everyone seemed to be pantomiming, with great exaggeration, awe, affection, disgust. In retrospect, the problem was very simple: I was wholly ignorant of the social scripts that governed large groups of females. All my mental energy was devoted to deciphering codes, analyzing unfamiliar words, and unpacking innuendo. I often felt the other girls looking at me, wondering why I was so quiet, but I never contributed anything because I was always a couple steps behind, still processing the last thing that had been said.

Over time, my curiosity gave way to bewilderment, and eventually to boredom. I became fatigued whenever I was forced to talk to more than one person at a time, overcome with a weariness that felt at times like mental blankness, and at others like acute physical exhaustion. I began eating my lunch in the library, under the pretense that I was catching up on homework, not realizing that this simple act of independence would damn me to full social opprobrium. Rumors made their way back to me—that I picked my nose in class, that I wore the same pants for ten days straight—which led me to retreat further. As a homeschooler, I had never felt lonely, even though my life consisted largely of solitude. It wasn't until I entered school that I understood for the first time the ache of seclusion and personal failure. We read *Frankenstein* that year in English. I didn't know then that the novel was in conversation with Rousseau, but I remember identifying with the monster's alienation. "Everywhere I see bliss, from which I alone am irrevocably excluded," he cries out in one monologue. "I was benevolent and good; my soul glowed with love and humanity: but am I not alone, miserably alone?"

I wish I could say that all of this passed like a bad trip, the way high school does for so many people. But to this day, it's rare that I end a social interaction without retracing the steps of those long walks home from school: convinced that everything I said was false, that authentic communication is impossible within the confines of social norms. I suppose I might be an angry person had I not, in the end, found my way back to Nature, or its closest analogue. It was during high school that I began writing. I transcribed conversations I'd overheard at school, observations about people, insights about the books I was reading. It became a habit that I came to depend upon, like nourishment, in the same way I craved solitude. The world was pulsing forward at a relentless pace, but the page was infinitely slow, infinitely patient. My first-person voice became my primary sense of identity—an avatar of words and air that I constructed each day and carried in my backpack like a talisman. Its private sustenance was less like a pastime than like the wilderness I explored as a child with total freedom, never exhausting its limits.

*É*MILE, OF COURSE, is not really a child care manual. It's a philosophical treatise that explores an intractable problem: how can one maintain freedom from society while also existing within it? Many of Rousseau's first readers missed this point and took his prescriptions at face value. In the years after *Émile* was published, parents frequently wrote to Rousseau claiming that they were raising their children in the manner he'd outlined. To one such father he replied, "So much the worse, sir, for you and your son, so much the worse."

Rousseau knew that the state of nature was a lost Eden where no person could return. Society put humans in a state of disunity: one's natural inclinations were always at war with one's social duties. But isolating a child would only heighten that sense of disunity. "He who in the civil order wants to preserve the primacy of the sentiments of nature does not know what he wants," Rousseau writes in the early pages of the book—a user warning for anyone tempted to try his methods at home. "Always in contradiction with himself, always floating between his inclinations and his duties, he will never be either [natural] man or citizen. He will be good neither for himself nor for others. . . . He will be nothing."

I suppose this state of "contradiction," or disunity, sums up my position today. I left my family's ideology somewhat late—in my early twenties, after two tortured years of Bible college—which ultimately made the exit more difficult. I wasted a lot of time mourning the loss, drinking, working lousy jobs. But despite everything I now know about the ideologies that informed homeschooling, I maintain mostly good memories of those years I lived in innocence. I sometimes credit homeschooling with the qualities I've come to value most in myself: a capacity for solitude and absorption, a distrust of consensus. It is tempting, even, to believe that my childhood inadvertently endowed me with the tools to escape it—that my mother's insistence that the World was conspiring to brainwash me cultivated the very skepticism that I later trained on my family and their beliefs. But this is circular logic, like someone saying they are grateful for their diabetes because it forced them to change their eating habits. Its wisdom resembles the hollow syntax of rationalization. If I've often found it difficult to speak or write about this ambivalence, it's because it's impossible to do so without coming to interrogate my motives and doubt my own independence of mind.

Last summer, I came across Tara Westover's memoir *Educated*, a story that in many ways held a mirror to my own experience. Westover grew up in rural Idaho in a family of radical Mormon survivalists who forbade their children to attend school or see doctors. In her book, she recalls working alongside her father in his junkyard, where she sustained several injuries that were treated homeopathically; listening to his conspiratorial rants about the Feds; and helping her parents prep for the end of days. The story hinges on the process by which she educated herself, in secret, so that she could go to college—first at Brigham Young University, then at Cambridge, where she got a doctorate in history. The manuscript was bought for six figures within twenty-four hours of hitting the market, and has since been published in twenty countries.

The whole idea of the book—its publicity budget, its book-club sheen—struck me from the beginning as evidence of bad faith. Americans maintain a voracious appetite for child-isolation narratives (*The Wolfpack*, *Room*). Unlike the readers of *Émile*, who delighted in the fantasy of native innocence, for Americans the allure of these cloistered children lies in the belief that they have been brainwashed; their entrance into society is not a loss of innocence, but a drama of liberation. Throughout her media tour, Westover was celebrated as a feral child who had crossed over, a symbol of American autonomy and self-governance who had, by dint of will, clawed her way out of a family that, incidentally, held fast to those same American virtues. Magazine profiles reiterated how "normal" she seemed. In interviews, she spoke of "psychological manipulation" and "reality distortions" with the authority of someone who had completed years of therapy. "All abuse is foremost an assault on the mind," she told *Vogue*.

Still, these talking points did not quell the collective anxiety that Westover maintained some confusion about her upbringing, and I suppose this is what interested me most about her story. Several critics found it unsettling that her parents were occasionally characterized, in her memoir, with a note of affection, and that the descriptions of her childhood landscape were undergirded by a sense of longing. One interviewer wondered "if Westover only really comprehended the difficulty of her childhood when she sat down to write." Reviewers noted this too, but dismissed it as an aesthetic choice. That she refused to "demonize" her family was not evidence of sympathy, but the result of her "matter-of-fact lyricism" and "characteristic understatement," a writerly restraint contrived to lend the darker moments of her story even more power.

Westover once hinted that the early iterations of her book had a lighter tone. When she first began writing, she confessed in one interview, she regarded her family's behavior as harmless and eccentric: "I don't think I had really appreciated how extreme bits of it were. I would write about the injuries a lot of times like comedies, and my friends thought, 'this undermines my trust in you because it doesn't seem like you understand the situation.'" One might argue that Westover understood her situation better than anyone, having lived it, but her authority as a narrator—and more fundamentally, as a witness to her own life—was for many readers discounted by the brainwashing she'd experienced as a child. The most popular comment on the book's Goodreads page spells out what many readers found troubling: "I do not understand why an educated and worldly individual would have difficulty understanding the horrible and violent upbringing that she experienced." In the end, Westover, who has described her life as a process of regaining "custody of my own mind," was subjected, again and again, to the insistence that she did not actually know her own mind.

This is the predicament of people who were raised in highly controlled environments: any ambivalence about your upbringing is proof of its success, a sign that you are not yet completely free. Homeschoolers, after all, are not the only ones preoccupied with autonomy. All of us in America are Rousseau's children: obsessed with liberty, terrified of those who would put restraints on our thinking. If stories like Westover's are unsettling, it's because they reflect the larger disunity all of us know to be our fate—that none of us live completely off the ideological grid, impervious to malicious systems of thought. We are all like Frankenstein's monster, victims of our own miseducations, a motley patchwork of the influences that have shaped us, sometimes without our awareness or consent.

It is impossible to anticipate how a person will interpret the lessons of her childhood, whether she will find in them an impetus for violence or a source of creative inspiration. In my own family, my siblings and I have proved the outcomes of my mother's pedagogy wildly unpredictable. Despite her best efforts to raise us deliberately, each of us has negotiated, in idiosyncratic ways, the legacy of our childhood, and our lives have veered down such divergent paths that when we are all together, it is difficult to imagine we were reared under the same roof. My mother raised a writer, a musician, a missionary, a hotel manager, and an accountant; a progressive, a centrist, two moral conservatives, and a libertarian. I do not have children, but my siblings have collectively produced half a dozen. All of them go to school. +

KEIRAN BRENNAN HINTON, *HOT WATER*. 2017, OIL ON CANVAS. 66 × 48". COURTESY OF THE ARTIST AND 1969 GALLERY.

WHAT GOOD IS LOVE?

Jill Crawford

AUD HAS TO WORK so Benji goes alone, in a huff, to drink mimosas and eat smoked salmon at his old flatmates' house in Watertown, where he lived through the end of his studies into this first year as visiting assistant professor without a whiff of tenure, where he lived until she came to him across the growing Atlantic. On his return from brunch to Calvin Street, she's sitting at the drop-leaf kitchen table, earbuds in, staring out of a cobwebbed window.

SHE IS LISTENING to Dinah Washington's "Is You Is or Is You Ain't My Baby?" while watching above the rim of her laptop as the neighboring couple, who of late ripped open the scrappy earth and stowed things in it, tend to their dizzying garden, which looks like a drug-induced hallucination, engorged with movement and gaiety. She does not move at the noise of the cowbell that clangs when Benji enters. From behind, he worms his arms around her ribs and nuzzles one side of her neck under the earlobe. He presses his mouth to her cheek and she flinches. A scent of fish lingers on his breath. She knows what it is he wants.

Won't you wash first? she asks.

He shrugs and walks away.

She calls after, through the archway, into the next room: I'm sorry, baby, but it's slightly gross. He doesn't speak, just unlatches the piano lid, rubs the edges of his mouth with his fingertips, drags his hand through his beard and hair. Her stomach twists. Off he goes again into that other place of his. She cannot work, just watches him with an eye. He never let her see the murk inside him, not until he got her neat inside his life

139

and distant from her own, which she seems somehow to have sacrificed without realizing. She did it as if she were born and raised to renounce herself. Was she raised to renounce herself? Not deliberately. But he has the power, or he seems to have the power; and because of this power he's not always nice anymore. She feels less without knowing why.

Benji wipes his hands on his sweater. He smears the keys of the piano as he plays, over and over, the theme music from *Death in Venice*. Or is it *Brief Encounter*? Something lugubrious and ardent. He's feeling awfully hard done by and sorry for himself. She's denied him what he's owed. He's pounding into his piano instead of into her. Is it because of his father or mother? Is it because he hasn't sisters? Because he's Roman Catholic or an academic? Because he's American? Anyway, she doesn't get it. His mood saturates the house. He drags like an anchor through her stomach.

What's that tune again? she says at last.

Mahler, he mutters, and changes to something else.

And this one? she asks, lightly, after a while. Won't you play the tune I love?

He played it in Paris the morning after the first night they fucked, played it while she showered in his cold and dirty flat near Bastille. His music had fretted beautifully at the wall while she cleaned her teeth with toothpaste and the tip of her index finger. In the cabinet above the bathroom sink, she'd discovered his inhaler, hidden behind a colossal bottle of mouthwash. She warmed to the covert fragility. Perhaps that was when she chose him.

Come on, baby! she teases. Play it for me. Please.

I don't feel like it.

He closes the lid, stands up from the piano stool. He is the king of huffs. There's something domineering in the huffing of an adult. Though she can still smell that smell that makes her want to puke, she follows him into the living room. He's seated in the armchair by the potted tree, reading Gilles Deleuze. She hasn't read Deleuze but is aware that Deleuze, like Benji, had problems breathing. In Paris, where they met, Benji took her on a pilgrimage to the flat, or the pavement outside the flat, where Deleuze ended his life. On the way home, along boulevard Saint-Michel, they watched a man and a woman post a small boy through a slit into the belly of a clothes bank, where the boy was expected to forage. He didn't look hesitant. He dove and wriggled in.

The boy's father held the mouth of the clothes bank open while the mother reassured her child through the chink.

She hovers by the arm of Benji's chair, rubbing a leaf of their rented olive tree between her fingers. The little branch stretches to her.

He looks up from *Logique de la sensation.*

Look, I'm sorry, she says, but I can't have sex with a man who smells of smoked fish.

It's my body and I'll do what I want with it, he replies.

I know and respect that it's your body.

She sighs. This has been going on since she flew in three months ago and they moved into the new place. He begged her to come. I can't live without you, he said. On her arrival, he met her at Logan International with flowers, his hair shoulder-length in a ponytail, yet another fad at 35. She said nothing about the hair, which he kept taking down and tying up in a rubber band till she lent him a snag-free bobble.

She impales him with her eyes: You are free to do what you want with your body, but if you do what *I* want with it, I'll do something for you.

He looks back, meek: You're a scoundrel.

Yes, I can be.

UPSTAIRS, HE RUNS HIMSELF a bath and unwraps a new packet of the soap he likes, Roger & Gallet, not wishing to grapple with the tadpole sliver that would slip from his hands. He sets the big smooth bar on the rim, steps in and perches, his feet hopping in sharp heat. He lowers himself, inhales and exhales steam, watches his pubic hair plump, his cock. He can guess what she meant, knows at once what he wants—he'll work up to that. Start simple, foreseeable, with lingerie. He'll ask her again for photographs for when they are apart, or to go to that "salon" he has mentioned only once so far. No, he wants to bathe with her, since she never lets him, always locking the door to keep him out, saying it's *a time for her*, which makes him jealous. He wants inside her every part. What's the point, otherwise?

He heads downstairs with sodden hair, towel about his groin. The basement door is open, and he can hear as the washing machine rattles, subdues, halts. Clunk of the door latch. A gentle collapse of contents into the yellow plastic washbasket, which has been in the family since he was a baby, the first son of sons. Here on the piano he keeps a photograph of his mother. She looks like a teenager—though she's only ten years younger than he is now—devoutly holding him in her arms. They had not yet come to America.

Aud clips up the basement steps with an armful of damp washing, face and torso concealed behind the mound, so he can only see arms and legs. He bolts the door behind her; she is scared of the basement.

Don't you open that trapdoor, he chants, *cos there's something down there.*

This is an allusion to a children's TV show she watched years ago and has shown to him on YouTube. They share a laugh at her expense.

She drops the pile on the dining table, where the cloth puffs and slumps: Shut up! she says.

As he fishes socks from the twisted heap, dangling them over backs of dining chairs, he watches her. She drapes heavy bed linen off doors. The hinges wince.

He moves close, pushes himself against her, revolves her around, eye in eye, mouth on mouth. Her freed hands skim across ribs to the small of his back, nestling there. The towel falls. He splays a hand against her breastbone, presses until she's curving back, holds her upright with his other hand on her spine, tugs at her bottom lip with his teeth.

I want, he says.

The fight is done. A duvet cover slithers off a door as they fuck on the sofa, curtains undrawn.

A FTER THEY ARE FINISHED, he says: I suppose I should take you out for dinner. Put on a pretty dress?

They go out for dim sum, smelling of each other's scent, but he has forgotten his wallet and she has to pay, which irritates her, which unravels him. He broods, striding home ten paces ahead, shoulders hunched, head set forward, casting back dark glances, wounded, *glowering*. Before being with Benji, she never saw a face eclipse for no good reason. This grim sulk will persist until tomorrow or the next day or the day after that. But he's always mislaying his belongings. She bought him a woolen scarf that he left at the yoga studio on its first trip out, going back to retrieve it when reminded and bringing home a different scarf, assuming it was the same. She had taken care in choosing that scarf in colors to suit him, albeit in the Irish shop in departures at Dublin Airport. It had cost her forty euros.

This scarf is from Scotland, she'd said. The one I gave you was from Donegal.

He's a pond into which things drop, vanish. He hates when she calls him the absentminded professor, sensing a prick in it. Do all Ivy League academics possess reverent, pragmatic spouses who manage the boring earthly acts of clothing and cleaning and child-rearing and pleasing that they might occupy themselves in probing knowledge? Bright souls can't wash a dish! His oblivion is self-serving, chosen, though bred into him as well. As a teenager, he was thought too rare and gifted to waste time on a Saturday job. What is it to only ever have been a pupil and a teacher, never to have served or had a boss? How on earth did she miss how delicate he was? He hid it well. He seeks, she thinks without awareness, to make an angel of her, an angel like his mother. I'm not your fucking angel, she wants to say. Don't you see that it has taken more to get me here than it took for you to get where you are? She cannot fit the emotion into words, doesn't yet know how. She loves him. He's the closest she has found. Is this the cost? Ah, she thinks too much. She must strive for softness. Other women, her friends, seem happier, more forgiving—perhaps one because the other. He behaves like this when she's pigheaded. He's tender otherwise.

At home, he ascends to the spare room. There he will spend the night alone. In the morning, he'll let her curl her body around him.

D URING THE NIGHT he comes in, which he's never done midargument. The bed heaves as he slips under, close. I hit a wall, he whispers. I'm here, she breathes, unsealing and resealing her eyes. They sleep, taking turns to hold each other's body, determined that, if they go down, they'll go together. She cannot let him go.

H E WAKES FIRST and brings up tea and buttered toast. When he proposed to her, he said: I'll make you breakfast every morning.

No way. Every morning? I don't believe you.

Every morning of every day for the rest of our life. I'm not fucking around.

Toast with marmalade? she'd teased. The vow was no less touching for being improbable.

Je t'aime. He kisses her now, his mouth fresh with spearmint, camomile. He's brushed his teeth.

Je t'aime, she murmurs, kissing back, stopping her own breath at the throat.

It's not always easy, he says. Sometimes I forget how.

I agree. We'll learn. We'll get better at it.

But it's passed. He gently dislodges some sleep from her eye.

So dumb. Let's pretend it never happened. Deal?

Today will be back to normal.

When he moves within her, they're nearly whole and innocent again. Yet at times, she glimpses a frantic tinge of yearning in his face that wasn't there before—or else she didn't apprehend it. Then he has the panicked eyes of a man who's clutching at something that's slipping from him, the loss inevitable. This struggle's his, she thinks. The abyss is beneath or in him.

THE APPETIZER IS SQUID they were meant to cook the night before. It oozes from limp plastic, plops onto the chopping board. They gaze at it, mauve and gray, slack and fetid. The reek of it catches in her throat. He coughs, swills some beer in his mouth. She squirms at his shoulder as he dissects it, crumbs it, and strikes a match to light the cooker.

You needn't think I'm eating that, she says.

It won't hurt you. Don't be fussy. He frowns, sets the matchbox on the chopping board. It slithers across goo.

Watch, will ye! She lifts the matchbox, rubs it with kitchen roll. The box is red, black, and white, an elephant inside two spheres. One corner is all blotched now. She tuts: Please use the gas lighter.

He shrugs: Look, they'll be here soon.

I told you these matches aren't cheap. They're mostly for decorative purposes, the odd candle. I have to order them from the special shop. Did what's-her-name text?

Not yet. She'll be getting in from the airport. The others are coming at eight.

Hope they're not early. I made up her bed, laid out a towel. Will she mind sleeping on the mattress? Should we give her our room?

No, he says. He takes salami out of the fridge, peels away paper as he crosses back, slams it on the chopping board, soots the surface with flour, carves into the flecked pork with the slimy knife. He holds out a piece: You want?

You're disgusting.

He eats, cuts more. A thick coin of marbled purple slithers across the counter and over the lip to the floor. He scoops it up, gobbles. Five-second rule, he says.

She stares at the tiles that haven't been mopped since they moved in: Are you looking for food poisoning?

Don't believe in it, he replies, setting his bottle back on the squid stain.

Don't put that there. She can just see him, spreading it throughout the house.

What, like this? He lifts the bottle, drinks, replaces it on the goo. I don't endorse your obsessive fixations, he says, turning back to his spitting pan, tossing in a ring and tentacle to test the oil's heat.

Charlotte arrives at last, via Uber, straight off the flight, fashionable, strangely neat, with a hard little mouth.

W HEELING HER CASE into the hall, Charlotte accepts a kiss on both cheeks from Aud, whom she's seen on Facebook, Instagram, Twitter, LinkedIn.

Sorry I didn't get around to bringing something, she says. Where is he?

He's in the kitchen, Aud replies. Come through.

Aud's voice is huskier than Charlotte expected, and she's thinner too, surprisingly tall. She doesn't seem to take a lot of pride in her appearance.

Thanks for putting me up, Charlotte says.

Benj? Aud calls.

Hi, he replies. I'm stirring—critical moment. Be there in a minute.

Charlotte follows Aud up to the guest room.

Folks will be getting here soon if you want to, uh, freshen up.

I forgot to bring toothpaste and, um, tampons, Charlotte says.

Oh sure, bathroom cupboard. Help yourself to whatever.

Thanks. As Charlotte smiles, her face feels tight, as though someone were pressing flat hands hard into her cheeks.

A UD LIGHTS TEA LIGHTS in jam jars on the coffee table, windowsills, fireplace. Benji comes in. She didn't bring wine, Aud says. Who comes to a person's house for dinner without bringing something to drink? Do you think it's a German thing?

She's not German, just lives there. She's from Las Vegas.

Well, I'll have to go out and get another bottle, at least.

Look, it doesn't matter.

Nothing worse than running out of booze. That's a sin where I'm from.

I'll go.

No, I'll go. She's your pal. I don't know what to say to her.

Aud yanks on boots and the long black coat Benji hates because it's shapeless, masculine. She steps out into the brisk dark. The cowbell jangles as the front door slams—the landlady is a Buddhist.

B ENJI PRESSES THE HEEL of the loaf he is baking; it doesn't bounce back. He closes it in the oven, sucks a scorched fingertip. Water is gurgling in the pipes. Charlotte is showering. He returns to his interrupted task of dabbing mushrooms clean with a kitchen towel. The bathroom latch. Her feet treading across the landing above his head. Strangulated croak of the guest bedroom door. If they don't mention it, didn't happen. Charlotte moves up there awhile and comes down looking put together: lilac camisole, neat-fitting trousers, hair slicked back and still wet, careful makeup. They don't touch. He doesn't even find her that attractive.

She seems nice, another exotic, Charlotte says. Where'd you find her?

Paris, OKCupid.

Scottish?

Irish. I didn't tell her anything.

I assumed.

That bra hoists Charlotte's tits so they look bigger than they actually are. It's a cheap trick. He toughens.

But hey, he says, one transgression is no great harm in the grand scheme.

Indeed. Charlotte smiles, face tight. What're you making? She prods the sporadically bubbling risotto broth with the wooden spoon, dips her face and throat in the steam to inhale. Her chest flushes.

Bitch, that turns him on. For the first time, he wonders if he erred in offering her the guest room. He hasn't seen her since Heidelberg, maybe didn't think this through, almost forgot it happened.

It was actually several transgressions, she says, looking out of the grubby window to a string of lights in the neighboring garden. Pretty, she observes.

He can smell her.

T HE OTHER GUESTS have arrived by the time Aud shuffles in with two bottles of good white. She kicks off her boots at the door, casts her mammoth coat over the staircase post. No time to change or to titivate much. She feels plain, narrow, slips up to put on lipstick.

Downstairs, Benji is seated at one end of the dining table, an empty chair to his right and left. Jesse is a no-show. Udoka and Davy are sitting opposite Charlotte and Luis. Molls is at the far end. They are discussing the humanitarian crisis in Haiti, where Udo's been working with Doctors Without Borders.

Aud, can you grab another bottle of wine? Benji calls.

Aud comes to the table with wine, takes her place between Charlotte and Benji, who dishes up. They eat, talk. First and second helpings. Then, cheese with bread and salad. Benji tells the others that Aud's family serves the cheese *after* dessert *with* coffee: horror. Aud pretends not to mind. When all the wine has been consumed, Benji delves into the landlady's liquor cabinet.

She said to help ourselves, Benji says, extracting a bottle of Bulleit. He knows she can't stomach whiskey.

C HARLOTTE HEADS OUTSIDE for a smoke while Aud clears the plates. The cowbell jangles as Charlotte opens the door. Nobody comes with her. She leaves the door ajar to feel part of things. After she's stubbed out, she heads up to the bathroom to wash her hands. She can't stand the stench once the pang is gone. She takes a tampon from Aud's bathroom cupboard, unpeels it, pees, and reads Aud's framed autographed photo of Luke Perry from *Beverly Hills, 90210*:

> To Áidrí, Love and peace,
> LP xo

What, did he ask her to spell out the freakin' name? Earnest people give her the creeps.

B Y MIDNIGHT, everybody else has gone.
School day tomorrow, Aud says, cling-filming leftovers, pongy cheese.

Benji lifts glasses, sets them in the sink.

Charlotte needn't help, Aud insists: Sure, you don't know where anything goes. And you've a big day ahead, presenting a paper at Harvard. What an honor!

When Charlotte has gone up, Aud comments: I'm surprised you can be a professor of African American studies and be white.

Soon after, they follow, moving between bedroom and bathroom, undressing, brushing teeth, trying not to make noise.

THE HALL LIGHTS GO OFF, a mattress strains. Whispers and the quiet of fucking, got to be. Charlotte gets up, nude, and opens the wardrobe, steps in, angles an ear near the wall to listen, taking care not to rustle the cheap wire hangers. She opens the bedroom door, which squeaks. They'll hear that. In the bathroom she pees, runs the tap to remind them she is here. The window sash is wedged up to let in four inches of navy air. Outside in the night, a low noise of crickets.

THEY FREEZE AND WAIT until all is still. Aud blows in Benji's ear.
Tell me? she says.

I want her to stand at our door and listen, he whispers. I want to call her in. She's at the foot of the bed. You go and stroke her legs, kiss her belly. She pushes you back, rough, crawls over. I watch, I watch, see you rippling together. You stoke her with your fingers and she takes me in her mouth and I kiss you while her little tits dangle in my hands.

Aud comes, then Benji comes inside her.

BACK IN BED, Charlotte listens to the languid afterward, drops a hand to pulse, pinches a nipple, comes without a sound, sleeps.

CHARLOTTE WAKES EARLY to read through her talk.
Breakfast is on the worktop: granola, rye bread, Bonne Maman apricot preserves. She's can't-eat-nervous and wearing a very snug pencil skirt, sheer stockings, heels—maybe trying too hard, but he likes it when women dress for him, something Aud doesn't seem to realize.

Benji appears and brews coffee, barely looks her way.

You should come to Germany for Oktoberfest, Charlotte says. You could stay in my guest room, both of you.

Thanks. Maybe we will. We're getting married.

Wow, Charlotte says. When did that happen?

A few months ago.

You've kept that quiet. Before Heidelberg?

When I got back.

How long have you been together?

A year and a half, long-distance.

Quick.

I want her here with me.

Shouldn't you give her a ring?

She won't wear one till I do. Shit, I'm gonna be late for class.

You haven't told people yet? I mean, nobody mentioned it last night.

No, we have. Our families. I just don't want to make a *thing* of it.

Worried about who might come out of the woodwork?

He ignores this: She'll be up soon.

I'll stick around to congratulate.

Don't bother. Well, good luck today. Maybe see you in Heidelberg, or at a wedding, right?

Benji leaves via the back door. Through the window, she watches as he unlocks his bike from the porch and exchanges a friendly word with the neighbor, who pauses at weeding. When Benji took his cock out to show her, he presented it as a trophy, like a proud boy showing off what he possessed. He couldn't stand for her not to know, fucked her as if he believed it was the one thing he was great at. No, he couldn't give that up, can't help it. He left her feeling restless, scooped out. There is no such thing as a neutral exchange; people give or take.

Charlotte is standing at the foot of the stairs. Above her, on the ceiling, a gray box winks. Her head swirls. She doubles forward and grips the banister's solid spoke as her stomach churns. She kneels on the first step. The carpet here is spare. It burns her knees. Her throat is pulsing like a frog's, her belly seething—something wants out. She seems to be a well, and baling twine is pulling up a rattly bucket. She creeps up the stairs, inch by inch, with limbs that are inexact, not hers, or rather her own not working with her, feeble and achy. Up she slithers to the top. Her ears echo. Aud is fast asleep and she's in Aud's home, sliming across the cold floor to the toilet. She tips up the seat. From the bedroom Aud will hear everything. She hovers over, lips open, gut pumping—to get what out? She gags, tries to gather herself, quietly spews over the toilet, splashing the seat, wall, floor, cistern, side of the bath. She spews again, specking hair and cheeks, her fingers webbed with saliva, acidic and foamy, muddled stuff. She'll never drink again, though she didn't drink that much. Impossible to stave off this loneliness.

Charlotte, you okay?

Aud's shadow is under the door. She didn't hear her move.

Uh, no, Charlotte says.

Can I help? I'll bring you some water. I can leave it here by the door.

Aud pads down to the kitchen.

Charlotte checks the lock. Thank god she didn't vomit all over the stairs. She yanks out ribbons of toilet paper, rolls her hand in them, squelches the wadding across puddles, spots. The spiral and bubble of the flush makes her want to puke again. She can do nothing but lie on her back on the floor in the reeking bathroom, her body a conundrum to her, always wanting and erring. When dizziness settles, she rolls onto her front, crouches in a ball. It doesn't mean anything.

But Aud is not alone, is she? Not crawling over Charlotte's floor, emptying out her insides? No, Aud is leaving a glass of water by the door. Aud does not need an engagement ring. Aud wants things to feel equal. What planet does this girl live on? How'd she get to be so hopeful, simple? Charlotte wishes she were less intelligent; it's a distorting gift, a perversion. She drags herself up to the toilet bowl again, coughing out bile and flotsam until there's nothing left in her but fumes.

I think you need a doctor, Aud says, when the deluge subsides. I'll call someone.

Charlotte sighs, exhausted, a husk.

Do you want me to phone the conference people?

I can't do it.

I know. I'll tell them you're sick.

They flew me here. I'm fucked. Charlotte hasn't cried in ages.

You can't help it.

A glob of drool falls out of Charlotte's mouth. Her throat is raw, lining bruised and jagged. She retches vainly. Nothing's left.

Sorry, she says, her voice a scorched wisp, a creak.

What crappy timing! If you open the door, I'll help get you into bed. You can lie in our room. It's closer.

My tights, Charlotte says. Her tights are pulled, flecked with fibers, smut.

We'll change your flight, Aud says. You can stay a bit longer.

Don't tell Benji!

Of course, not yet. Aud goes into her bedroom, comes back out: Who should I call to cancel?

It's in my phone. We texted yesterday. The code's, um, 2046. Dr. Olawale.

AUD RETURNS to the bedroom and texts Benji:
C is vomiting What if we poisoned her?
I'm fine. We ate the same thing. You?
I didn't eat the squid What do I do?
Don't tell her about the squid. Pharmacy? Am tied up with seminar.
Can you come at lunch? I've a meeting Don't feel right abandoning her
Dunno. Can you reschedule?
Fuck Benj, that's not fair!
Your work's more flex. We're a team, no?
Will phone the doc
Chicken soup?
Ye kidding? I don't like touching raw chicken
Don't be a wimp.
Fine You're cleaning the bathroom See you asap, yes?
Home by 7.
7!
Sorry, baby, best I can do.

BENJI'S OFFICE HOUR has been uneventful—even the suck-up didn't show today. He flicks through webpages: on Rate My Professors, a new review calls him *funny*. It's not a word he'd have used. He suspects it was written by one of the two girls who sit at the front of the class, occasionally braless, bare legs. They try to fluster him. When he's getting off, he sometimes pictures the taller one with the slow eyes. She can't be more than 20. Oh, he's really not that guy, but it doesn't hurt to think about it. He's been given a red chili for hotness. He looks up his colleagues. He can't fathom how Jonathan Delgado got a red chili. Jonathan Delgado just got tenure at Columbia, but he's an aberration, a genius like Benji's father, born that way, hardly deserves credit.

He goes through his mail. There's a postcard from the quiet Native American kid to thank him for the extra lessons. It felt good to help someone for no other reason than to help someone, not thinking about oneself for once. He'll do half an hour of Catullus and some marking before class starts. After that, he'll mull the Charlotte problem. Would have liked to have swum before dinner; that's fucked. Where will he get tenure? He wants them to stay on the East Coast, not end up in Nowheresville.

He sends Aud a thoughtful WhatsApp:

If we have a baby girl I'd like to name her Laure?

Laure's sweet, she replies.

Wish it could happen by accident.

Fuck sake, Benj You don't make a mistake You decide A child is an epic responsibility

Just saying.

And apart from Auntie Lil, my fam' are miles away

We'd work it out. Mom would come help.

Have to go At Wholefoods, buying chicken

Benji locks his door, takes his phone off Wi-Fi, and flicks onto YouPorn, Teen category. They're probably not teenagers, though they look fresh, beautiful. He takes a quick five, *time for him*. If Aud were to let him have pictures, he wouldn't look at porn as often. She says no, because of Jennifer Lawrence—what if? They are getting hitched and she doesn't trust him yet. Charlotte sent him a photo.

When Aud plucks the wiry black hairs from the moles on his back, she claims: This is my expression of love. I'm grooming you.

Like an ape?

Yip, like an ape.

Ow. That hurts!

If we ever split, she said recently, you'll tell your next woman your wife did this, and she'll think I was cruel, and you'll hate me for it.

We won't split, he replied. I want you forever.

Once they are married, he'll try, really try, to wind down the porn, and he must stop sleeping with other women. He discussed it with his mother and his married brother. He told them everything, or enough. They were surprised but agreed that what she doesn't know won't hurt, best not to come clean, she doesn't need to know. Honestly, he would rather unburden. Except for these fitful scraps that don't count, he tells her everything. But he can't be too hard on himself, his mother said: he needed, he needs, and now he's suffering. And if he can't ever tell her, he'll suffer indefinitely. That's a sizable sacrifice to make for any person. He'd do anything for Aud, to keep her. He doesn't really have her yet.

He needs them to have a child. Things will be clearer then. He should text Charlotte:

Hey, sorry you're ill. Hope A is helping out. B

SOME BOYS ARE SAUNTERING up ahead as Aud walks back from the supermarket. They wear backpacks. One has a rolled-up towel under his arm. Their heads are damp. They push each other, talk loudly, speaking rubbish. One leaps to swipe the branches of a magnolia tree. One's keen to show the others something, asks his friend to call him. They crumple into whoops and giggles as the phone croons and whimpers, making sexy noises. They are about 11, wee boys who haven't had their growth spurts. At the traffic lights, the kid with the towel says bye and the others wave, go on. His mum rounds the corner in an SUV. An older girl is up front. He climbs into the back seat, slams the door, which doesn't shut properly. His mum looks back, hasty, tells him to do it again. Again, the door does not close tight. His sister has to hop out and do it for him. Once their seatbelts are clasped, the car goes.

AUD STOPS AT THE CROSSING and sets down her shopping bag. It's heavy: roast chicken, Pepto-Bismol, club soda, loo roll, bleach, and oranges. She stretches her achy arm. It's too early to be sure. She doesn't feel anything yet. Wouldn't she feel something by now? Every body is different, reacts differently. Please don't let it be yet. She isn't ready, they aren't ready. She should have told Benji. She can't.

Hale, vivid flowers have come up through chinks in the pavement, as if they were needle-hard instead of yielding stem, sepal, petal, so craving the sensation of sun, wind, dust, winged things that they've pierced the tarmac and swollen to crack it open. Her mother would know these flowers. Her folks are far away. Maybe it will be all right. Fishing in her pockets, she pulls out her iPhone to take a photo to send to her mum, ask her about the flowers. Shit, she's lifted Charlotte's phone, too.

CHARLOTTE IS LYING on Aud's bed. Nearby a train streaks past, hauling her out of sleep. Her limbs are heavy. Her bra is squeezing her ribs. Breath won't sink deep inside her, barbs in her throat. An insect hums against the mesh of the small square window, wanting in. Otherwise, the room is bare, peaceful, a faint smell of dust. She doesn't want to go home yet.

Before he heads to the seminar, Benji pokes about in his desk for the bottle of Xanax his mother gave him, since he hasn't been sleeping well. He swallows three capsules with the dregs of the morning's coffee.

Aud opens the text to Charlotte from Benji. She scrolls up the chain of messages they've exchanged. Under her breastbone, there's a lump of cold dough. When she finds the photo, sound falls out of her ears, a hand flies to her mouth. She drops to her knees on the pavement. No—she gets to her feet, bolts back in the direction of the shop, away, anywhere, gripping Charlotte's phone. She stops, twists around, goes back, twists again, keeps going. She. She doesn't know what. Her knees hurt, she will not cry. This is not her story. This is not it. She walks into a warm coffee shop, walks straight out again. Everything she's doing is a cliché—excruciating. She is not this person. Where should she go? She doesn't have anyone here. Her shopping bag waits on the pavement at the crossing. The chicken is cooling in its foil pouch. Its salt skin puckers in congealed juice. She rings Auntie Lil in New York.

Can I come? I'll catch the train tonight.

Of course, Lil says. I'm in Patagonia, but Raúl will let you in.

Thank you. You're saving my bacon.

You know, Lil says. This is not a death.

On Riverside Drive, over Skype, she listens as he spills. Sobbing, he tells her of the two, three, five, nine women he's fucked since saying that she was his person, since asking her to love him and have their children. She senses there were more. How many women, men? Does he know how not to lie? Strange encounters come to mind—at Harvard Square by the newsstand, in Trina's Starlite Lounge—each woman stunned to meet her, disturbed that she existed. Now she sees it all. Stupid. Stupid. Stupid. Her eyes stored each encounter to taunt her over what she missed. Her fingers pick at stickers on pomelos in her aunt's fruit bowl. She can't stay here. She digs a nail: the scent of acrid, soapy rind. Quite young, she was told, *It'll fall to you to say no.* That, she'd thought, was the olden days. She said yes and watched herself being taken over, slowly altered, having invited Benji in, at first innocent, then complicit.

I'll do anything, he pleads, when all's supposedly confessed.

She opens the fridge and cracks a beer. A sip won't do any harm. It hurts to see his pain, a chord between them still. Could she stay and give him a chance? People aren't one thing. She isn't perfect. It doesn't have to make sense.

He says: I can't be too hard on myself because I hated lying to you and I've suffered a lot. There's relief in his expression.

When did you last have sex? she asks. Was it in our house? Is she still there?

His face malfunctions. He looks caught.

Ha. A memory trickles and she bursts, shielding her mouth with her hand, laughing, laughing.

What? he asks.

There's spittle on her keyboard, small bubbles on the screen.

Uncertainty in his face, he smiles.

She drops her hand and shakes her head: Do you remember kissing on that street corner by *métro* Parmentier after eating in the specious Brazilian place?

Oh, the bum? He snickers.

Yeah, the bum with the bum—ludicrous. She's suddenly crying. She gasps: I should've known then that this was a joke to you.

Aud, I'm so sorry.

Why?

I don't know. I don't even know. He sighs and looks inside her instead of at her, and she almost recognizes him. I tried, he says. I can't explain it. I got lost. It got worse and worse till I couldn't feel. I did it and I couldn't tell you, or undo it, or make it better without telling. From the first time, the first mistake, it was over, I'd spoiled it. I thought I could pretend it hadn't happened and it would, well, you wouldn't know, and I'd never do it again. Lots of people do that. But I felt terrible, terrible. Lying was painful. I was so angry. I mean, I wanted to forget or fix it, but I couldn't. I kept doing it. There was no escape. I couldn't look at you without seeing myself, how ugly I'd made it. Your lovely trusting face was torture. I didn't know what to do. I don't. I love you. I'm drowning, Aud. I'm drowning.

Stop. I can't bear to listen to this. You're not a victim here.

I'm just sick of suffering and hiding from you. I've lived you like a dream.

For fuck's sake, Benji. I'm real, I've always been real. Catch yourself on. You wanted me and her and everything you wanted. And you felt, you feel, you still feel, that you are entitled to that. Don't you? Don't you? What makes you think that way? You're just a man. You thought you'd get away with it. Own up.

You're wrong, he says. Shit . . .

What?

Light's coming up outside. I have to sleep.

Are you serious?

He smears his hands across his eyes. Can we do this later? Please. I've work soon. I'm exhausted.

Fine, she says. It'll be a pig of a day.

IT'S ALMOST SIX. She shuts her laptop. He doesn't get it. He only knows how to feel for himself. She hates him. She intends to hate him. He's coiled about himself. Why did no one teach him that lies eat indiscriminately? Every grown-up knows that.

She walks across the apartment and looks out through the three large windows that face New Jersey. Madness. The daybreak's honey, tangerine, magenta. How did he not know that? Is he warped, stunted, doolally? Madness. She's so fucking tired, so full and empty, so everything nothing. But she's away and she'll never go back because it wouldn't make sense. Could she go back? She hates him. She's never loved anyone so much. What if she never loves anyone as much? She unlatches a window that is really a door. A gust pushes in like a person who's dying to enter to get something done. Madness. Once it was precious. It really was unlike anything. How did they mess up something so good? It was hard to remember since they'd gone all King Lear.

She looks down from the seventeenth floor. Down down down down down down down down down down down down down down down—no, she'd never do that. Not judging though, not judging, just not the genre of person, doesn't have it in her, more the type to choose to die gradually if it came to despair. The river's a very delicate pink, the shade that dishwater goes when you wash a knife with which you've sliced beetroot. It's so pretty she could howl. Her Skype rings.

If it's him, and it is him, then it's too late and too early. She won't answer. No, he's lovely and she hates him. She'll kneel down here and have a little violent sleep on the carpet and then, and then, and then, she'll pee and stay or go back, go back or stay or go. Madness. If only she could hear only what was in her head and not feel anything, she'd be mended. Her phone keeps buzzing. Why is she still worried about him? She plucks the phone from a crevice in the couch and throws it out of the window that's a door, down down down, bending her head over the rosy indelible emptiness, watching the phone fall, checking that it doesn't hit some innocent person. What if he calls again? So what. The pavements are lonely anyway.

She draws her head back in and shuts the door and shivers. She rubs her eyes. What did she expect? Dinah warned her all about it. But she didn't hear when she was listening. Dinah Washington is always singing, always fantasizing about the awful glowing madness that scatters through your life and makes no sense and makes sense utterly. He's wrong and she's wrong and it's wrong and everything's wrong. It's the only blazing thing and impossible at the same time. Now she knows. Now she hears. Now she's alive. And what will she do now that she's raw energy? Not everything she had is gone if there's a child. And does she really have to tell him there's a child? Better to keep a child apart from a greedy, fragile liar. And yet he had such promise. What a relief!

She takes the stairs down, down, down, down, down, down, down, down, down, down, down, down, down, down, down, down, down to the foyer and the sidewalk and the corner and another corner. She keeps walking, all the way to where she is going. When she gets there, she buys a cheap mobile phone—pay as you go. She heads to the next place, a pharmacy. When she comes out, the siren goes off. She runs up Broadway, hoping they'll run after her, though she didn't steal. Nobody bothers, lazy fucks.

Back in the apartment, she sets up her new phone, locates the number, and calls, but there's no answer. She texts:

Hey, you in town?

She hasn't seen Dev since he left Belfast, what, five years ago. She runs a bath and steeps, het up, high, electrified, pure disgust in her veins. After nearly an hour, the phone pings. She wipes away the condensation with a hand towel.

Who this?

It's Audrey

His reply comes within a minute: *Where?*

Here. She shares her location. *Let's go dancing.* +

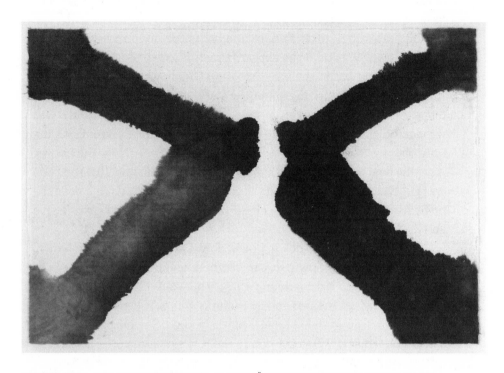

SUH SE OK, *PERSON*. 1998, INK ON MULBERRY PAPER. 24.3 × 35.8". COURTESY THE ARTIST AND LEHMANN MAUPIN, NEW YORK AND HONG KONG.

THE PAINFUL SUM OF THINGS

Pankaj Mishra and Nikil Saval

The writer V. S. Naipaul died on August 11, 2018, at the age of 85. The correspondence below took place over the following week.

DEAR PANKAJ,

I saw the news about Naipaul. I was expecting it: I had heard he was seriously ailing as far back as 2015, and since then I have returned intermittently to his books, rereading several, with a strange uneasiness or sense of preparation.

Now that he has died, the preparation feels insufficient: the uneasiness remains. I suspect you feel it as well: how to speak about a writer whose work has been meaningful—in my case, profoundly so; I could not imagine my life without it—as well as a source of frustration or real pain. I have admired Naipaul as much as I have found him difficult to admire, a murky admixture that I find difficult to explain or clarify, and which I find with no other writer to anything like the same degree. (Edward Said referred to his "pain and admiration," and dissonant phrases of that kind are scattered through appreciations of his work.) I know, too, that you knew him, which I did not. I don't know if that makes him more or less difficult to appraise.

Perhaps it would have been better for me to work all this out before he died, but since it gives an occasion like no other, I thought I'd write you.

Yours,
Nikil

DEAR NIKIL,

Yes, I thought several times in recent years while hearing news of his ill health: I should write something, put together a more complex record of my debt to him, and also of the ways in which his vision was constricted and constricting. For many aspiring writers from modest backgrounds, in the West as well as in Asia, Africa, and the Caribbean, he was the first writer who made us think that we, too, had something to say, and that we, too, had an intellectual claim upon the world. He was a great enabler in this sense, starting the underconfident and less resourceful among us on long journeys. In societies and cultures where the idea of a whole life devoted to writing and thinking is confined to the privileged members of the population, Naipaul's example—that of a man making himself a writer through sheer effort—was a great boost. His novelistic gifts were so great, endowing even very minor characters in *A House for Mr. Biswas* and *A Bend in the River* with dignity. His harsh critiques of India, in particular, and postcolonial societies, in general, came as a bracing revelation—that this kind of writing is possible, even necessary.

This was the first phase of my engagement with his writing, when Naipaul as an example and innovator was hugely important. But this relationship was to change—inevitably. Over time the larger political and social contexts in which a writer writes and is read and receives acclaim start to become visible, and one's own work starts to be clarified. I read all of Naipaul, introduced two volumes of his essays, and briefly entertained the idea of writing his biography. For many years, however, I have felt closer to Stuart Hall than to Naipaul.

All best,

Pankaj

DEAR PANKAJ,

It's interesting you bring up Hall, whose posthumously issued memoir, *Familiar Stranger*, I read last year. Hall brings up Naipaul in the context of attending Oxford and listening to the BBC radio program *Caribbean Voices*, in which Naipaul participated alongside other great figures—George Lamming, Derek Walcott, et al. Thrown into relief, Naipaul comes across as unpleasant, self-loathing—unwilling, in a way, to be seen to participate in the collective project of fashioning a Caribbean identity in the new island home. By institutionalizing the study of diaspora cultures (among other achievements), and making it possible for countless others to do the same, Hall modeled a more generous attitude to the place he came from than Naipaul did. He was also much closer to—was central in founding—the academic study of the postcolonial world. I was introduced to both of them at the same time, when I was in university in the early 2000s.

And yet I read Hall's memoir wincing with the same kinds of recognition that attend my readings of Naipaul (especially his travel books on India), and I feel that they share commonalities obscured by their divergent careers and their obvious political differences. Hall was a child of the small African diaspora bourgeoisie who adopted an ersatz version of English society in Jamaica; Naipaul of an impoverished Hindu family, his father notoriously frustrated in his desire to achieve literary success. Both of their self-narratives shift relentlessly: from a sense of identity with others to a sense of alienation from the people they are expected to identify with. Hall wrote of how, growing up in privileged surroundings, he never knew the "other, darker Jamaica of the multitude"; but then, having moved to England, he *became* part of this multitude. He remembers the shock of seeing black people at Paddington Station in the 1950s in England. "What I thought I had left behind as an unresolved dilemma—the difficulties my family background had bequeathed to me of neither wanting any identification with my own social stratum, nor being able to feel present in my own homeland, conscious of the chasm that separated me from the multitude—had turned up to meet me on the other side of the Atlantic," he writes.

Scenes like this are classically Naipauline. I was rereading the section "The Journey" from *The Enigma of Arrival*—the most beautiful of his books—and was struck again when, on the ship from New York to Southampton, the stewards ask a wealthier black passenger to share a room with Naipaul. Both understand the moment immediately. "It's because I'm colored you're putting me here with him," the black man says in anger. Naipaul, too, tries to avoid the moment of identification, and mulls it later:

In Puerto Rico there had been the Trinidad Negro in a tight jacket on his way to Harlem. Here was a man from Harlem or black America on his way to Germany. In each there were aspects of myself. But, with my Asiatic background, I resisted the comparison; and I was traveling to be a writer. It was too frightening to accept the other thing, to face the other thing; it was to be diminished as man and writer. Racial diminution formed no part of the material of the kind of writer I was setting out to be.

Were the passage to end here, it would be empty, politically and morally: Naipaul wishes to be a Writer, a raceless figure, and he views it as an achievement to be that. But then he doubles back from the vantage point of the present:

Thinking of myself as a writer, I was hiding my experience from myself; hiding myself from my experience. And even when I became a writer I was without the means, for many years, to cope with that disturbance.

He recognizes the limits on solidarity, recognizes the aspects of it that he hides from, recognizes the trauma of it—unmistakably colonial. And yet he stops at the recognition. I am not certain that he ever found the means to cope with the disturbance. He could only return to it.

Hall excavated the same ground. ("Over and over something would remain / Unbalanced in the painful sum of things." —James Merrill, "For Proust.") But Hall found the intellectual resources, among colleagues, European and English and diaspora theorists, the multiracial movement on the left against Thatcher. (From the pages of *Familiar Stranger*, one gets the sense that it was never quite enough.) Partly to his detriment, Naipaul was thrown constantly back on himself, as if he had nowhere to turn—as if that were the only path available to a writer, to find what appeared to be one's own way. "You sense that the curve of evolution in his own work comes from within himself and is something he alone fully understands," Hilary Mantel wrote, in one of the most succinct, perceptive essays on the writer. It is unclear whether figures like the narrator of Teju Cole's *Open City*, who rejects a fraternal gesture from an African cabdriver ("I was in no mood for people who tried to lay claims on me," he says), could exist without the Naipaul prototype: the sacked newspaper reporter; the mimic man; the servant in unfamiliar surroundings in Washington DC; Naipaul himself, in India for the first time, thinking: "To be a member of a minority community has always seemed to me attractive. To be one of four hundred and thirty-nine million Indians is terrifying."

The question is whether this fundamental dissonance had to find the toxic resolutions that it did: his Islamophobic comments that gave succor to Hindutva; the current of antiblackness that courses through his work; the consistent disregard for women writers and editors. Illiberalism became for him a reflex, in the classic manner of reactionaries—though in the time when I was reading him, the US commenced its "war on terror," and I was dispossessed of the idea that liberalism made a stable foundation for toleration and pluralism. I am not certain that he adopted a colonial view, as others said he did; as late as *The Enigma of Arrival*, the degree of estrangement from this view is enormous. Nor am I certain that his most wretched provocations are revealing. But it has taken me some time to come around to feeling in Naipaul what Adorno recognized in Wagner: that what is damaged and wounding and reactionary in him is essential, a critical part of the work, not something ancillary or disfiguring.

Yours,
Nikil

DEAR NIKIL,

A news report today said that the new editor of the *Daily Mail* was summoned to Naipaul's deathbed by his wife, and together they read Tennyson aloud as the man slipped into oblivion. I find this tableau full of unbearable ironies—that the editor of Britain's most xenophobic tabloid should minister to the greatest postcolonial novelist of our time with the lyrics of the bard of British imperialism. From what I know of Naipaul's last years, they were full of rich and powerful people paying court to him and making him feel cherished. Of course, this is consistent with the choices he made when he was alive and well—and, as you say, such choices go back to his early days in London, when he distanced himself from his West Indian peers; turned his back not only on political community, but also on other ways of feeling love and solidarity (companionship, children, ordinary friendships); and embarked on this perilous project of extreme individualism with a half-romantic, half-bourgeois notion of what it means to be a writer.

You are right to think that this project, with its built-in dis-satisfactions, could only have terrible political and emotional consequences—racism, Islamophobia, misogyny, and general misan-thropy. There is an incandescent essay by Vivian Gornick on Naipaul and Baldwin—on why the latter opens up new places for reflection and action while the former closes them down. She concludes that Bald-win's unavoidable engagement with the tormented history of African Americans saves him from the sterile despair she identifies in Naipaul's nonfiction writing. This is a very important point—and complements one that Mantel makes about the endlessly self-referential quality of his work. Naipaul did not have an equally profound stake in any society he knew—or in the societies he condemned for failing to be more like the civilized West. He was embraced early in his career by Britain's white literary establishment; he retreated to the countryside but took little interest in British politics and professed disdain for the political struggles and intellectual endeavors of people like Stuart Hall. He was embarrassed about his origins in the small island of Trinidad and hoped to achieve a generous identity through his ancestral country. But an evi-dently weak and intellectually confused India disappointed and shamed him until the Hindu nationalists emerged on the scene and India began to look like a superpower-in-waiting.

It's interesting that you mention Wagner, who followed a some-what similar trajectory: the aspiring provincial in the metropolis who retreats from private humiliations into grandiose fantasies of self and nation. Naipaul's own fears and compensatory fantasies of strength probably developed early in his journey to the imperial metropolis, and during a pretty relentless experience of racism in England in the 1950s and '60s. Perhaps success of the kind he longed for and often received was no salve for these early wounds. He seems never to have ceased to feel a dissonance between the private and public self—that distortion he first began to feel on the epochal journey he describes in *The Enigma of Arrival*. He features, for instance, in Anthony Powell's diaries, inven-tively insulting Arabs or some other dark-skinned minority. I often wonder if Naipaul hated this side of himself even then—the performer from the colonies amusing a white audience that knows nothing or very little about his background. It may be why he turned so violently against Powell, his greatest early friend and supporter in England. In abandoning and betraying his friendships, he seems to have been running away from reminders of his shameful performances, his discarded selves, and into the security of wealth and power, where he could be cherished (a favorite word of his, incidentally) as a singular and matchless writer.

I also find it interesting that honesty for Naipaul too often meant the untrammeled expression of extreme prejudice—of the kind the far right today wants to legitimate in the name of free speech. It never amounted to an inquiry into the sources of prejudice. For instance, why did he never explore the reasons behind his loathing of writing by women? Of course, anyone who knows a little bit about Trinidad, the Indian subcontinent, or the Hindu caste system knows that his dislike of black people was rooted in the communal politics of the island, the Hindu distrust of Muslims, the feudal-patriarchal view of women as best confined to the domestic sphere, and the Brahmin's disdain for the swarthy alien. Naipaul took these primal fears of an insecure but entitled Indian minority to different parts of the world, enacting and elaborating them in very different contexts. This is why his travel books are best read as records of his own neuroses.

I think my own early admiration came to be qualified as I discovered his weirdly intransigent isolation and his failure to break it through worldly success. I grew up in India, in a very dense web of social relations, aware of the histories of diverse populations around me, and with several oral and literary cultures as my own inheritance. The world was not divided for me, as it seemed to be for Naipaul, between those who have achieved the summit of civilization (the modern West) and those in half-made or unmade societies who are trying but failing miserably to get there. There was enough postcolonial idealism around for us to reject the neoliberal, there-is-no-alternative notion that "the world is what it is" and people who don't find a place in it are nothing. The activists, writers, and thinkers I knew thought that such an unjust world could be changed; at the very least they wished to explore how the world came to be as it is. Naipaul's uncompromising individualism was indeed inspiring in a climate that did not encourage individual expression, let alone writerly ambition. But as I began to write, its limits came quickly into view. I began to see, too, after first traveling to the West in the mid-'90s, how Naipaul—or, more precisely, the idea of Naipaul as a brutally honest witness to the third world's absurdities—was a product of the cold war's intellectual culture.

All best,
Pankaj

———

DEAR PANKAJ,

What you say about Naipaul and the cold war rings true. It is obvious in the reception of his work: it seems fatuous that so many reviews upheld him as a reliable witness to the convulsions of third worldism. People found confirmation for what they wanted to see. India, Argentina, Central Africa: so it was not going to work out after all. Naipaul himself appeared conditioned by the reception, increasingly ready to play the fluid, mobile reporter—colonial but also cosmopolitan, brown but also *déraciné*—that was required. But it is less clear to me that he set out to be this person. The first two books on India are clarifying in this regard. In the second, *India: A Wounded Civilization*, Naipaul performs the sententious figure of caricature: one stentorian pronouncement follows another; entire worldviews are spun out from casual remarks dropped by supposedly representative figures. It is an unpersuasive book.

He is a more ruminative character in the earlier record, *An Area of Darkness*, and the book stands out to me less as a portrait of India than as the record of an encounter—a diaspora Indian "returning" to a country he imagined, an experience that repels the original image and turns his back on the self that conjured it. In the section "Fantasy and Ruins," he comes close to articulating the source of the isolation that you mention. He details an Indian "philosophy of despair, leading to passivity, detachment, acceptance" and then identifies it as his own:

> It is only now, as the impatience of the observer is dissipated in the process of writing and self-inquiry, that I see how much this philosophy had also been mine. It had enabled me, through the stresses of a long residence in England, to withdraw completely from nationality and loyalties except to persons; it had made me content to be myself alone, my work, my name (the last two so different from the first); it had convinced me that every man was an island, and taught me to shield all that I knew to be good and pure within myself from the corruption of causes.

This can be read in different ways, it seems to me. It could be a moment of awareness whose resolution is not yet ordained. In the paragraph that follows, he acknowledges the "colonial humiliation" that he did not fully recognize in Trinidad—that he could only encounter in India. And there is much acute writing later in the chapter on the omissions, silences, and repressions of 19th-century English fiction with regard to the empire.

But in another sense, the awareness is false, or is a half awareness—if only because we know that it became something of a credo for him, even if he often betrayed it. (About his loyalty to persons we know; his withdrawal from nationality was not so complete as he supposed.) There is something delusional about the phrase *corruption of causes* (one he would repeat): an anti-ideological feint that is characteristic of cold-war thinking, familiar from Nabokov, the self-regarding artist who is at pains to avoid groups, beliefs, positions. The historian Sanjay Subrahmanyam has also pointed to the legacy of neo-Hindu reformism that had taken hold in Trinidad, identifying Naipaul as in some sense a product of this larger historical process: "It was into this expatriate culture—envious of the West and its superiority, suspicious of Islam and Muslims, often with a healthy contempt for many of the practices and 'superstitions' of the old motherland that had been left behind—that Naipaul was born."

Still, there is the "enabling" aspect of the writing that you mention. I carried Naipaul with me—it was the collection of reportage *The Overcrowded Barracoon*—on my first return trips to India as an adult, in the early 2000s (my parents had moved back for a time). It was a horrid time: the emergency measures taken after the attack on the Parliament, the tenth anniversary of the destruction of Ayodhya, the pogroms that Modi presided over in Gujarat, "India Shining," et cetera. Over everything there was a pall of smugness and self-satisfaction, this feeling that the country was at last shaking off the accumulated centuries of dispossession to achieve itself. I could not stomach it, could not face up to it, could not feel myself to be part of the place.

Out of ignorance, I did not know what the living Naipaul thought of the situation, and so I read his early writings on India as if they were contemporary: as if they were describing the situation I saw transpiring around me. The other tonic was Arundhati Roy, whose seething book *The Algebra of Infinite Justice* I found in a bookshop in Bangalore. Whatever the misprision, these writings were twinned for me: they gave me the language to speak about India, a country that was not strictly mine, but that was also not not mine, that I could find my way into a sense of anger and betrayal about nonetheless. It was the beginning of political feeling. Naipaul was part of it.

In the tradition of community organizing in which I have been trained, I was taught the mode of regarding my past—any humiliations and shame and anger and privations—as something to be dug up, narrated, and ultimately politicized. Family and friends, schooling, stories from childhood: these were the source not just of politics, but the obstacles to politics—behaviors that keep one from organizing, that keep from one power and solidarity. Everywhere in Naipaul's writing, there are routes into the political world that are diverted back into the self; humiliations that lead into humiliations of others. "These people want to break my spirit," he wrote in a letter to his first wife, Patricia Hale, describing the British. "They want me to forget my dignity as a human being. They want me to know my place." This could have been the beginning of an entirely different trajectory. The result instead was—and this is to tell only part of it—the terrible humiliation of his wife and the abuse he meted out to Margaret Gooding. Nothing can excuse it. But I think Naipaul was often trying to find just such an excuse, without ever examining what he was doing, and to whom.

I have often thought of Naipaul alongside the great Kenyan master Ngugi wa Thiong'o. Perhaps it is because two of their important nonfiction books have opposing titles: Naipaul's *Finding the Center*, Ngugi's *Moving the Centre*. But Ngugi, himself a fierce critic of the postcolonial state, the compromises of its leaders, and the corruption of its society, found his way to a different sort of intransigence: a Maoist approach to the novel form, written in a subaltern language that had no tradition in the novel. He called for the abolition of English departments—the sort that would eventually find room for Naipaul (as well as Ngugi's own early work). He found himself forced into exile, and then in various positions at American universities. The closeness of Ngugi to the university mirrors Naipaul's distance from it—just as scholars were developing new ways of coming to terms with postcolonial societies, Naipaul was increasingly marking his remove. I recognize the impulse, but it captures another aspect of the thinness of his analytic mode late in life, and the nature of the reception he garnered: as if, far from the political strictures of academia, he alone could see the truth. It was another cost of his isolation, with deleterious consequences for him and the discourse he contributed to.

Yours,
Nikil

―――――

DEAR NIKIL,

You are right: Naipaul did not seek this role of the uniquely positioned reporter on the third world. He found himself in it, and much of his complicated and tormented relationship with his subjects was bleached out, especially in his writings on Muslim countries. This has at least partly to do with the Anglo-American (and very un-Continental) cult of the no-bullshit, empiricist intellectual—the man who exposes himself to unpleasant or dangerous reality and tells the truth about it, using the clearest of prose. Orwell was the first great figure in this pantheon of cold-war liberalism, and what Raymond Williams said about him in *Culture and Society* could also be applied to Naipaul.

It is worth quoting Williams on Orwell at length:

> He is genuinely baffling until one finds the key to the paradox, which I will call the paradox of the exile. For Orwell was one of a significant number of men who, deprived of a settled way of living, or of a faith, or having rejected those which were inherited, find virtue in a kind of improvised living, and in an assertion of independence. The tradition, in England, is distinguished. It attracts to itself many of the liberal virtues: empiricism, a certain integrity, frankness. It has also, as the normally contingent virtue of exile, certain qualities of perception: in particular, the ability to distinguish inadequacies in the groups which have been rejected. It gives, also, an appearance of strength, although this is largely illusory. The qualities, though salutary, are largely negative; there is an appearance of hardness (the austere criticism of hypocrisy, complacency, self-deceit), but this is usually brittle, and at times hysterical: the substance of community is lacking, and the tension, in men of high quality, is very great.

Williams then goes on to define Orwell as a vagrant, and tries to understand the nature of his appeal, and this applies to Naipaul as well:

> Orwell, in different parts of his career, is both exile and vagrant. The vagrant, in
> literary terms, is the "reporter," and, where the reporter is good, his work has the
> merits of novelty and a certain specialized kind of immediacy. The reporter is an
> observer, an intermediary: it is unlikely that he will understand, in any depth, the
> life about which he is writing (the vagrant from his own society, or his own class,
> looking at another, and still inevitably from the outside). But a restless society
> very easily accepts this kind of achievement.

I think mainstream intellectual cultures in cold-war America and Britain in the '70s and '80s were prone to accept very easily Naipaul's reporting and analysis of Asia, Africa, and Latin America. It was so much easier to warm to a writer who downplayed the profound damage imperialism inflicted on many non-Western societies; almost entirely ignored the two world wars, genocide, slavery, the many crises of capitalism, and other self-inflicted calamities of European and American societies; warned against the glamor of victimhood; and claimed that the failures of Asians and Africans were largely the result of their own intellectual confusion and political incompetence. It of course also helped that a large part of Naipaul's nonfiction is infused with Western assumptions of modernization theory, and notions of individual responsibility and private entrepreneurship that were subsequently sacralized by the Reagan-Thatcher revolution in the 1980s. Remarkably, these decades when Naipaul became the prime witness to the third world's abortive modernization were also the time when a range of writers and scholars were breaking with dominant Western modes of knowledge and offering new epistemologies—from Lévi-Strauss and Syed Hussein Alatas to Ashis Nandy and Samir Amin and, of course, Ngugi. But their insights were yet to be absorbed—and still are—in mainstream discourse.

Naipaul's reputation as a bold truth teller about the postcolonial world peaked around 1981, with *Among the Believers*, just as postcolonial studies got underway with the publication of Edward Said's *Orientalism*. Naipaul's response to this intellectual revolution, which focused attention on how the "East" had been misrepresented, and how many intellectuals came to be complicit with imperial power, was to pretend not to have heard of Said, deliberately mispronounce his name, and claim that the postcolonial academy generates a lot of "babble." The latter charge was of course not without truth—Said himself complained about some of his unreadable disciples—but it took a great deal of intellectual obtuseness to deny the pathbreaking work of many historians and anthropologists, such as those identified as members of the Subaltern Studies Group.

Naipaul's own reputation began to split: postcolonial academia took a far more skeptical view of him than the *New York Review of Books* or the *New Yorker*. The literary value of Naipaul's work did not diminish, but his reportage now had to coexist with, and often be challenged by, more rigorous and sustained scholarship in academia. For instance, it was too easy for a historian trained in the academy to point out that Naipaul's analytical framework in *India: A Wounded Civilization* was a particularly lurid cliché of colonialist historiography—Muslim invaders wounding Hindu India—and that he was naively projecting into the inhabitants of the 10th century a very modern and deeply politicized idea of who is a Hindu or Muslim. Said brutally dismantled the central argument of *Beyond Belief*: that converts to Islam are a uniquely damaged people.

All this did not matter much outside academia, especially in mainstream Anglo-American journalism, where Naipaul's reputation was secure and his corrosive view of Muslim societies, amplified by people like Bernard Lewis, had many more takers than anything written by Said. But even for writers like me, who felt greatly enabled by Naipaul, and who were writing for the mainstream and not academia, it felt imperative to develop a very different method. As I said before, *An Area of Darkness* was for me a bracing shock, just as his essays were for you—living in a small town, surrounded by all the absurdities and cruelties of Indian society, I had simply not realized that they could be written about in this stringent way, or that my own experience could be described so uncannily well. The book liberated me as a writer. At the same time, I could not write like Naipaul—could not visit the Iranian Revolution, for instance, have a series of fascinating individual encounters, and draw vivid tableaux, but fail to discuss the shah's regime. There was no way I could go to Kashmir and not write about the Indian military occupation of the valley. I had to engage with its political and economic realities, often through the work of other writers. I could not pretend to be this singular, omniscient observer—the exile, the vagrant, the reporter—who takes accurate readings of society simply by showing up and talking to a few people, and then judges them for having failed to modernize/Westernize/Indianize sufficiently.

Time, too, was passing. Naipaul's last substantial work, *A Way in the World*, was published in 1994. His major work was done by the late

1980s—thirty years ago. He had no second wind like Philip Roth or John le Carré, and he became known to younger readers largely for some outlandish public pronouncements. His reputation briefly flowered after September 11, when cold-war liberalism made its last attempt to define itself against a formidable enemy—political Islam—but has been in rapid decline since. Reading Naipaul today, one would have very little sense of why the United States—in which he placed his hope for a universal civilization devoted to the pursuit of individual happiness—is the way it is today. There remains, of course, the myth of Naipaul. "A writer," he himself wrote, "is in the end not his books, but his myth," and "that myth is in the keeping of others." What is the myth of Naipaul, who maintains it today, and can it survive our tumultuous present? It certainly can't serve any progressive politics—young socialists and feminists in America and Britain are unlikely to have any time for the man who depicted socialists as frauds and claimed that women writers were inferior to him. Unlike many writers with ugly prejudices against women and minorities, Naipaul failed to finesse his public persona. The myth of Naipaul today is largely in the keeping of middle-aged white male liberals and neoconservatives—people seeking ideological validation as the world in which they exercised unchallenged hegemony fades away. After Naipaul's death, a *New York Times* writer hailed him as a great defender of "Western civilization" and quoted liberally from a speech of his to a right-wing think tank in New York in 1990. But we know that Western civilization today does not need stout defenders so much as critical interpreters—and here Naipaul does not provide much illumination, having insisted throughout, with very few and muted reservations, that the West was best.

All best,

Pankaj

———

DEAR PANKAJ,

There is a question that stands out to me in our correspondence, regarding the nature of the knowledge that a writer like Naipaul provides. As a traveler, he came to rely on the idea of immediate experience, of an analysis born from personal encounters with exemplary individuals, whose speech exuded the symptoms of some civilizational malady. He came strenuously to deny the extraordinary prejudices he brought to the enterprise, and to conflate the ideological traps his subjects and characters fell into with a suspicion of all ideology—to imagine it as pure illusion.

This was part of his appeal to some. Joan Didion's defense of Naipaul on this score is typical: "He is a writer for whom the theoretical has no essential application, for whom a theory or an ideology is superficial to the phenomenon it attempts to describe, something no more than a scaffolding, something to be 'erected' or 'demolished'; something 'imposed' (a word Naipaul often uses in relation to ideas) on the glitter of the sea, the Congo clogged with hyacinth, the actual world." This is a sour brief in favor of anti-intellectualism, not unknown in Didion's own work (the resonances between the two are striking; they developed very similar kinds of writing in isolation), and it unintentionally captures the failings of Naipaul as well as a more interesting aspect of his work, especially demonstrated in his novels. He was suspicious of the postcolonial national idea, and showed us nations that could not integrate the diverse populations they housed: nations that would elevate some and subject others. It is thus—perhaps against the grain—that the aphorism from *The Mimic Men*, "Hate oppression; fear the oppressed," can be read. What we used to call the third world had been ransacked by colonialism ("oppression"); but some of the leaders and forces that emerged ("the oppressed") approached the task of decolonization with blindness, venality, and worse.

The foundational mistake was not to suspect the same of the West, something he was in a position to do; he may have come close in the writings on the imperialist imagination in *An Area of Darkness*, and, more obliquely, in the estranged countryside of *The Enigma of Arrival*. (Admittedly, to call it a mistake is to euphemize, since it seemed essential to the coherence of his world.) The Western figures who populate Naipaul's midperiod novels are fantasists of a more palpable sort than the naifs of Greene or le Carré; one has the sensation, as a person of color, of listening in, as it were, on a private discourse. The dialogue of Bobby and Linda barreling through a disintegrating country in *In a Free State* ("She said, 'If I weren't English I think I would like to be a Masai. So tall, those women. So elegant'") has all the disturbing glibness, the insouciance with which Westerners still think of the countries of the South, to the extent that they think of them, with whose fates they can forever be unconcerned. There is an elective affinity between these narratives and those of the rageful midperiod Ngugi, who excoriates the

Kenyan bourgeoisie, with their golf clubs and other ersatz re-creations of the colonial world they once abjured. There is a good deal of this in Naipaul, and in the end too little of it.

When Naipaul received a knighthood, the cycle of humiliation made its final turn. He praised the universal civilization that granted him one of its highest, most nostalgic honors. There was the heir to Conrad and Dickens—Dickens who proposed, in response to Indian killings during the 1857 rebellion, "I should do my utmost to exterminate the Race upon whom the stain of the late cruelties rested"—receiving the sign of grace from the queen of the United Kingdom and the other Commonwealth realms.

It is the nature of the societies we live in never to let you forget your luck, to point to any individual success as a sign of those societies' ultimate justice, to make your rage against them seem like ingratitude. In the end, to an extent that I find debilitating, Naipaul was grateful. I know that the feelings of personal injury and grievance that arise in recalling these fundamental aspects of his life and art are disabling. Such feelings might one day be transmuted into something different: a necessary distance. But I have yet to manage it.

Perhaps it is because I linger with his observations of places and people for whom developing societies had no use—injured, abused, discarded, futureless—and think of Naipaul as one of the first to notice, one of the few for whom these could be the subject of literature. As in the unprompted glimpse of a cabdriver in the "Traveller's Prelude" to *An Area of Darkness*, on the docks in Alexandria:

Not far away, below a lamp standard, stood a lone cab. It had been there since the late afternoon; it had withdrawn early from the turmoil around the terminal. It had had no fares, and there could be no fares for it now. The cab-lamp burned low; the horse was eating grass from a shallow pile on the road. The driver, wrapped against the wind, was polishing the dully gleaming hood of his cab with a large rag. The polishing over, he dusted; then he gave the horse a brief, brisk rub down. Less than a minute later he was out of his cab again, polishing, dusting, brushing. He went in; he came out. His actions were compulsive. The animal chewed; his coat shone; the cab gleamed. And there were no fares.

Yours,
Nikil

DEAR NIKIL,

Yes, I can think of many episodes in Naipaul's writing where, reminded of his own experience of poverty and insecurity, he moves to a compassionate understanding of the insulted and the injured. There is a moment in *India: A Million Mutinies Now* when he is visiting poor Muslims in a frequent setting for anti-Muslim violence in Bombay and suddenly achieves an insight into what many liberals too dismissively call "identity politics." He begins to feel that "if I had been in their position, confined to Bombay, to that area, to that row, I too would have been a passionate Muslim. . . . I knew that . . . the grimmer things became, the more you insisted on being what you were."

There is an even more unexpected moment in *Among the Believers* when he can plausibly be read as outlining Islam's creative potential: "I could see how Islamic fervour could become more than a matter of prayers and postures, could become creative, revolutionary, and take men on to a humanism beyond religious doctrine: a true renaissance, open to the new and enriched by it, as the Muslims in their early days of glory had been." I suppose Naipaul was enthused by a similar possibility about Hindu nationalism when he approved of its "passion."

As we seem to be reaching the end of this exchange, let me try to sum up my thoughts. I have been critical of Naipaul's weakness for such obviously lethal projects as Hindu supremacism, but I also think it partly reflects what is by any measure the most interesting aspect of his work: the acute tension between his attraction to the "early days of glory" of Islam and Hinduism and his staunch belief that convergence with the modern West is the only plausible and desirable option for non-Western societies.

In retrospect, his analysis of the failings of postcolonial states and societies does not seem unique; it could seem unprecedented only in the West's intellectually underresourced and politically partisan mainstream press. Naxalite and Dalit movements in India, for example, had further-reaching critiques of what went wrong with the newly independent states and their elites. But they were not likely to be published by the *New York Times* or Knopf, and Joan Didion wouldn't have come across them. Your quote from her reminds us of the very provincial and self-regarding intellectual culture of cold-war liberalism (which is struggling to make sense of Trump right now) and the fact that cold-war liberals warmed to anyone who attributed ideological—and therefore suspect—motives to those they deemed illiberal (or knew little about), while claiming perfect rationality for the free world, along with aesthetic and moral superiority.

Naipaul was indeed vehement, as you say, in his rejection of the white colonialist romance with Asia and Africa. He certainly wasn't an apologist for imperialism—an accusation many of his left-leaning critics level against him. And I think his critique, however sporadic or fleeting, of the self-seeking white savior still holds, and has become more pertinent. But the most fascinating aspects of Naipaul's work are the recessed repudiations of secular liberalism and the openness to other human possibilities—those that do not stress individual ambition and achievement and are not obsessed with securing "glory." There is his regard for Gandhi, after all, the man who dismissed modern Western civilization as a "good idea"—a regard that grows throughout Naipaul's life, and manages to overcome his distrust of religious figures. One can also find instances in Naipaul's writings of his attraction to premodern peoples, who in his imagination had the virtue of wholeness and a non-instrumental relationship with nature. (When I pointed them out, he told me that this was the most neglected side of his work.)

These contradictory commitments also marked the first generation of Asian thinkers and writers. One of Naipaul's spiritual peers, I have often thought, is Lu Xun, someone who despaired of his countrymen's uncritical adherence to tradition but was attentive to its creative potential, and who while exhorting a full embrace of modernity was deeply skeptical of its possibilities of liberation. Perhaps it is this Janus-faced self of Naipaul's, rather than the one-dimensional Western supremacist beloved of white liberals and conservatives (and loathed by the progressive left), that will reward intellectual inquiry in the future. It certainly matches our own ambiguous experience—and that of many others in the age of rapid mobility and profound psychological disorientation—of several different, clashing worlds. Naipaul's uncommonly divided life, work, and legacy tell us that though we may think that we write or speak out of our own experience, the meanings we impose on it are not secure or stable, and this experience, manifold and complex by nature, will always overflow the stern categories in which we seek to imprison it.

All best,

Pankaj +

WHAT IS OUTSIDE IS INSIDE.

Ace Hotel New York @acehotelnewyork
Stay over with code **KEEPREADING** for a smart deal

REVIEWS

A. S. HAMRAH
We Can Still Think Our Own Thoughts

Crazy Rich Asians

IF YOU GO TO A BACHELORETTE PARTY ON AN island and the other guests put a huge bloody fish head on your pillow, you are in a horror movie, not a rom-com. Maybe at this point in the history of capitalism there's not much difference. *Crazy Rich Asians* looks more like a glossy tourist magazine produced for an international economics summit than a movie.

While Henry Golding just misses the mark at being an actual Anglo-Asian Cary Grant (maybe next time), Constance Wu, playing an Asian American everywoman, comes off generic, a paper doll dressed first as a professor, then as a Disney princess. Among the too numerous cast, Ronny Chieng and Victoria Loke stand out as a sarcastic, mean-spirited young husband and wife who despise each other, unlike the unmemorable Gemma Chan and Pierre Png, who play a more prominent, unfunny version of the same thing. I would gladly watch an entire movie about Chieng and Loke's shallow, disrespectful, well-dressed irritants wasting their fortune while struggling to maintain their status.

BlacKkKlansman

THE FILM IS FRAMED by a satirical lecture featuring Alec Baldwin as a John Birch Society racist and documentary footage of the 2017 Unite the Right rally in Charlottesville, Virginia, in which Heather Heyer was killed by someone who could be this Baldwin character's grandson. What comes in between is an action-comedy that supposedly takes place in Colorado and mixes together, in standard Spike Lee style, police investigations, black-history lessons, ruminations on genre cinema, and a dismantling of *The Birth of a Nation*.

Complaints that *BlacKkKlansman* valorizes cops are moot, since this film could not exist without them any more than a Sidney Lumet film like *Serpico* or *Prince of the City* could. Just like in those films, the cops here are a rogues' gallery of New York types, now transposed to Colorado. Their dialogue slips into a version of, "Eyyy, I'm John Turturro's brother, are we gonna get these Klan scumbags or what?" Adding to this Brooklyn feeling, a triumphant scene takes place in Sunny's waterfront bar in Red Hook. Lee establishes the scene with Sunny's red-and-green anchor-and-dolphin neon sign, showing us that this is just one of those nautical-themed saloons you find a county over from the Rocky Mountains.

Lee made the didactic *BlacKkKlansman* to move audiences, which he succeeds in

doing despite the feeling that the film has been stitched together from everywhere. If the love scenes between John David Washington and Laura Harrier fall flat (unlike their period hairdos), it's because they are the bland good people in this movie, which foregrounds actors like Ashlie Atkinson, who plays the self-deluded, racist wife of a Klan goon like she's a transplant from the Bensonhurst of *The Honeymooners*. The film works well when Washington puts on his white voice to prank call Klansmen. He aspirates the word *white* with the precision Diane Keaton brought to the word *wheat* in *Love and Death*, without the crutch of being dubbed by a white comic as in *Sorry to Bother You*. His phone routines could have gone on longer, which would have added to the satiric intensity of the movie more than Alec Baldwin's slideshow meltdown.

Mission: Impossible–Fallout

ALEC BALDWIN is everywhere in 2018 as a bigheaded, squinty illustration of American authority's collapse. In the latest *Mission: Impossible* movie he returns as Tom Cruise's boss, the leader of a spy agency more rogue than the CIA. His confrontations with Angela Bassett, as the CIA's head, are tepid. They distract from Cruise's epic struggle to maintain his status as an action hero, a fight Cruise wins via grueling stunt work on the roofs of the world. Cruise is a live-action testament to his own ability to take punishment, a kind of human sacrifice. He is undiminished by both time and all the semi-comedy around him, which is the story of his career and his life.

Mission: Impossible–Fallout begins with a harrowing dream sequence, like *Vanilla Sky*. Called into question at his wedding as a failure who puts his loved ones in jeopardy,

Cruise spends the rest of the film trying to make up for it by putting random people in danger, up to and including everyone in China, India, and Pakistan—a third of the world's population and a substantial market for films like this. Everyone who is not in Cruise's squad is formidable: Vanessa Kirby as a British arms dealer more threatening and coolly appealing than any woman in a recent Bond film; Sean Harris as a Steve Bannonesque alleged mastermind strapped to a chair. Watching Cruise relentlessly pursue and destroy Henry Cavill's double-crossing CIA hunk, whose dialogue seemed dubbed, was really satisfying. If anyone has earned the right to victory over a British superhero actor twenty years his junior with a porn mustache, it's the movie star who has managed to avoid the trite universes of DC and Marvel, even if it took being in that mummy film to do it.

The Equalizer 2

IN THE FIRST *Equalizer*, Denzel Washington played an ex–intelligence agent working at a Home Depot in East Boston, Massachusetts. What made that movie work was how real Washington and director Antoine Fuqua made employment at Home Depot feel, as if someone involved had done time in the PVC pipe and lumber aisles. They had the layout down.

The new one starts with Washington disguised as an imam on a train in Turkey, with a big beard, a white skullcap, and black-frame eyeglasses, a look he pulls off better than anyone else in the past thousand years. While this is a change from working at Home Depot, *The Equalizer* 2 is not quite a *Mission: Impossible* movie. Soon he is back in Boston, where he now works as a Lyft driver and still lives alone in a small

apartment. During one of his shifts, he breaks into the hotel room of a drunken misogynist fare, a finance bro, to teach him and his buddies a lesson.

Between the train scene and the Lyft driving, *The Equalizer* 2 begins with a lot of momentum. It dissipates as attention shifts to Washington's former spy colleagues. Confrontations with them in a suburban driveway and at a beach house in a deserted seaside town during a hurricane indicate movement away from the working class, toward the kind of real estate ex–intelligence agents are more likely to inhabit. Fuqua stages it all with a kind of Anthony Mann intensity and attention to space, but *The Equalizer* 2 will probably end up being the only action movie to ever leave me wanting more scenes of the protagonist working for a rideshare app, or at least the only one since Jamie Foxx invented Uber in *Collateral*.

Leave No Trace

WILL (BEN FOSTER), a veteran with PTSD, and his adolescent daughter, Tom (Thomasin McKenzie), live hard-core off the grid in a state forest in the Pacific Northwest. After yuppie hikers discover their lean-to and report them to the rangers, Will and Tom are relocated to a tree farm in an isolated community with a church and a school. There, Tom is exposed for the first time to people her own age. She makes contact with a dude who looks like a refugee from a Gus Van Sant film, or a guy from a grunge band like the Screaming Trees, a name that makes sense in this context. Tom wants to join 4-H with him so she can learn to take care of animals. Will, however, cannot abide the confinement of the small house he and his daughter have been assigned, nor can

he tolerate the war-battle noise of the heli-
copters that haul away trees to be sold at
Christmastime. "We can still think our own
thoughts," he tells Tom when they move in,
but the conformity of the simple life blots
out thought for him, a man for whom peace
of mind is impossible in human society.

Debra Granik's *Leave No Trace* is the
director's belated return to feature filmmaking after *Winter's Bone* in 2010. Like
Captain Fantastic from a couple of years
ago, but with much more art, grace, and a
sense of actual danger—perhaps because it
is set among the homeless, perhaps because
it was made by a woman—*Leave No Trace*
restates the male Gen-X narrative of protecting children from the outside world
and their eventual reintegration into it. For
Foster's Will, there is no redemption, unlike
Viggo Mortensen's character in *Captain
Fantastic*. Will is a permanent exile who
turns his back on the world, too damaged
to change despite the chances offered him.
Foster plays him somber and unlikable, in
a performance of confusion and quiet self-
righteousness that leads him to expose his
daughter to frostbite, rides from truckers,
and housebreaking. When Tom finally abandons him, he slinks back into the woods, a
hermit turning his back on the film he's in.
Granik pulls away to a God's-eye view of
this figure as he disappears.

Gavagai

THE ENIGMATIC American filmmaker Rob
Tregenza's last feature film before *Gavagai*
came out twenty years ago. As in *Leave No
Trace*, in *Gavagai* a man (Andreas Lust) goes
into the woods alone. Unfriendly and embit-
tered, he arrives in a remote Norwegian town
and hires a driver (Mikkel Gaup) to take him
farther north for reasons he doesn't explain.

This is not a road film in which two men wax
philosophical and overcome their differences
on a journey through the European countryside, like in those *Trip* movies and TV shows
with Steve Coogan and Rob Brydon, "from
acclaimed director Michael Winterbottom."
Tregenza shoots quiet people in long takes
with complicated camera moves. The two
men barely speak and never quite bond. Tregenza is not sketching the wistful unhappiness of the moneyed creative class so much
as staring into the divide between souls.

The man's journey comes to an end short
of his destination. In the rain on a cliff over-
looking an expanse of forest, he rips up his
late wife's translations of the Norwegian
writer Tarjei Vesaas and flings them into
the wind. His anger, destructive and futile,
seems to compound his wife's death by
destroying what's left of her work. *Gavagai*
is a film about the impossibility of closure
and the endlessness of grief. The title comes
from the analytic philosopher W. V. Quine's
Word and Object, in which Quine invents
the word *gavagai* to use as an example of
that-which-is-untranslatable. Tregenza and
his coscenarist Kirk Kjeldsen have translated, it seems, the poems of Vesaas into
mood and atmosphere. The poems haunt
Gavagai in this confrontation with the void.
Sometimes they appear in the form of the
man's wife, a ghost who shows up as an awkward memory-in-translation. In the end,
the man and the film are both wise to abandon this image and return to life around a
fire at dusk.

Let the Corpses Tan

THIS BELGIAN genre film, a delirious,
unpleasant mash-up of a *poliziottesco* and a
spaghetti western, shot in Corsica, is as violent as it is arty. A heist-gone-wrong set in

and around a villa and a cave, it features a cast of treacherous, criminal zeroes, bohemians, and cops, and it doesn't let up on the violence or the artiness.

While adapting Jean-Patrick Manchette novels for the screen is as inevitable as it is desirable, this one seems to exist only as a music video for Ennio Morricone's score. As a music video, it's a shocker but too long. As a feature film, it's pointless and repetitive, especially the squeaking-leather-pants sound effect that recurs over and over again. Manchette's novels are latter-day *séries noires*, fast-paced, destructive critiques of capitalism from the era of urban terrorism in Europe. Few of their characters survive. In *Let the Corpses Tan* none do, and the grimness is not ironic or critical, just maggoty. The film does give off that "I'm on drugs" feel (specifically of bad speed), but it's so labor-intensive that, like many a trip, it should have ended a long time ago. Elina Löwensohn's presence as a witchy bisexual and often-nude painter is almost as mysterious as Morricone's contract must have been. I hope Löwensohn made money, because busy-bee deconstructionists with many-itemed shot lists like codirectors Hélène Cattet and Bruno Forzani should pay their actors by the frame.

Mandy

THE CINEMA IS moving in all directions as endless new content crams itself into every available space. This is leading to new kinds of international cross-border weirdness, as films, more than ever, are shot wherever the money is. It's not just Belgians in Corsica imitating Italians, or Brooklyn playing Colorado, or North Carolina as California, or Toronto and Vancouver as anywhere else. Now, in *Mandy*, we get Belgium as both the

Pacific Northwest and the bowels of hell, starring Nicolas Cage.

Emerging from the same cross-contaminated genre swamp as *Let the Corpses Tan*, *Mandy* achieves its goals with blunter and larger instruments, which is all the better, because where *Corpses* fails, *Mandy* succeeds. If *Corpses* was a music video, *Mandy* is a whole doom-metal opera in poisonous Technicolor, with an album cover depicting a landscape of magenta, indigo, and golden-yellow ruins. The film is like that Bell Witch album that only has one ninety-minute-long track.

It opens with King Crimson's "Starless" on the sound track, playing before a clip from a Ronald Reagan speech about "spiritual awakening." It's 1983 and Cage, a lumberjack, lives in the woods with his girlfriend (Andrea Riseborough), a weird-fiction fan who works in a tiny country grocery store and speaks like Patti Smith reading the poem at the beginning of "The Revenge of Vera Gemini"—a British person's version of unaffected Americanness. Riseborough's slight New Jersey inflection points to where *Mandy* lets in real life. One of the film's principle pleasures is that for all its splashy-morose color schemes and arty dissolves, its death cult maintains the feeling of unemployed oafs from Neptune, New Jersey, worshipping Satan in Ramapo Mountain State Forest.

The film is pure acid trip with a macaroni-and-cheese commercial thrown in. (TV commercials are the worst thing to see on hallucinogenic drugs.) Cage howls in pain and screams in despair, breaking out in occasional intelligibility only to say things like, "Don't be negative." By the end, as a grimy, wounded Cage stands with a chain saw in front of a burning car and still hasn't avenged his girlfriend or saved anyone else from the drug-addicted demons/private-press recording artists, it becomes obvious what director Panos Cosmatos has delivered here: a parody of "the hero's journey" on par with Kanye West's use of that phrase in the Oval Office while describing Donald Trump to himself.

Burning

PANOS COSMATOS knows a lot of things about making movies, including that you show the burning cars. And yet he's no Lee Chang-dong, who fails to fully reveal a burning Porsche that's an important plot point in his new film. Lee does show Donald Trump, however, on a TV in the protagonist's apartment, using the original Cheddar Goblin to add to the sense of unease in this unique serial-killer mystery. And unlike *Let the Corpses Tan*, *Burning* raises actual questions about money and its effects on people's lives.

Burning, like *Psycho* and *L'avventura*, starts off as a film about a woman, Hae-mi (Jeon Jong-seo), who appears to be its subject and star. While working her job hawking cell phone accessories in a miniskirt, she reconnects with Jong-su (Yoo Ah-in), a poverty-stricken aspiring writer she knew in high school. After they hook up, she leaves for a solo trip to Africa and returns with a new friend, Ben, played by the American actor Steven Yeun in a subtle, nuanced performance that shifts between friendly-classy and "I'm a secret arsonist." Ben is a young member of Gangnam's idle class, and neither Hae-mi nor Jong-su fit in there. After Hae-mi begins to date Ben, she disappears again. Jong-su quizzes Ben about her absence and slowly comes to realize something isn't quite right with this slick, fashionable dude who starts reading Faulkner because Jong-su mentioned him, one of the film's slyest condemnations of rich-person poaching.

Burning refuses to reveal what actually happened to Hae-mi, or what kind of person Ben really is, if he is any type at all, which leaves Jong-su in a terrifying moral limbo. All three of the film's main characters are dispensed with by Lee in this unsentimental movie that shows human connection as fragile and masked when the friends are unequal. Hae-mi, dismissed from the film the earliest and seemingly with ease, in a way gets off the easiest of these characters, because there's no way to know what happened to her. She's kooky and a searcher but also just an innocent victim. But of what? With the men it's all too clear.

Decline and recline

CINEPHILES IN New York have noted the difference between how 2018 began and how it is ending. In January it was possible to see a movie a day in almost any theater for $9.99 a month using MoviePass. It was possible to stream thousands of classic and foreign films at home through FilmStruck for about $8 a month. Now, out of the blue and with little explanation, but as the result of its monopolistic deal with AT&T, Time Warner has shut down FilmStruck. MoviePass still exists, but barely. For a while it managed to do something that seemed impossible: it changed theatrical exhibition for the better. Now it has (more predictably than the shuttering of FilmStruck, it must be said) become some new kind of con in which only the most mediocre and longest-running movies are available to see, and only three a month. Suddenly we are plunged into a world of $16 movies at theaters in a city with no video stores.

The cancellation of both services, at this point, seems like the end of the long tail. The blockbuster model has reasserted itself and as usual seeks to muscle everything else out of the way. At the height of corporate capitalism you pay full price for bad movies improperly projected in ugly theaters whose business is selling large sodas at a 1,000 percent markup. If you want to watch a movie at home, there's Netflix, now mostly a streaming television service, or Amazon. It's all an insult to cinephiles and to film history. Going mass means living in the moment and throwing away what came before. The moment is crap.

To rub it in, the large theatrical chains have implemented reserved seating policies, which, by slowing down ticket buying at the box office, herd filmgoers into making electronic purchases for which they have to pay an additional fee. Reserved seats are antithetical to moviegoing, which traditionally and democratically has been first come, first served. You could move to a different seat if a weirdo (or anybody) was sitting too close. This new nonegalitarian system is fancy and inappropriate. It takes too long and it huddles people together. Let's just go to the opera at this point, instead of seeing *The Girl in the Spider's Web* pinned in place next to someone texting "wyd?"

Meanwhile the ads shown before movies have gotten more aggressive about copping to how terrible and disgusting their products are. The one for Diet Coke with Netflix actress Gillian Jacobs is a masterpiece of the passive-aggressive come-on. "Look," Jacobs begins, like a pundit on a TV news show, "here's the thing about Diet Coke: life is short." As well as nasty and brutish. Next she implores people who want to live in yurts to "yurt it up" and "just do you." Yurt dwellers may not drink Diet Coke, but they still have rights. She concludes with a simple confession: "Diet Coke: because I can."

Has freedom of choice ever seemed less appealing? At least that particular ad wasn't made by a film student. The worst, most dystopian Coke ads shown in theaters—each one a little nightmare from a society that has gone full *Clockwork Orange*—are now also promos for higher education. They are contests that inculcate their lucky film-student winners into a world of meta-shilling, where the theatrical experience is reconfigured as an excuse to slurp Coke under dim lights. Doing that is so satisfying that the actors onscreen envy the soda guzzlers in their cushy seats with cup holders and reach out to grab their giant sodas.

This kind of audience flattery is a form of permission to use cell phones while the movie is on. If the actors are just dorks like you who need a Coke so bad, there isn't any need to pay attention to them. When I went to see *Crazy Rich Asians* my date and I sat next to three other couples in a row with eight seats. The young women in the other couples texted throughout the movie (which was sold as an important cultural event) while their boyfriends, careful not to mess up a date, sat passively and stared at the screen as if their girlfriends were watching the movie with them instead of paying attention to other people who weren't there.

I saw an Ingmar Bergman film at the Museum of Modern Art recently, where I was seated one row over from a family of four. The father texted throughout the first half hour of the movie, impervious to the nearby MoMA regulars hissing at him to stop. When they began turning around, jabbing their fingers in his face, and threatening to take his phone, he stood up, grabbed his children's hands, and marched out of the theater in a huff, his wife trailing behind. Somehow, he had been wronged. Similarly, at the New York Film Festival screening of *Burning*, a man seated a couple of rows ahead of me texted on and off for the first twenty minutes of the film until someone got an usher to shine a flashlight in his face and threaten to remove him. I understand why the texters went to see *Crazy Rich Asians*. I do not understand what they were doing at MoMA and the New York Film Festival.

It's true that excellent new theaters that show good movies have opened, and are opening, in New York City. They sell discount cards, and anyway, there are many different ways to see movies, some of them legal, without FilmStruck and MoviePass. But cash outlays for those discount cards are not small and the prices without them are steep. And when *Venom* came out last month to universal pans and no human being who liked it could be found anywhere, it still cleaned up at the box office. It's still playing. I looked just now and it has passed $200 million in ticket sales. It must be a great movie for texting.

Wobble Palace

A JOURNEY TO the end of the night set in Los Angeles, like *Faces*, *Wobble Palace* is an anti-rom-com of debasement. Unlike *Faces* its characters are petulant, underemployed young whiners instead of confused, middle-class, middle-aged drunks. Times have changed in Los Angeles. No longer Cassavetes's city of nice houses with big dining rooms, *Wobble Palace* reveals LA living as downscale and codependent, even in open relationships. Scrolling text messages take up part of the frame sometimes and add to *Wobble Palace*'s mood of smarmy irritation. One gets used to them on-screen, where they are better than in the audience, but not to the artificial *click-click* sound of the keys. Put your shit on silent.

The Halloween night 2016 setting aids the film, as writer-director-star Eugene

Kotlyarenko goes full Herzog's Nosferatu as his costume choice for the scenes before the final breakup. It's more flattering than the "fat Skrillex" look he is accused of sporting earlier. Costar and cowriter Dasha Nekrasova also gets to say things like "We're gonna have our first female president soon" in her distinctive world-weary drone of postironic predisappointment. Like Viva's bored drawl in the late 1960s Warhol films and in Varda's LA-set *Lions Love*, Nekrasova's voice is the voice of a generation—in tone at least. It is so distinctive I wish she would record the service interruption announcements on the subway so that the true sound of the stalled and waiting would come through the speakers.

Support the Girls

"NO DRAMA" is posted as rule No. 1 for the servers at the Hootersesque restaurant in strip-mall Texas where *Support the Girls* takes place. Andrew Bujalski highlights his film's commitment to that as a concept, even as star Regina Hall, as the restaurant's manager, admits that banning drama is impossible with her half-dressed staff of twentysomething women. But when they get too provocative, she reminds them, "We are mainstream! We are mainstream!" Drama is mainstream, porn is not. Mumblecore isn't either, so Bujalski, who is now one of the best directors of actors in American filmmaking, has designed this unique, low-key film as a vehicle for Hall, the excellent actress from the *Think Like a Man* and *Scary Movie* movies who was overshadowed by the discovery of Tiffany Haddish in *Girls Trip*.

While the film descends into a bar-top riot and ends with women drinking and screaming in rage and frustration on a roof, it is men who are more likely to violate the

"No Drama" rule. The restaurant owner (James Le Gros), for instance, subjects a captive Hall to his pointless fury as they speed in his truck, with boat attached, to pursue another driver who has annoyed him on the road. When Hall and her staff move over to a corporate chain restaurant called Man Cave, an HR manager, played with polished friendliness by Brooklyn Decker, reveals the true drama of our time. "We've built this super-well-thought-out culture of respect," she explains, "and we have a whole team of attorneys who are paid a crazy amount to make sure we lay that out clearly."

Like the manager she plays, Hall is a team player to the end. I'm not sure the ensemble cast doesn't overshadow her. Lea DeLaria as Bobo, a dyke regular at the bar, steals every scene she's in. Shayna McHayle, a.k.a. the Brooklyn rapper Junglepussy, draws attention away from everybody else with nothing more than baleful stares and a self-contained sick-of-it-all attitude. If someone put McHayle and Dasha Nekrasova in a movie, they would become a bored, indie Richard Pryor and Gene Wilder, at least for South by Southwest and Bushwick, if not the mainstream.

The Queen of Sheba Meets the Atom Man

RON RICE'S LAST film, unfinished at the time of his too early death, is an essential document of bohemian New York City in 1963 as it was lived and thrashed in cheap apartments and on the streets. Taylor Mead, its star, the ultimate weird boho-hipster of the second half of the 20th century, finished a final cut of *The Queen of Sheba Meets the Atom Man* in 1981 after having screened other versions around the world for almost two decades. Mead's version has now been restored by Anthology Film Archives.

The film's black-and-white images demonstrate what the camp/avant-garde nexus meant in the Manhattan of Andy Warhol, Jill Johnston, and Frank O'Hara. The film was shot a year before Sontag's "Notes on Camp" was published, but Rice's movie is a living, breathing, leg-humping enactment more amusing, friendly, and connected to daily life than Jack Smith's *Flaming Creatures*. Smith, one of Sontag's inspirations, appears in the movie and almost takes over its second half from the coy, shier Mead and from Winifred Bryan, the implacable, overweight black woman who is the Queen of Sheba to Mead's Atom Man. The film, having established the bizarre relationship between these two mismatched oddballs, can't stray too far from them no matter who piles on. *The Queen of Sheba Meets the Atom Man* should be projected twenty-four hours a day somewhere in Manhattan, so that before we're all pushed into the sea off Rockaway Beach people can be reminded of the strange form of life that once lived here.

The Jerry Lewis Gar-Ron movies

IT TURNS OUT that self-conscious cinematic camp was not exactly invented by Jack Smith in New York. In an unimposing suburban home in Pacific Palisades, California, Jerry Lewis, unbeknownst to the avant-garde, had begun in 1951 to shoot black-and-white movie parodies and pre-Warholian color screen tests during his nights and weekends off from Paramount Pictures, where he and Dean Martin were employed as the nation's most popular comedy duo. Shown only once to friends at premiere parties at the same house where they were filmed, Lewis's Gar-Ron productions (named for his sons) remained unseen by anyone else until this past October, when the Lewis estate and the Library of Congress debuted them at the Museum of Modern Art. These films, which combine borscht belt humor and *Mad* magazine–style parody with vulgar put-downs and gay panic, reveal Lewis as a comic auteur and "total filmmaker" almost ten years before his official directorial debut, *The Bellboy*.

The Gar-Ron movies, like *The Queen of Sheba Meets the Atom Man*, also document their time and place, which in this case is the sunny Southern California of Hollywood movie stars partying at home. If you had been waiting to hear Dean Martin, Janet Leigh, Tony Curtis, or Shelley Winters utter words like *orgasm*, *cock*, *shit*, and *vomit*, your wait was over if you made it to MoMA this past fall.

The series combined featurettes, shorts, and home movies from this period in which Jerry Lewis and America were both on the rise. Lewis's well-known neuroticism and aggressiveness are less hidden and more integrated in these productions than in the Freudian constructs Paramount put together for him and Dean, or in the later work for which he was solely responsible. In fact, these movies present a happy Jerry, not the lugubrious interviewee America got to know from his films in the 1960s, after he became an auteur and a philanthropist. One home movie, shot at a 1920s-themed jazz party in the Lewis rec room, is positively giddy, with Lewis and Patti, his wife, and Curtis and Leigh doing the Charleston in boaters, spats, and flapper outfits late into the night.

The films themselves present popular movies of the day in "Jewish" versions. *Sunset Boulevard* becomes *Fairfax Avenue*, the story of a handsome young delivery boy (Curtis) from a kosher deli forced to write a screenplay for a washed-up star of the silent screen (Leigh, caked in face powder). In *Come Back Little Shiksa*, Martin is a doctor "struggling to avoid sobriety." Each is like

a Kuchar brothers film with big stars in it, too weird and offensive for TV sketch comedy, an emanation from a hip demimonde that only existed in Lewis's house when Curtis and Leigh dropped by. The Milton Berle screen test, which poses Uncle Miltie against a bright-red backdrop as it scrutinizes his face so Lewis can pepper him with rude, absurd questions off-screen, is more out-there than any Warhol screen test. I'd say it's one of the best films of the 1950s, and it clearly demonstrates Lewis's way with color and his ability to capture stylized discomfort on-screen.

Slaps to the face

IN THE MOMA lobby between Jerry Lewis screenings, a basketball-stomached older man wearing a large newsboy cap introduced himself to me as Slaps Donovan. He cornered me to tell me he used to be the film critic on Jackie Mason's radio show. Now he had a Broadway play and a reality TV series he was developing. "Hal Prince," said Slaps, "has my play on his desk, but he's booked up for the next three years." This play, a musical, takes place during the Woodstock rock music festival in 1969, but doesn't use any of the songs. It's all new, original music that Slaps has written. His TV show, *Celebrity Séance*, involves unsuspecting contestants speaking to famous dead people through the medium of Slaps's voice impressions, which he will provide off-screen.

At the very moment Slaps asked me, in the voice of Jerry Lewis, about getting some nookie, I got a text on my phone. A woman I know who works for Netflix was in town for the New York Film Festival. She was inviting me to meet her and two filmmakers for dinner at a fancy restaurant near Lincoln Center. While Slaps imitated Jerry Lewis and I looked at this text on my phone, a Brazilian artist named Romero Britto walked by dressed in a multicolored homemade suit and stopped to pose for photos fans of his wanted to take with him. The clowns had been sent in, and I was among them.

I couldn't go to dinner. There was another Jerry Lewis movie in half an hour that I planned to see, and besides I wasn't dressed for that kind of thing. If I had gone to meet my friend and two glamorous strangers, I would have become the Slaps of the dinner, explaining how I was a film critic.

That night, instead, I had committed myself to the bizarre and the asinine. Slaps exited onto 53rd Street, still doing his Jerry Lewis voice, and I went and sat down in the lobby to wait for the next show. A lady in a burgundy tracksuit sitting across from me pulled a container of macaroni salad out of a crinkly plastic shopping bag, pried off the clear plastic lid, and began eating it with a big metal soup spoon she had brought with her to the museum. At least I wasn't wearing a funny hat.

The Other Side of the Wind

A TRUER SÉANCE of dubbed voices, forgotten faces, and witchy art, Orson Welles's *The Other Side of the Wind* brings a lost work back to life. By the time of his death in 1985, Welles had been working on the film for fifteen years and hadn't finished it. Now it arrives complete, fully formed, a masterpiece and a shock to the system, courtesy of Netflix and all the money they have to burn. It is not a fragment like Welles's *It's All True* or *Don Quixote*. It is done. Never has a movie been as overwhelmed by the history of its production as this one, "this circus of scattered souls . . . a desperate venture shared by desperate men." That doesn't

matter anymore. The desperate men and the scattered souls are now on the screen.

Near the beginning of the film, a busload of partygoers on the way to the desert house of the film director Jake Hannaford (John Huston) passes a drive-in theater where the huge marquee advertises two movies: I EAT YOUR SKIN and I DRINK YOUR BLOOD, fitting titles for this exposé of Hollywood vampirism. It's filmed alternately like *Zabriskie Point*, random Eurotrash, Kenneth Anger–ian avant-gardism, 1970s porn, Cassavetes, and cinema verité. Like *Faces* it is another SoCal journey to the end of the night; like the Jerry Lewis home movies, it inhabits a vulgar-sophisticated world of homosexual panic, here partially masked by lots of naked hippie hetero sex in a steam bath, in a moving car, and on a back lot in Hollywood, abandoned and in ruins.

In *The Other Side of the Wind*, Welles purposefully synthesized every film style that had come along since the late 1950s, in a bid for relevance the film mocks when Hannaford is accused of doing the same. Where Hannaford crashes and burns, Welles succeeds with brilliance, adding to the sense of tragedy surrounding the film. It should have come out in its time.

The film swings wildly between tones and tempos, black-and-white and ultra-vivid color. Michel Legrand's score and the other music in the film add to this. In the psychedelic film-within-a-film, Blue Cheer dominates the soundtrack like Can tried to at the beginning of *Inherent Vice*. In the party scenes, we hear the hip jazz pianist Jaki Byard, his music piped in as drunks spill booze on each other and sing "Glow Worm" in a haunting scene lit only by candles.

The film was cowritten by Welles's companion, Oja Kodar, who also costars. She is often nude and plays a mute Native American who is mocked as "Pocahontas" while an underage blonde girl (Cathy Lucas), a nonactor in an ARCHIE BUNKER FOR PRESIDENT T-shirt, is passed from Peter Bogdanovich, as a director in the flush of success, to Huston's Hannaford, a director who can't get his film made in the New Hollywood of the time. It's a sick, glorious movie that ends at another drive-in, a graveyard of the cinema with a train running past it, where Kodar, projected on the screen, stabs with scissors at these men's fantasies and dreams. +

JEANNE-MARIE JACKSON
On New Zimbabwean Literature

Panashe Chigumadzi, *These Bones Will Rise Again*. Indigo Press, 2018
Novuyo Rosa Tshuma, *House of Stone*. Atlantic Books, 2018

TO LOVE ZIMBABWE FROM AFAR IS AN ALL-consuming task. Your virtual tool kit includes Twitter, Facebook, and an endlessly bleeping string of WhatsApp groups, each of which you curate to have overlapping but nonidentical networks of people in the know. You refresh each medium on loop as you get word that something shady is afoot in the usually laid-back capital city of Harare. Your eyes burn; hours melt; a familiar delirium seems to radiate from your phone. And this is just basic access. At minimum, to keep up, you will need working knowledge of two languages from among English, chiShona, and isiNdebele, the three most widely spoken in the country. Ideally, you'll have the whole suite. If you are a Zimbabwean writer, you may capture some choice phrases in a novel or story. Soon after its publication, you may be greeted by furious Twitter debates about whether you were right to italicize and/or translate and/or appropriate African languages in your mostly English text, and whether you have done justice to their local contexts. These threads will be interspersed with frank confessions of despair over the future of democracy given the Zimbabwean leadership's latest broken promise, and perhaps the occasional photo of a lion shot by an American dentist.

It's not easy to be a Zimbabwean writer abroad: in addition to having to answer familiar questions about who speaks for whom, writes to whom, and by whom their books are published, writers in the diaspora have to negotiate citizenship from a distance. And the line between "here" and "there" is unusually blurry for Zimbabweans. Because of the country's economic and institutional collapse over the last two decades, there are around five million Zimbabweans, out of a total population of seventeen million, living and working abroad. While not unique, the extent to which the Zimbabwean economy is not just connected but actually *outsourced* to its diaspora is a singular trait. According to the Reserve Bank of Zimbabwe, diasporic Zimbabweans contribute upward of $750 million a year in remittances to the flailing GNP. It is difficult, as a result, to make a case that Zimbabweans who leave have less claim on what happens in the country than those who stay. But their experience is profoundly different. Over the past decade, a new generation of Zimbabwean-diasporic writers such as Petina Gappah and NoViolet Bulawayo have gained much-deserved international prominence and "world writer" status, publishing with major transnational conglomerates and signing lucrative contracts. Meanwhile, their peers at home face a bare-bones national publishing infrastructure and, as of 2015, a 40 percent import tax on books. A few small presses—Weaver, in Harare, and amaBooks, in Bulawayo—persist as costly labors of love, publicizing titles online in hopes of selling them to other small presses elsewhere. For better or for worse, those who have "made it" and those who have not converge in the digital commons, where the prestige economy of global literature meets the more frenetic literary scene of the World Wide Web. This convergence is both a blessing and a curse: a blessing because it makes diasporic Zimbabwean writers some of the most interesting thinkers about the role of virtual worlds in intellectual life, and a curse because of the surging, even manic pace it entails.

THOUGH OFTEN overshadowed in its international reception by South Africa, Zimbabwe has long been a literary powerhouse. From the 1970s through the '90s, Zimbabwean writers made important and, for a time, widely read contributions to an African postcolonial canon in English, most of them published in Heinemann's now defunct African Writers Series. Charles Mungoshi's *Waiting for the Rain* and Stanlake Samkange's *The Mourned One*, both published in 1975, explored the tension between rural enclosure and industrialized, racist modernity by juxtaposing a conflicted, Western-educated protagonist with a brother who remains behind in his village of origin. *The House of Hunger* (1978), by Dambudzo Marechera—the enfant terrible of Zimbabwean letters famous for exclaiming, "If you are a writer for a specific nation or a specific race, then fuck you!"—took aim at both Rhodesian township malaise and Oxford social niceties. Chenjerai Hove's *Bones* (1988) and Shimmer Chinodya's *Harvest of Thorns* (1989) chronicled the devastating effects of the decades-long Liberation War, or Second Chimurenga ("struggle"), leading up to the creation of an independent Zimbabwe in 1980.

When it comes to the long, hefty novel, Zimbabwe's women writers have always shone brightest. Doris Lessing's steely dissection of white supremacist psychology, especially in *The Grass Is Singing* (1950), won her a Nobel Prize in 2007. In 1988, Tsitsi Dangarembga's Shona bildungsroman *Nervous Conditions* became an international classroom sensation, helping to define a generation of writers seeking to move beyond both colonial rule and the patriarchal nationalism marshaled for its defeat. Yvonne Vera, perhaps Zimbabwe's most sophisticated prose stylist, broke taboos of women's depiction in her fluid and unsparing novels *Butterfly Burning* (1998) and *The Stone Virgins* (2002).

The new wave of Zimbabwean-diasporic literary stars has drawn on this legacy, marrying historical excavations of the country's long struggle against racism with searching questions about the toll this struggle exacts. Modern Zimbabwe's foundational displacement forces writers to imagine connection from dispersion; Zimbabwe is a place whose writing cannot but be *both* global and ambivalent about globalization. Its rising generation of diasporic writers is united by the contemplation of distance: the distance from the rural countryside to Rhodesian cities; from Zimbabwe to South Africa; from the African continent to Europe and North America. Their writing naturally toggles between hyperlocal and dizzyingly "global" registers. In her poem "Song of Yobe" from *Beating the Graves* (2017), Tsitsi Ella Jaji describes the "principle of uncertainty" through which a flame in a Harare science classroom spurs her empathy for Nigerian students lit aflame by Boko Haram. In *We Need New Names* (2013), NoViolet Bulawayo jumps from Matabeleland, in southwestern Zimbabwe, to Detroit without formal transition, returning to her book's point of origin only through the unsatisfying fits and starts of Skype. In *The Maestro, the Magistrate, and the Mathematician*, published one year later, Tendai Huchu follows three Zimbabweans living in Edinburgh as they bob and weave through a connected narrative, unbeknownst to any of them in their ill-fated individual plotlines.

In these works, there is neither Afropolitan fetish nor a clear path to tradition, heritage, or home. All, however, adopt a strategy of naivete or limited perspective to trace the fault lines of extraterritorial Zimbabwean life. Two recent books by Zimbabwean-diasporic writers, both published while their authors were under 30, show us something different: a narrator overwhelmed by awareness. *These Bones Will Rise Again* by Panashe Chigumadzi and *House of Stone* by Novuyo Rosa Tshuma advance the best parts of Zimbabwe's legacy without shying away from its uglier aspects. Both writers were educated outside the country—in a recent conversation in the *Johannesburg Review of Books*, they recall their shared experiences of Wits University in Johannesburg—and now live in the United States. (Chigumadzi has just begun a doctoral program at Harvard; Tshuma, a graduate of the Iowa Writers' Workshop, will soon receive her PhD from the University of Houston.) Conditioned by digital media–induced reflexivity and "infomania," and also wary of it, both affirm a critical yet strong sense of belonging while tackling head-on the points at which this belonging tips over into new forms of exclusion.

The question of what it means to be *from* Zimbabwe versus still living *in* it has gained new urgency since Robert Mugabe left office last year. (As most readers will know, the now 94-year-old leader was finally ousted from power by his own ZANU–PF party after a numbing 37-year reign.) Given Zimbabwe's status as perhaps the

world's most infamous gerontocracy—the "youth league" of Mugabe's ZANU–PF party is known to have members well into their sixties—Chigumadzi's and Tshuma's achievements mark a timely changing of the guard. In the wake of Mugabe's retirement, as the country is caught between its own delayed historical reckoning and the need to curry favor with global institutions, they bring a feminist and self-reflexive acumen to fundamental questions of who owns Zimbabwe's history and, thus, its future. Both novels are notably concerned with questions of ancestry. Through careful excavation, these books dispense with the familiar radicalism of violent breaks to sift, instead, through the dust of previous generations.

FOR CHIGUMADZI, the quest for ancestry takes the form of an idiosyncratic memoir-essay—what might be called a "record of search"—linking the life of her own paternal grandmother to that of Zimbabwe's most famous spiritual medium, the incarnation of the ancestral spirit Nehanda in the woman Charwe, also called Mbuya Nehanda, who was hanged for her role in a 19th-century anticolonial rebellion against the British South Africa Company. *These Bones Will Rise Again* is a reflection on medium in two senses of the word, both as the name for a real person through whom ancestral spirits offer guidance and as the name for a technology by which information is conveyed. The first traffics in eternal truths, the second in ephemeral content, yet both raise similar questions. When can one separate the truth from the telling, or the ancestral spirit from her fallible human vessels? And how does one negotiate between a "timeless" message—of freedom, say—and its historically specific modes of transmission?

Chigumadzi refracts these questions through the of-the-moment challenge of how to account for deep spiritual reality from within the fleeting, fickle norms of the internet. Tension between essential truths and awareness of their contingency is a central part of her own coming-of-age story, which she relates in bits and pieces across three time periods: her South African present, her recent trip to Zimbabwe, and Zimbabwe's more distant history. "Having grown up in South Africa, away from my extended family, I've always been at a physical remove from my culture," Chigumadzi tells us. As a result, she has created her own record of Zimbabwean life from any number of sources curated by others, across evolving media, from analog to digital. (For example, she "discovers" the legendary Chimurenga musician Thomas Mapfumo via a physical copy of his *Greatest Hits* album and then on YouTube.)

Chigumadzi's presence in her book thus serves to underscore her distance from the thing she nonetheless *is*. Though Shona by birth, she must work to make her Shonaness "real," to unearth the sounds and impressions through which it can have meaning. As part of this process of excavation, she frequently translates Shona phrases, at once carving footholds for the reader and chronicling her own efforts to maintain a hold on the language. "My maternal grandfather Sekuru Douglas Chiganze, or 'Teacher Chiganze', a primary school teacher, would often buy us Shona school readers," she writes. "More than just basic literacy, this was a way for me to get to read and hear some of the stories and fables that my grandmothers would have told me had I grown up with them close by." In this way, Chigumadzi fulfills a dual function of speaking to Zimbabwean readers and filling in foreign knowledge gaps. Like her publisher, the brand-new, UK-based Indigo Press, run by the Zimbabwe-born industry veteran

Ellah Wakatama Allfrey, she is split between cultures and continents.

And yet the deeper she goes into her history, the more it seems to elude her. The present and recent-past tenses of the book are structured as vignettes of her encounters with defiant or reluctant sources. Her most forceful, felt connection to a line of Zimbabwean women, the proof of her belonging, is a treasured photograph of her paternal grandmother, Lilian Chigumadzi. After losing the photo during a school presentation, she is forced to reconstruct a secondhand version of her grandmother's life, whose funeral, for reasons of geographical distance, she is unable to attend. A similar process plays out across her meetings with other Zimbabwean elders, both family and not. At one point, an effort to trace her Shona clan—a group descended from a shared ancestor, each of which is associated with a *mutupo*, or totem, as well as a *chidawo*, or praise name—reveals to Chigumadzi the complex intermingling of Shona and Ndebele origins.

This narrative is true on a broader historical scale: as Chigumadzi points out, *Shona* is shorthand for a related but diverse collection of smaller, regional languages and identities, consolidated only in the 19th century. But *These Bones Will Rise Again* is a creative work, not a scholarly history of the region. The real significance of Chigumadzi's search-for-origins narrative is the way she employs it to muddle narrative convention. Traveling around Zimbabwe, endeavoring to trace the lineages of her grandmother and of Mbuya Nehanda, she is met time and again with skepticism or uncertainty. "I have found myself frustrated and even exasperated by the many meandering and often contradictory histories of Nehanda that I have heard when consulting spirit mediums, traditionalists, and books," she writes, "making it feel as if the single version that I initially tried to grasp . . . is constantly slipping through my fingers like water."

What Chigumadzi offers is an exercise in reconciling the divergent media—human and virtual—by which "Zimbabwe" is transmitted, weighing the demands each makes on her in counterpoint. This negotiation, in turn, models a mode of historical engagement concerned less with "story" than with how to keep multiple stories in play without sacrificing the possibility of unified political resistance. "*Zvimwe hazvibvunzwi*," she keeps hearing: "Some things are just not asked about." She feels an uncomfortable voyeurism in prying information from her own relations. Searching for other incarnations of Nehanda, she shows up at the home of one previous medium, a stranger, and is met with intense suspicion (the home is enmeshed in the ZANU–PF power structure, and Chigumadzi does not come with the party's blessing). More importantly, she is struck by the incredible time and knowledge required to maintain a spirit's presence. She is told that a little girl has been identified as a new medium for Nehanda, but that "it is necessary to allow time for her to gain enough strength and maturity to carry all the weight that Mbuya Nehanda's spirit brings." This is a long, slow process, demanding a patience nearly impossible to cultivate through the moment-to-moment updates by which Zimbabweans are virtually bound together around the world.

And yet *These Bones Will Rise Again* circles back again and again to the virtual conditions in which this seems impossible. "As I watch the inauguration on my phone's screen, it feels a farcical gesture," Chigumadzi writes of Emmerson Mnangagwa officially becoming Zimbabwe's president last November. During the remainder of the "Fourteen-Day Revolution" that followed

his ascension, she writes, she is "glued to my phone and laptop." Describing her daily routine, she baldly states, "I spend a lot of time scrolling through my Twitter timeline." As a description of how Zimbabwean news circulates, this is dead-on: anyone with ties to the country is well aware, as Chigumadzi notes, that "Twitter knows everything before everyone else." The book's larger point, though, is that she needs both kinds of knowledge—the singular and slow, and the always-already-happening—to make meaningful advances in her understanding of this real yet scattered place.

The book does not treat social media as a microcosm of existing Zimbabwe—it is missing too many voices to fill that role—but as a tool for distilling the challenges of its own partiality. Social media, for all its virtues, is rigged to favor its own communicative norms. "In this moment of great upheaval," asks Chigumadzi, "who has time to listen? I have to still the world around me. There is much confusion and much noise, so I struggle to hear the bones of Mbuya Nehanda and Mbuya Chigumadzi rattling in my heart." For readers who are themselves trapped in the dichotomy of media frenzy and media detox, there is value in her record of social media's give-and-take. The result of the book's bouncing between the depths of knowledge of the mediums she traces in the flesh and the dizzying surface speed of their virtual counterparts is humility, essential to any long-view movement building. This is Chigumadzi's Zimbabwean inheritance, and the rest of us would do well to take notice.

NOVUYO ROSA TSHUMA'S four-hundred-page novel is also centered on ancestry: the bones of the victims of Zimbabwe's Gukurahundi (loosely, "early spring rains") massacre, in which members of the country's Ndebele minority were killed by the Shona majority in the mid-1980s. *House of Stone*, named for the English translation of *Zimbabwe*, offers the most challenging account to date of the Gukurahundi killings. In sentences that sting like whips, Tshuma excavates her young country's original sin: the ZANU–PF-led murder of approximately twenty thousand Ndebele "dissidents" in Matabeleland between 1983 and 1987. As Tshuma's graphic prose reminds us, the view of Zimbabweans as a "peace-loving people" was forged by guerrilla soldiers in the flames of burning huts.

Yet this roguish, self-interrogative book is only partly historical fiction. Tshuma's confrontation with her first home's past is also a way of questioning claims to its unmediated access in the present. Like *These Bones Will Rise Again*, *House of Stone* explores the fraught interplay of medium, message, and self-construction. But while Chigumadzi turns to the device of auto-narration—not autofiction per se, but a sort of hybrid memoir—Tshuma prefers the still more ambitious canvas of the realist novel *about* auto-narration. Her book is narrated by the 24-year-old Zamani, who lives on the property of a couple he considers to be surrogate parents. It is 2007, and they have lost their real son, Bukhosi, in the chaos of a recent Ndebele separatist rally. From the start, it is clear that Zamani's zeal for the tales he tells is both his gift and his liability: "I am a man on a mission," he announces. "A vocation, call it, to remake the past, and a wish to fashion all that has been into being and becoming."

Zamani's yearning for family belonging bleeds into a desire to inhabit Zimbabwean history during its period of liberatory idealism. Plying his father figure, Abednego, who is also his landlord, with drugs and alcohol to loosen his tongue, Zamani draws out the details of his new, made-up ancestry.

Abednego and Zimbabwe, though—a new father to mark the birth of a new nation—keep throwing up barriers to the young man's desire for attachment. His description of his surrogate parents' photographs of their missing child captures the deep, heart-pinching allure of the exclusive parent-child bond he longs for and is unable to attain. "It overbrims with life, the baby album, it holds in its pages the measure of seventeen years of living," Zamani observes enviously. "There is baby Bukhosi on the first page at just three weeks, his tiny, walnut face peeping from a Super Mario blanket, his emerald eyes ashimmer, his mouth pinched around Mama Agnes's teat." This scene, one of the novel's most evocative, delicately represents the inherent slipperiness of staking one's future on vicarious experience, whether loving or traumatic. At the same time as he overidentifies with things that he did not live through, it is impossible for the reader to turn away from the fresh life he gives to the pain of those whose lives he channels. The more he is confronted with his lack of access to Bukhosi's past, the greater his desire to usurp it.

The central problem of the novel has to do with how much weight to give accounts of violence recounted years after-the-fact, by people who weren't there, in contexts of present political aims. How can we trust unavoidably partial, partisan narratives of events? But at the same time, how can we not? In this light, *House of Stone*'s treatment of the Gukurahundi killings can be seen as part of a larger Zimbabwean contest over who can speak for history. The Chimurenga war for liberation from Rhodesia thus looms behind the novel's more immediate focus on Gukurahundi, placing these ostensibly opposed national-origin stories—one claimed by the Shona-led government, and one foisted upon the minority Ndebele by the Shona majority—in an uncomfort-ably parallel relation. Both of them, that is, raise questions about historical access. "He never got the honour of experiencing com-bat up close," Zamani notes of Abednego's past. And yet, "just like that, history found him anew and declared him a war hero." As Chigumadzi's narrative unfurls from a miss-ing photo, Tshuma's circles around a collec-tive tragedy doubly recounted by Abednego and his young confidant.

Characters come vividly to life in Tshu-ma's writing before she reminds us that their pasts are in large part made-up, usually by laying bare the device of Zamani's shifty and ultimately infantile persona. ("He shuns me, my surrogate dada," he whines, "now when I need him more than ever.") This is especially true of Zamani's attachment to Abednego's first love, Thandi, who is killed in the Guku-rahundi attacks. Taking cues from what we are told are Abednego's memories, Zamani takes off on flights of "disnarrative" fancy, to use Gerald Prince's coinage for things that might have happened but didn't. Remem-brance and embellishment commingle in Tshuma's narrative world. Recounting Abed-nego's recounting of his plans for a future with Thandi, in a house "where they would place his TV and her gramophone and watch late-night feature films," Zamani inter-jects with his own, present-tense desire for the now deceased woman. "How I wish to spend many hours folded into my inamorata," he exclaims in parentheses, "tucked in her mature bosom!" The description of Thandi picks up steam from there, as we greet the intimate nooks and crannies of Abednego's intended "love-nest." The reader tours a non-existent home: "And then, shuffling ahead, through another doorway, ah, this would be the kitchen; there wasn't the present chalky smell of cement but instead the future aroma of Thandi's cooking, the scene of rosemary

and oregano and simmering stew." Zamani's liberties with a past that is not his own thus push Tshuma's own prose to new but fraught heights, as he interjects himself between his-torical narrative as such and its vivid person-alization. It is based on fictions, after all, that we care so much when Thandi and her son are imagined "dancing to the tune of gun-fire before tumbling to the ground puppet-like." Tshuma skillfully makes us question our most visceral responses—horror, sadness, rage—suspending her reader before torn-up flesh only to wink at the ill-got sincerity of our sympathies.

This ethical footwork is trickiest in the novel's treatment of violence against women. Zamani spares no detail in his description of Thandi's murder at the hand of Black Jesus, a horrific figure based on Perence Shiri (who uses the nickname "Black Jesus" himself), Zimbabwe's former air force commander and current minister of lands, agriculture, and rural resettlement under President Mnangagwa. As Shiri was, Black Jesus is here commander of Zimbabwe's Fifth Brigade, the military unit responsible for the Guku-rahundi massacres, and in Tshuma's telling, he also becomes a point of personal fixation for Abednego. After burning children alive in a hut, Black Jesus slaughters Thandi with a scythe, opening her pregnant stomach. "Thandi lay in the dirt," Zamani tells us, again in the present tense. "Beside her spilt belly. Beside her intestines, her colon, her stom-ach. Beside her pancreas, her spleen, her liver. Beside her twitching foetus."

Were Tshuma not so gifted a writer, the violence here might verge on the gratuitous. But her expertise is too abundant, her invest-ment in her city of origin's past too palpable for "appropriation" to seem like a meaning-ful framework. Instead, she gives her reader no choice but to confront the bloody graves atop which Zimbabwe's current government stands, denying her the luxury of separating state from scythe. And yet all the while, we are attentive to Zamani's instability and fictive machinations. This is true at yet another narrative level in the book's second half, when Zamani switches from channeling Abednego's past to channeling Abednego's wife's. At this point Tshuma reveals Abednego's violence toward her, but spins the revelation into Zamani's confessional narrative and ploy for sympathy. "What kind of family hi-story would it be, anyway, that chronicles the surrogate father without also ushering forth the voice of the surrogate mother?" he queries the reader, before making reference to "a force bordering on the primal, to the mother-child bond, in particular the mother-son bond," which he has, of course, exploited. With each new twist in the multipronged plot, poignancy is leavened by doubt.

House of Stone thus proceeds along two tracks: one in which Matabeleland's history is put on piercing and timely display, and one in which its presentation is undercut. Like Chigumadzi, Tshuma makes room for the additional challenge of virtual dissemination. She introduces the Rhodesian farmer who is thought to be Abednego's biological father through a reference to his blog, which he maintains with "ambitions of attracting a large enough following to turn his Life and Times into a TV series." Farmer Thornton, determined to "Make Rhodesia Great Again!," gains readers through his own pained narrative of the Gukurahundi genocide, in particular one viral post in which he describes his wife "having been raped and strangled by the dissidents."

The effect here is most obviously to show that many wrongheaded angles on history can seem "true" if they are rendered persuasively enough to enough people. But aside from that, social media introduces a faintly absurd dimension to the grave material of the novel. Something about online discourse is self-satirizing, Tshuma seems to say, and yet so unavoidable as to have even old Rhodesian farmers in its ether-like grasp. In a similar vein, Zamani is beholden to a set of cherished devices. He gazes plaintively at a selfie on his phone and makes nervous reference to an omnipresent MacBook. The Southern African histories of Rhodesia and apartheid are the 20th century's most vaunted stories of racial oppression and liberation, laden with grandiose themes and iconic political leaders. And yet here they are, refracted through the same endless stream of memes and petty grievances and cat pictures as everything else in our lives. This might, in part, be a good thing, with everything now up for everyone's critical grab, and no one able to stand on sanctimony. But as Zimbabwe "opens for business" under a still repressive ZANU–PF, these books might also give us pause, as we reflect on the gap between appearance, reality, and the tricky virtual third spaces that now act as intermediaries between the two.

As Zamani channels and embellishes his would-be family's stories, he remarks on the various mediations that they already contain. "It seemed to my surrogate father that it was this, the narrative of war rather than war itself, which incensed Thandi," says this unreliable narrator of another man's views on a woman who is already dead. The reader has too many options for how to read this line, and at the same time none at all. We can neither take Zamani at his word nor ignore the voices to which we have no other access. War is real, and yet its telling is always partial, its relation after the fact somehow skewed. In this way, a troubled recounting of someone else's reflection on yet one *more* ghost's relation to an originary trauma mirrors a virtualized public sphere in which, through constant contact, we move apart as often as nearer to one another. And in a world of endless refraction of the most real pain, Tshuma asks, how on earth will we go about telling the difference? +

GEORGE BLAUSTEIN
My Fellow Prisoners

John McCain and Mark Salter, *The Restless Wave: Good Times, Just Causes, Great Fights, and Other Appreciations*. Simon & Schuster, 2018.

THERE IS A RIGHT WAY TO SWEAR, A RIGHT way to spit, a right way to roll a cigarette on the deck of an aircraft carrier, a right way to drink wine on the retreat from the Battle of Caporetto, a right way to get gored by a bull, a right way to dismantle a welfare program, a right way to blow up a bridge, a right way to taunt your captors, a right way to catch a bonefish, a right way to lead, a right way to serve, and finally there is a right way to die.

The right way is the heroic way and the manly way, which happens also to be the moral or ethical way, which happens in turn to be the picturesque way. You will sometimes fail to follow the right way, in which case there is a right way to grimace and a right way to atone.

"MOST CURRENT FICTION bores the shit out of me," said John McCain in 2006, surprising no one. He always gravitated toward the lost generation, Ernest Hemingway above all. If we are to believe McCain's account, when he was 12 (this would be 1948) he found two four-leaf clovers in the yard and ran inside to preserve them in the pages of a book. From his father's shelves he happened to grab *For Whom the Bell Tolls*, and his eyes lighted upon this:

"What are you going to do with us?" one asked him.

"Shoot thee, Pablo."

"When?" the man asked in the same gray voice.

"Now," said Pablo.

"Where?" asked the man.

"Here," said Pablo. "Here. Now. Here and now. Have you anything to say?"

"*Nada*," said the *civil*. "Nothing but it is an ugly thing."

This is the scene in which Pablo, leader of a band of Republican guerrillas in the Spanish Civil War, kills four policemen and has the town's fascists flailed to death.

The mature McCain who relates this anecdote admires Hemingway's "austere glare at the savagery that war can coax from even good-natured people," and notes that the scene "should disabuse the most immature reader of any romantic notions about the nature of organized bloodletting." There is a wrong way to kill fascists. But young McCain was beguiled: Hemingway's account of the Spanish Civil War "gave flight to a boy's romantic notions of courage and love, of idealistic men and women ennobled by their selflessness and the misuse and betrayal they suffered for it."

The protagonist, Robert Jordan, is an American professor of Spanish who has come to blow up a bridge for the Republican side. He falls in love with a girl named Maria. Despite Pablo's treachery and the mission's increasing risk and his own doubt that blowing up the bridge will really accomplish anything, Jordan does his duty. Old McCain recounts his younger self's breathless page-turning:

Hemingway, the rascal, allows the reader a brief moment of hope with a quick feint toward a happy ending as the hero nearly escapes his fate and rides to a better life with his new love. . . . I, still smug because I had penetrated the story's early mysteries, fell for it and cheered silently.

But instead of a happy ending we get a picturesque death, which, young McCain realizes, is an even happier ending. Jordan is injured by an explosion, orders to safety the Spaniards he has come to love, drags himself to a tree, and waits there with a gun. "The world is a fine place and worth the fighting for and I hate very much to leave it," he thinks as he dies. That line gave McCain the title for his second memoir—*Worth the Fighting For*—in which he fondly recounts this romantic reading. "How great it made me feel as I closed the book and charged on with my young life," old McCain remembers, "aspiring to Jordan's courage and nobility and certain I would possess it someday."

It must be nice to have a favorite book, and to have it remain your favorite book your whole life. McCain reread *For Whom the Bell Tolls* many times, but the first impression of a 12-year-old looking for models of greatness and manly exertion—"how and why to be brave, how a real hero lives and dies"—remained the truest impression. No older, wiser reading could supplant it. To read Hemingway and fall for it, to enjoy falling for it, to think it is your destiny to fall for it—maybe this is how Great Men read books: like boys.

MCCAIN'S IMPENDING death was an oddly public event, an extended civic ritual. He was diagnosed with brain cancer in July 2017. He flew from Arizona to Washington DC for one last Senate performance, saving Obamacare but not really saving Obamacare. He then flew back to Arizona for treatment. News spread that he was planning his own funeral, a rare luxury, and

that Donald Trump was not invited. Eulogies were written and published in advance. They were always eulogies for something larger: for nondespicable Republicanism, for "regular order," for compromise, for another America. It was hard to parse what died with McCain from what was already dead and what still lived. Those eulogies in turn elicited anti-eulogies, reminding us that the real McCain betrayed the virtues he was pre-eulogized for embodying.

The interesting thing about McCain was not his politics, which were, by and large, predictably Republican. His sanctimony masked nepotism, self-interest, and political expediency. His concrete political legacy is not the timeless virtue of sacrifice, but catastrophic war. Yet for decades he has remained interesting as a figure of myth, and that mythology invites something like a literary analysis. One is speaking here less of McCain himself than of McCainology. It is a slippery subject; McCainology usually says as much about the McCainologist as it does about McCain. The aura of a unique ordeal followed him from his captivity in Vietnam into politics, and McCain himself (the first and most devoted McCainologist) cultivated that aura. The question of *authenticity* has been McCainology's main preoccupation, but it is a red herring. I am asking other questions: If McCain were a fictional character, which he kind of was, then what is his story about? And when was it written? And why did we read it?

THE BEGINNING is always the same. McCain was shot down over Hanoi on October 26, 1967, on a bombing raid. He broke both arms and one knee as he ejected the plane. When he landed in a small lake a crowd pulled him out, smashed his shoulder, and bayoneted him in the groin. He was taken to the Hanoi Hilton prison. His injuries were not treated for days, and never treated properly; thereafter he could never raise his arms above his shoulders. He spent five and a half years as a prisoner of war. For the first two years he endured solitary confinement, interrupted by torture and interrogation.

Because he was the son of an admiral, McCain's captors offered him early release, which he refused. In his memoir of the experience, *Faith of My Fathers*, he recalls debating the decision with the prisoner in the next cell. They communicated via coded wall taps, which the book renders as spoken dialogue:

"You don't know if you can survive this," he argued. "The seriously injured can go home."

"I think I can make it," I replied.

McCain refused out of adherence to the US Armed Forces' Code of Conduct, which demands that prisoners be released in the order they were captured. He knew an early release would be fodder for enemy propaganda. He also figured that his captors would taunt the remaining prisoners with the tale of the pampered admiral's son. His refusal brought worse torture and three more years of captivity.

For four days he was beaten every two hours. He tried to hang himself with a shirt but was stopped by the guard and beaten again. The memoir is matter-of-fact on this point: "I doubt I really intended to kill myself. But I couldn't fight anymore, and I remember deciding that the last thing I could do to make them believe I was still resisting, that I wouldn't break, was to attempt suicide. Obviously, it wasn't an ideal plan, but it struck me at the time as reasonable." Finally, broken, he signed a false confession. In what will become a common McCain motif, he cannot forgive himself this dishonor, but it is offered in such a way that the reader

forgives him. And he in turn can forgive other prisoners who are similarly broken.

On March 14, 1973, McCain and 107 other American POWs were released. But the climax of *Faith of My Fathers* comes not when the hero regains his physical freedom, but rather when he accepts his captivity and understands it as a form of grace: "In prison, where my cherished independence was mocked and assaulted, I found my self-respect in a shared fidelity to my country. All honor comes with obligations. I and the men with whom I served had accepted ours, and we were grateful for the privilege."

CAPTIVITY DEFINES McCain as much for what he missed as for what he experienced. The assassinations of Martin Luther King Jr. and Robert F. Kennedy; the Prague Spring; the Tet Offensive; Lyndon Johnson's withdrawal from the 1968 election; Democrats in Chicago and George Wallace in Alabama. McCain was in prison through Richard Nixon's election *and* reelection, and through the entire television run of *Laugh-In*. The My Lai Massacre and its exposure; "Vietnamization"; the bombing of Cambodia; the lottery phase of the military draft; the American Indian Movement; Valerie Solanas shooting Andy Warhol; Miles Davis going electric; Woodstock, Altamont, and the Isle of Wight; *Portnoy's Complaint* and *Planet of the Apes*; Norman Mailer's absurdist bid for mayor of New York ("Vote the Rascals In"); the Kent State shooting; the trial of Angela Davis; the founding of the EPA; *Roe v. Wade*; John Kerry asking the Senate how they could "ask a man to be the last man to die for a mistake"; *The Joy of Sex* in its original, hirsute coffee-table-book form; *The Godfather*; *Gravity's Rainbow*; the first Earth Day; the last *Bonanza*.

It is intriguing which glimmers of the era make their way into McCain's account. At the Hanoi Hilton the day began with a half-hour radio propaganda breakfast from Hanoi Hannah, broadcasted on the Voice of Vietnam. The prisoners heard about "anti-war activities and incidents of civil strife" and speeches by "prominent American opponents of the war." In 1972, Hanoi Hannah unwittingly let the cat out of the bag about the moon landing (the moon landing!), broadcasting "George McGovern chastising Nixon for putting a man on the moon but failing to end the war." The prisoners became cultural time capsules.

McCain was born in 1936, a decade before the baby boomers whose defining experiences he did not witness. His captivity compounded this generational distance. It is not enough to say that he "missed the Sixties." Captivity insulated him from both the counterculture and the counter-counterculture. He became more filiopietistic while the rest of the culture rebelled against their parents. Their disillusionment coincided with his reillusionment.

Draft evasion was as essential to the boomer experience as the war itself. For McCain, who was both older and born into a military family, the draft was not an issue. Nor was he one of the boomer-age conscripted soldiers who actually had to fight the war that the privileged could avoid. He thus had little in common with the figure of the traumatized veteran, wrecked by the war, spat on (though this is a myth) by anti-war protesters. His character resonated with neither the powerful *First Blood*, in which the Vietnam vet John Rambo breaks down and weeps, nor the crude *Rambo: First Blood Part II*, in which Rambo asks, "Do we get to win this time?" As a senator, McCain pushed back against the Rambo fantasy that POWs remain in Vietnam. This caused discord with some veterans and some Republicans, for whom the unsaved missing-in-action were a symbol of the war's nonresolution.

To have been a POW was, at least, an insulation against being ordered to murder en masse for the state. McCain's dishonor was to break after four days of torture. His forced confession admitted to "crimes against the Vietnamese country and people." But he was spared the guilt, shame, or trauma of having committed the crimes themselves. His confession could remain false.

The congregation of POWs could keep the faith while the rest of the country lost it. In *Faith of My Fathers*, their captors taunt that they'd been "abandoned . . . by a country busy with a war that wasn't going well and too torn apart by widespread domestic turmoil to worry about a few forgotten pilots in Hanoi." Those pilots became heroes and martyrs, with allegory-ready names like Mike Christian, who sewed an American flag into his shirt, was beaten for it, and began immediately to sew another. "We clung to our belief, each one encouraging the other," McCain writes, "with a steady resolve that our honor was the extension of a great nation's honor, and that both prisoner and country would do what honor asked of us." The "great nation's honor" was never lost. The center held.

FEW FORMER POWS have entered national politics, and McCain was the only one to run for President. In 1977 he began the shift from a military career to a political one, serving as the navy's liaison to the Senate. In 1980 he divorced his first wife and married into the Arizona beer aristocracy. His second wife, Cindy, is the daughter of Jim Hensley, whose beer distributorship grew up with the Sunbelt; the millions who moved to the Southwest from the 1950s onward washed down their Republican votes with a cool Anheuser-Busch beverage brought to them by Hensley & Company.

Cindy bought a house in Arizona's First Congressional District the minute a seat opened there in 1982. McCain, who had not grown up with the Sunbelt, faced the charge that his Arizona roots were only as deep as his rich wife's strategic purchase of property. He had a ready answer: military families, he snapped back, lacked the luxury of a stable, rooted upbringing, and that "as a matter of fact, when I think about it now, the place I lived longest in my life was Hanoi."

McCain told his POW stories many times, and he heard them repeated back to him many times. It becomes rote. Consider a forgotten detail from the 2008 election. It is October 8, a month before the vote, and McCain is speaking in Bethlehem, Pennsylvania. Behind him are his running mate, Sarah Palin, and his daughter Meghan, both looking bored. McCain gives his standard stump speech, peppered with antique refrains of "my friends" and "my fellow Americans." He's supposed to say, "This is the agenda I have set before my fellow citizens," but instead he says, "This is the agenda I have set before my fellow *prisoners.*"

The snap judgment at the time was that old man McCain was "losing it." But a Freudian slip is not a sign of senility or madness; it reveals a deeper truth. Captivity is the master trope of McCain's life and career. Over the years, he faced the charge that he was irreparably damaged by his time in prison: that he suffered from PTSD, that he was nuts, that his famous temper was a sign of mental injury. He'd say the opposite was true. In 1999, before his first presidential run, he let a select group of journalists look through fifteen hundred pages of his psychiatric records. They revealed that in 1973, a navy psychiatrist had observed that McCain had "adjusted exceptionally well to repatriation." Not only did he emerge with his faculties intact; captivity comes across as a kind

of therapy. McCain "has been preoccupied with escaping being in the shadow of his father and establishing his own image and identity in the eyes of others," the psychiatrist wrote. "He feels his experience and performance as POW finally permitted this to happen." McCain "felt that he had profited by his experience and had changed significantly" and had "learned more about himself, about others."

In our era, captivity makes McCain unusual. He is less unusual the further back we look. *Faith of My Fathers* is a belated entry in a foundational American genre: the captivity narrative. McCain's fellow prisoners include John Smith, the founder of Jamestown, who was captured by Powhatan and rescued by Pocahontas in 1607, as well as Mary Rowlandson, who was held for three months by the Wampanoag, Nipmuc, and Narragansett in 1676. The genre stretches forward to Daniel Boone among the Shawnee and beyond. Captivity narratives were so common in colonial history that Benjamin Franklin wrote a parody version.

It is instructive to read *Faith of My Fathers* alongside Rowlandson's *The Sovereignty and Goodness of God*, which was published in 1682 and reprinted many times over the following century. As American items—movies, the flag—become sacred to McCain in the Hanoi Hilton, so relics of Englishness bolster Rowlandson through her harrowing "removes" from civilization. Captivity narratives are suspenseful not because the captive won't be saved—she lives to tell the tale, after all—but because of the violations and betrayals she may have to endure and commit along the way. Religious conversion offers the profoundest resolution, and Rowlandson's and McCain's are both conversion narratives. The journey from captivity to redemption tracks the journey from sin to salvation.

Captivity narratives are also terribly unreliable, written after-the-fact. (McCain's was coconstructed with Mark Salter, his all-purpose Boswell.) They make something coherent out of a perhaps unnarratable trauma, or a chaos, or what Rowlandson calls "that distressed time." What brings order to such experience is divine providence. Rowlandson, like McCain, ponders suicide, but "the wonderful goodness of God" keeps her from using "wicked and violent means to end my own miserable life." Providence guides her fingers to just the right page of the Bible, a Bible also delivered to her by providence. McCain is given similar revelations. "Once I was thrown into another cell after a long and difficult interrogation," he recalls. "I discovered scratched into one of the cell's walls the creed, 'I believe in God, the Father Almighty.' . . . I felt God's love and care more vividly than I would have felt it had I been safe among a pious congregation in the most magnificent cathedral." Cosmic coincidences will lend his tribulations an air of destiny and design. He will refuse early release on the very same day his father assumes command of the navy in the Pacific: the Fourth of July, 1968.

The captive becomes a proxy for her society as a whole: John Smith stands in for all Britons, Mary Rowlandson for Puritan New England. They chronicle harrowing experiences on the empire's frontier and make those experiences meaningful to the center. Rowlandson's is an allegorical ordeal in the wilderness, preserving Englishness against savage violation. John McCain, privileged son cast into mortal danger, can likewise represent America itself. The imperial hegemon is no longer a hegemon but a scrappy underdog, held in bondage. His prayers become your prayers. Whatever war or conquest of which the captivity was an episode can therefore be redeemed as well.

Captivity gave McCain a mystique. But it was also a hurdle: he was not the kind of politician who could represent or embody common experience. The experience he embodied is absolutely uncommon. His political appeal depended on a spectacular and terrifying experience few will have and no sane person would want. An elite navy brat has no obvious constituency in a representative democracy; nor, paradoxically, does the redeemed captive. The captive is a proxy for the polity, not a participant in it. The timeless virtues of the congregation of captives—courage, service, mission, honor, sacrifice—carry one only so far in a battle of interests and distributions. And someone else's impossible sacrifice can be off-putting.

IT IS CUSTOMARY to speak of a "Vietnam syndrome" in American foreign policy. Ronald Reagan used the phrase to identify an American reluctance, born of guilt or defeat, to deploy military might, and he saw a renewed bellicosity as the cure. George H. W. Bush said after the Persian Gulf War, "By God, we've kicked the Vietnam syndrome once and for all." As a member of Congress, McCain embraced Reagan's cold war, but not as overcompensation for defeat in Vietnam—or at least not principally. After the cold war ended, McCain was instrumental in normalizing relations with Vietnam, alongside the draft-dodging boomer Bill Clinton and the veteran-turned-antiwar-activist John Kerry. But he was otherwise critical of the "self-doubt" he saw in Clinton's foreign policy, and he attributed that self-doubt to "the mindset of a culture formed in opposition to the Vietnam War."

McCain had even less patience for the '90s-era reckonings of the war's original architects. The wartime secretary of defense Robert McNamara turned confessional and apologetic in his 1995 memoir, *In Retrospect*, in search of whatever wisdom "the lessons of Vietnam" might hold. In 1997 he convened a conference in Hanoi of aged American and Vietnamese statesmen to rehash the decision-making on both sides. The transcripts, gathered into a book called *Argument Without End*, amount to a revealing and frustrating document. Neediness characterizes the American side: a need to be thought well-intentioned, a need to convince the Vietnamese that we had not in fact been "neoimperialists." Our anti-imperialist mind-set was genuine; our belief in the domino theory was real. We were "wrong, terribly wrong," but not evil.

Mind-set and *tragedy* are important words for McNamara: once you've admitted that your enemy had a mind-set you didn't understand—for instance, that the Vietnamese were driven more by anticolonial nationalism than by pro-Soviet Communism—you can then lament misunderstanding as "tragic," and take solace in misunderstandings at least being *mutual*. This leads McNamara to clunky formulations like this one: "I am damn certain we didn't understand that that was your belief. So I think it's a tragedy that we allowed that misunderstanding to exist."

Is false consciousness interesting? One answer to McNamara is that the US could be an empire without having an imperialist "mind-set." The Vietnamese, for their part, could respond to murky mind-sets with bracing clarity: "You are wrong to call the war a 'tragedy,'" General Vo Nguyen Giap says to McNamara on the first day. "Maybe it was a tragedy for you, because yours was a war of aggression, in the neocolonialist 'style.' . . . You wanted to replace the French; you failed; men died; so, yes, it was tragic, because they died for a bad cause." McCain chose bracing clarity over hand-wringing retrospect. "What," he asks in *Worth the Fighting For*, "did Robert McNamara expect

to learn from his former foes?" Undignified and soft-boiled, McNamara's delegation deserved the cool reception they got. There is a wrong way to lose a war.

McNamara suffered existentially but not physically; McCain had suffered physically but not existentially. His second memoir cuts through McNamara's argument-without-end with a fond portrait of Nguyen Co Thach, the foreign minister of Vietnam with whom McCain had worked on diplomatic normalization. Thach, it so happened, had been imprisoned by the French in the very same prison where McCain would end up—he is another of McCain's fellow prisoners—and he sometimes met McCain while wearing a tie embroidered with little heads of Adam Smith. They could laugh about it. That's where real history is, where a personal bond between former foes means something, damnit, where you might lose your temper about war reparations but then drink it out and resolve a diplomatic impasse with a hard-boiled joke: I bet the food was better when it was a *French* prison!

MCCAIN'S OWN reckoning with the legacy of the Vietnam War was both contradictory and somehow uncomplicated. He admitted that the war would have been better left unfought, yet he also insisted that it was winnable. He held to the line, common in the military circles that despise McNamara, that a more aggressive effort would have prevailed if the US had pursued it and not lost "the will to fight."

One can imagine a toxic version of this, but McCain held to it without apparent bitterness. He could afford to do so because national honor was affirmed rather than eroded in the Hanoi Hilton. The war was, for him, not a generational event but a familial one. Such is the tightness of the McCain family drama that his own father was commander in chief of the Pacific. Admiral John Sidney McCain Jr. pushed hard for renewed attacks on the territory of North Vietnam and bristled for years against politicians' "half measures." The US halted bombings of North Vietnam in 1968; bombing resumed in March 1972, in response to North Vietnam's Easter Offensive. The POWs in McCain's account welcomed the bombing as a sign of American commitment: "As the bombing campaign intensified, our morale soared with every sortie." The father orders the bombs that might kill his captive son; the son in turn narrates this as the noble carrying out of a duty.

This is not to say that there was nothing for McCain to resolve in the legacy of Vietnam, only that he gravitated toward a particular kind of resolution: vivid and novelistic, gestural rather than ideological. There is a right way to lose a war. He first returned to Vietnam in 1985, for a CBS documentary. "There was a great deal of pain here, a great deal of suffering, a great deal of loneliness," McCain says in his old cell in Hanoi. "There was also a lot of courage displayed. And a lot of love, love for one another, that I think Americans are uniquely capable of." (Americans: uniquely capable of love!) He returned again in the '90s: "Curiously, I felt little emotion at all beyond sympathy for the poor bastards who were living there now," McCain wrote in *Worth the Fighting For.* "It had been a long time. What's past is past."

The climactic resolution comes not in his old cell but in, of all places, Ho Chi Minh's vacation villa. During McCain's captivity a prison commander told him about a place in Ha Long Bay "that Ho had used to relax." As a senator, McCain hints to a Vietnamese vice foreign minister that he'd like to see it. Sure enough, on one of his diplomatic trips, his hosts arrange him a stay. "And a few nights later," he writes,

as I breathed the warm breezes off the bay that blew through the unshuttered windows, snuffed out the candle on the table next to me, and laid my head on the pillow, in the bed, in the house where Ho had slept, I knew I had received all the recompense I was likely to get for the nights in Vietnam I had spent in less comfortable circumstances, many years ago. There was nothing more I could gain by revisiting the war with my former enemies.

The prose gets a little awkward, the hard-boiled woven with the mildly platitudinous, but it's still pretty good:

Better to enjoy the evening and in the morning see to more promising pursuits, among which was helping to build a relationship with Vietnam that would serve both our peoples better than our old one had. In that endeavor, I pledged to keep the bullshit on both sides to a minimum. I think the memory of fifty-eight thousand dead Americans and three million Vietnamese dead deserves to be honored with the truth.

Truth and minimum bullshit. Sleep, don't tell. McCain, again a proxy, enacts with one metonymic good night's sleep in Ho's villa the resolution that the feckless hand-wringing of a dozen McNamaras could never achieve.

GOOD STORY, BUT is it true? What we're dealing with, what we're always dealing with when we talk about McCain, is myth. One turns to McCain not for fact but for drama and resolution. The redeemed-captive-turned-senator returns intact—nay, stronger and wiser!—to the site of his primal ordeal. Not only does he *not* suffer from Vietnam syndrome, he pulls a story of redemption from a war that lacked it. Instead of a generational agony, he offers an individual destiny.

In the Hanoi Hilton and the villa on Ha Long Bay, McCain was alone yet still performing: for us, for himself, for History.

Destiny! Even his jokes buttressed this mystique. He and his predecessor in the Senate, Barry Goldwater, performed this snappy little routine in the 1980s:

> GOLDWATER: If I had been elected president in 1964 you wouldn't have been a prisoner of war in Hanoi.

> MCCAIN: True. I would have been a prisoner of war . . . *in China!*

The joke lands because it suggests that even in the alternate histories, McCain would have been shot down and captured somewhere or other. That's just how destiny works.

McCain entered Congress in 1981, as part of the Reagan wave. He was hawkish in all things, though in his first year in the House he disagreed with Reagan about keeping US marines in Lebanon. He voted against Martin Luther King Jr. Day in 1983, but for sanctioning apartheid South Africa in 1986. That same year he was elected to the Senate. Though he took over Goldwater's seat, he was temperamentally more of a backslapper and a crony (navy liaison to the Senate had also been that kind of job). In 1989, during the savings and loan crisis, McCain was one of the Keating Five, senators who took money from banker Charles Keating when they were supposed to be regulating the industry. Only after that scandal did McCain take up the issue of campaign finance reform, although he continued to deregulate the finance industry and to reap money.

He acquired the sobriquet "maverick" in the mid-'90s, a decade after Tom Cruise played Maverick in *Top Gun*, another short, dickish, hotheaded navy fighter pilot with unresolved father issues. *Maverick* signals individualism; it was originally a term for unbranded cattle. But it is the wrong word for McCain. His individualism had more to do with individual atonement—with having been branded, burned, dishonored, but then redeemed. Often these atonements would performatively rehearse his captivity. The Keating Five was that kind of episode: McCain admitted the error and histrionically likened the ordeal to his time in Hanoi. Campaign finance reform was the redemption. The pattern is familiar: a moment of dishonor, a trial, a grimace, an atonement. McCain wanted these performances to be the definitive markers of time. Once you have the scar tissue, there's no point in discussing the wound.

Or he was called a maverick when he was really just generationally out of step. He was a reliable Republican company man, to be sure, rewarded with predictable millions from the NRA. But even as a Republican he channeled rustier orthodoxies. He took over Goldwater's Senate seat but not Goldwater's mantle of ideological conservatism. He invoked Teddy Roosevelt's rustic-progressive strenuous life while Reagan attacked the welfare state. He thrilled to Roosevelt's *Rough Riders* while his party tuned to Hayek's *Road to Serfdom*. McCain wasn't really a neocon because he'd never not been a hawk. (He could thus oxymoronically call himself the "original neocon" when boosting the Iraq war.) When challenged from the nativist Republican base, he claimed Reagan as his political idol, but with a protesting-too-much ardor. He even interpolated Reagan back into his tale of captivity, claiming that he and his fellow POWs were psyched to gather snatches of information about the then governor of California. (They heard about Reagan, but not the moon landing?)

McCain is best understood less as a reactionary than as an anachronism. An anachronism does not merely evoke another era; he is literally *from* another era, like a Rip Van Winkle sleeping through the American Revolution, or a Captain America retrieved from the ice. McCain's generational otherness allowed other generations to project meaning onto him. He satisfied our nostalgia and our need for narrative. He also capitalized on that need, and being an anachronism shielded him from criticism.

His generational out-of-step-ness was particularly appealing as the 20th century closed. Here at the end of history was a figure who had been *present* for history yet curiously insulated from its disillusionments. His hair had gone prematurely white in Hanoi, but he'd emerged from the cold war with something like a youthful energy. Profiles from this period routinely describe him "bounding" somewhere or other, and they note that he looked older in person than on television but was more energetic and impatient.

One writerly account stands out, though it is often misunderstood. David Foster Wallace's profile of McCain for *Rolling Stone* appeared in April 2000, at the height of McCain's crossover appeal. This was during the Republican presidential primary and the maiden voyage of McCain's tour bus, the Straight Talk Express. McCain had become a darling among journalists because he was willing to say the religious right was evil and shoot the shit, freestyle, for nine hours a day.

Was he real? It took Wallace twenty-five thousand words to arrive at an anxious *I hope so.* McCain's captivity, at least, was irreducibly real. Wallace fixed on those "five-plus years . . . in a North Vietnamese prison, mostly in solitary, in a box, getting tortured and starved. And the unbelievable honor and balls he showed there." This experience imbued McCain with "something riveting and unSpinnable and true."

That unSpinnable *something* was "underneath politics" and therefore a foundation for politics. (Wallace has to remind himself that McCain says some "scary and rightwingish" shit when he's not being "cool" and "nondweeby" and suffering from authentic chronic pain.) McCain's impossible nonexpedience was everything that politics in the 1990s — "midmorning in America's hangover from the whole Lewinsky-and-impeachment thing" — wasn't. Bill Clinton was all triangulation, pseudosincerity, and boomer smarm. He claimed to feel your pain, but McCain's pain was bracingly truer than any pain you've felt, and he chose to endure more of it. Wallace even exaggerated the ordeal: two years in solitary confinement became five years in Wallace's account, and the torture was ceaseless.

This says more about Wallace than about McCain — or rather, Wallace clung to McCain on behalf of Generation X. "Since you're reading *Rolling Stone*," the essay begins, "the chances are you're an American between say 18 and 35, which demographically makes you a Young Voter. And no generation of Young Voters has ever cared less about politics and politicians than yours." Wallace himself was 38 at the time, handing down a redemptive wisdom to slightly younger readers: Be cynical, but not too cynical. It was McCain's peculiar fate to speak for no generation, but now, for a moment, he appealed to one.

If McCain is sincere, can I be sincere? And am I being sincere when I'm aware of how sincere I'm being? The Generation X predicament is a maddening, self-chasing loop. Wallace made it seem like an equation has finally been solved:

> If you . . . have come to a point on the Trail where you've started fearing your own cynicism almost as much as you fear your own

credulity and the salesmen who feed on it, you may find your thoughts returning again and again to a certain dark and box-sized cell in a certain Hilton half a world and three careers away, to the torture and fear and offer of release and a certain Young Voter named McCain's refusal to violate a Code.

McCain's solitary suffering speaks across a divide of thirty years. His fellow prisoners are absent; the war itself is strangely absent. The argument depends on McCain's atavistic singular weirdness: on a character and a courage that awakens the "corny American hope" we might all still have, the hope "lying dormant like a spinster's ardor." The wounds that matter to Wallace are emotional and semiotic: "we've been lied to and lied to, and it hurts to be lied to." McCain's physical wounds are a saving truth, hence the visceral prose when Wallace writes about them. The reader who has only suffered emotionally or semiotically is brought to McCain's story and made to imagine a groin wound. ("Imagine: *groin wound.*")

MCCAIN LOST that primary, but he lost it the right way. That the opposition had been so dirty redounded to his own dignity. Republicans in South Carolina received phone calls that asked, "Would you be more or less likely to vote for John McCain if you knew he had fathered an illegitimate black child?" (The McCains have an adopted daughter from Bangladesh.)

McCain could then, for a moment, become the political maverick he had played on television: a figure who really would vote against his own party. The McCain-Feingold campaign finance reform bill passed in 2002. (The Supreme Court gutted it in 2010.) And a maverick Republican could be at least a tepidly climate-friendly one: McCain and then Democrat Joe Lieberman introduced a market-friendly cap-and-trade bill. McCain was so popular (and the Democratic Party so craven) that in 2004, John Kerry wanted McCain to be his running mate.

But the avenue of McCain's ambition was not independence from party. It was the war on terror. His push for war began immediately after September 11, 2001, and he styled himself a hard-boiled, war-is-hell hawk rather than a war-will-be-easy hawk. "War is a miserable business," he wrote that October. "Let's get on with it." Air strikes in Afghanistan had already begun; McCain, channeling his father's disdain for "half measures," was arguing for full commitment, for not repeating the strategic errors of Vietnam. He pushed early, too, for war in Iraq: "Next up, Baghdad!" he yelled to sailors on the USS *Theodore Roosevelt* in January 2002, joining the chorus of the war's neocon boosters, all of whom had avoided the draft in Vietnam.

McCain tied his political fate to the Iraq war: its success would be his success, its failure his failure. It is tempting to see a tragic grandeur there, as if McCain were fated to replay the drama of his own father, calling in vain for more troops and more surges, all the while insisting that "Iraq is not Vietnam." But even to say it that way is to fall into the trap of McCain's self-mythologizing. There was tragedy in it, yes, but no grandeur—only error and opportunism.

Self-deception is still deception. As the catastrophe wore on, McCain was in the curious position of saying that the war was just and winnable but also that doomed causes were noble and picturesque. Robert Jordan returned. The memoir containing McCain's reminiscences about *For Whom the Bell Tolls* was published in 2002, and in subsequent years Robert Jordanism became McCain's compulsion. Aides would remind him that Jordan is a fictional character. It is a powerful fantasy: to read *For Whom the*

Bell Tolls as an allegory for the war on terror figures America not as a brutal and bumbling empire, but rather as a scrappy foreign fighter in other people's liberations. McCain could then romanticize doomed causes as a "beautiful fatalism," as if Iraq and Afghanistan were not Vietnam-like quagmires but modern-day Spains.

One irony of McCain's fondness for Hemingway is that McCain would have cut a ridiculous figure in every Hemingway novel besides *For Whom the Bell Tolls*. Robert Jordan is the exception, after all: he dies for a doomed but beautiful cause, but most Hemingway heroes don't die in a war. They walk out into the rain and live on as hardboiled men, wounded men. They scorn statesmanly pieties and take up fishing, bullfighting, boxing, or literature. "I was always embarrassed by the words sacred, glorious, and sacrifice and the expression in vain," says the narrator of *A Farewell to Arms*, an ambulance driver in World War I. "Abstract words such as glory, honor, courage, or hallow were obscene beside the concrete names of villages, the number of roads, the names of rivers, the numbers of regiments and the dates." But *glory*, *honor*, *courage*, and *hallow* were McCain's favorite words. The second irony is more bitter. The war on terror made McCain less like Robert Jordan and more like the unnamed, ignoble figures who sent Robert Jordan to die.

BY 2008, WHEN McCain chose Sarah Palin as his running mate—his only generationally ahead-of-the-curve political move—he had retreated from all that endeared him to non-Republicans. He had called Jerry Falwell and Pat Robertson "agents of intolerance" in 2000, but now he courted conservative evangelicals and gave a graduation speech at Falwell's Liberty University. Palin was a young favorite of the religious right, and a "heartthrob" to neoconservative insiders like William Kristol. That she was young and unknown made the pick seem "mavericky"—one of that year's exciting new words, along with *photobomb*, *fatberg*, and the verb *unlike*—but it was the logical end point of partisan calculation.

Beyond the religious right, the governor of Alaska was a relative unknown. Palin introduced herself at the Republican National Convention as a real American from the small town of Wasilla, population ten thousand. "We grow good people in our small towns, with honesty, sincerity, and dignity," she said, citing "a writer." This was remarkable not only because the writer was Westbrook Pegler—the '30s-era John Bircher, anti-Semite, and isolationist who lives on in the far-right quotations of our era—but also because John McCain wasn't grown in a small town or even in a state: he was born in the Panama Canal Zone when the Panama Canal Zone was a US territory. He grew up hearing his father recite Victorian poetry about empires and civilizing missions; now here he stood with a witless reactionary whose folksy-seeming family soon devolved into a reality show. He invoked Kipling; she foreshadowed *Duck Dynasty*.

The McCain/Palin campaign slogan, "Country first," handily contained this alliance. On one hand, it recalled McCain's romance of captivity and redemption, his valor and sacrifice in an unpopular war that was definitely, emphatically not at all like the endless, unpopular war that he still championed. On the other hand it channeled the old fascist slogan "America first."

Palin remained a sin for which McCain did not atone. In his third and final memoir, *The Restless Wave*, published this past April, he wrote, looking back to 2008, that he was losing in the polls and therefore needed a "game-changer," but that he should have chosen Lieberman instead. "I don't like not doing what I know in my gut I should do." Well, who does?

THAT 2008 ELECTION is remarkable for being the only one in the past thirty years not to feature a boomer candidate. (Dismal fact: Bill Clinton, George W. Bush, and Donald Trump were all born in the summer of 1946.) McCain was older than the boomers, and a hallowed war hero; Obama was younger, too young to have faced the military draft or dodged it. This meant that the Vietnam War was, for the first time in a generation, not at issue in a presidential election. Without guilt or shame, Obama could praise McCain's wartime heroism while consigning him to grandfatherly obsolescence.

Rarely noted, though, is a deeper consonance between McCain and Obama. Nonboomers both, they were also both cosmopolitans, born on the margins or former margins of an American empire. McCain moved through the military establishment from the frontier to the center: from Panama to the Naval Academy to Hanoi to Arizona to Washington. Obama's route was also circuitous: from Hawaii to Indonesia and back, and then through the academic establishment, from Occidental College in LA to Columbia and Harvard Law; and then from Chicago's South Side to Washington. Both wrote compelling family memoirs in the 1990s. McCain's *Faith of My Fathers* and Obama's *Dreams from My Father* stand as twin codas to the "American Century." McCain came to understand the faith of his ever-present fathers while in captivity in Vietnam. Obama came to understand his ever-absent father on a personal pilgrimage to Kenya.

McCain was cosmopolitan the way Rudyard Kipling, born in India, was cosmopolitan, and he channeled that antique sense

of imperial mission. In a 2007 statement of foreign policy for *Foreign Affairs*, he wrote that "our unique form of leadership—the antithesis of empire—gives us moral credibility, which is more powerful than any show of arms." He meant the antithesis of European-style empires, but "antithesis of empire" is one of those phrases that really suggests its opposite, and not only because McCain was born in the Panama Canal Zone. He also wrote paeans to Alfred Thayer Mahan (the father of the modern navy), Billy Mitchell (father of the air force), and Theodore Roosevelt.

Though he would not put it in these terms, empire was McCain's source of order, anecdote, poetry, and noble death. The usual foreign-policy labels—*hawk, neocon, interventionist*—don't quite capture that view of the world. We need a label that befits an anachronism, something like *pre-postcolonial*. His view of the world did not need new epistemologies to comprehend the subjectivities of colonized peoples; he did not wonder whether the subaltern can speak.

Obama, by contrast, stirred a hope that the world was already postethnic, postracial. His more paranoid critics imagined that he was born elsewhere, or that he inherited his father's anticolonial politics. But Obama's rhetorical genius lay in absorbing his cosmopolitan sensibility into a liberal variant of American exceptionalism: to narrate a world in which the wounds of race and empire had somehow already been healed. Where McCain was pre-postcolonial, Obama was post-postcolonial.

Both were fictions. Obama did not end the war on terror, though he spoke as if he did. McCain, for his part, clung to the story of Robert Jordan with ever more devotion. His key gesture in the Obama years was the international trip: the senator as foreign fighter. "They are my heroes," he said of the anti-Gaddafi forces he visited in Libya in 2011. He made a surprise trip to Syria in 2013 and posed necktie-less for photographs with armed leaders of the Free Syrian Army. The politician-as-Hemingway-hero needs to be *there*, whether *there* is Syria or Libya or Baghdad.

Arizona, the state he ostensibly represented, meanwhile thrust monstrous figures into the national arena. McCain did not hide his contempt for Phoenix sheriff Joe Arpaio. But in 2010 he voted against the DREAM Act, earlier versions of which he'd sponsored, and he supported Arizona's Support Our Law Enforcement and Safe Neighborhoods Act, a repressive law that required police to ask people for immigration documents during stops, detentions, and arrests. In a campaign ad from that year, when McCain faced a primary challenge from the right, he walks beside a sheriff who warns of the "illegals" who come through Arizona. "Complete the danged fence," McCain says. "It'll work this time," the sheriff replies. "Senator—you're one of us."

THE END OF the American Century feels like the end of something else: a novel, maybe, that we thought would end differently. Trump's victory struck many people as implausible, but plausibility is as much a measure of narrative as a measure of politics. What kind of story do you think is being told? Where are we along its narrative arc? What is believable in the plot and what is beyond the pale of plausibility? Which reversals or twists would be in keeping with the genre and which would break the genre's rules? Does the story have a moral?

Obama and McCain were the American Century's last literary statesmen, and they presided over its decline. Both catered to the desire to see America as a text, as something legible, and both assumed its futurity.

Obama was the narrator whose every speech added a paragraph to the American story, moving all of us, the expansive *we* of "Yes we can," ever nearer a promised land. McCain was not a narrator but a character—a hero rather than an everyman, but no less literary for being heroic. He summoned Hemingway's foreign fighter above all, but also older archetypes: the captivity narrative of the 17th and 18th centuries, the imperial adventures of the 19th. His heroism was always twice-told, never not an old book. In every Obama story, something is transcended; in every McCain story, something is preserved.

Hence the constant hallowing. McCain's memoirs are peppered with tributes to uncommon men he admired and emulated—Ted Williams, Mo Udall, Emiliano Zapata as played by Marlon Brando—as well as figures from the imperial past, Great Men and the occasional woman who did things the right way. Fictional characters, too. McCain believed firmly in an afterlife of that sort: one measures the health of a body politic by how well or poorly the honorable dead are honored. Pantheons need custodians, especially when you want to be in that pantheon. In that sense, McCain had been planning his funeral since he was 12 years old.

These narrative postures live on in the Trump era, but they feel like obsolete rituals. Obama still shares on Facebook an annual list of books that inspired him, as if all will be well and another shelf can be added to the bookcase. McCain, on the occasion of his last memoir, likewise hallowed his literary favorites in an interview with the *New York Times*, and of course they were books from an earlier age. He reminisced about his childhood readings of Sir Walter Scott, *Treasure Island*, Mark Twain. He liked W. Somerset Maugham's "cosmopolitan sensibility, his feel for the personal and social dramas provoked by clashing cultures." He

recommended classics of military history and the biographies of Great Men. The one book the President should read, he said, is Carl Sandburg's six-volume biography of Lincoln. (Isn't that six books? "If he doesn't have time to read all six volumes, he could make do with the one-volume edition published in 1954.")

Couldn't they see the wreck? Maybe not. Trump doesn't fit. He is too narrow and inarticulate to be one of the diverse points of view that Obama would embroider into the American story. The paranoia of birtherism is unassimilable. In a McCain plot, Trump would most resemble the torturer. Torture unmakes the world, as Elaine Scarry argues in *The Body in Pain*. It obliterates language and narrative. Trump offers no future to achieve, nor a future from which to hallow our heroes. There is only the excruciating present of someone else's joyless real-time narcissism.

"He's not a war hero," Trump said of McCain in 2015. "He's a war hero because he was captured. I like people that *weren't* captured." Deflating the sacred mystique of McCain's captivity, and the captivity tale as a genre, is fully consistent with the illiterate nationalist profanity that Trump embodies. He is the least cosmopolitan rich man of all time. McCain's hallowed literary archetypes—the captive's redemption, the imperial picaro's adventures, the foreign fighter's sacrifice—only matter if the rest of the world matters, or if the margins matter, or if you can read.

MCCAIN REGAINED some of his old romantic stature during the Trump presidency, and not only because of his approaching death. It was also because McCain has been his era's foremost advocate for the Great Man theory of history. It's quaint, both boyish and grandfatherly, to believe that a pivotal figure's moral fiber determines the course of human events. Such theories are out of fashion among professional historians, but they are very much in fashion, in an unacknowledged way, in daily political life. The recurring liberal fantasy that some or another Great Man or Woman will come to the rescue is a sign of how terribly and perversely true that theory of history has become.

In July 2017, having been diagnosed with brain cancer after undergoing a craniotomy, McCain flew back to Washington with a sharp black line of stitches over his left eyebrow and the fate of the Affordable Care Act in his hands. "Stop listening to the bombastic loudmouths on the radio and television and the internet!" he admonished his fellow senators in a much-lauded speech. "To hell with them!" He spoke of greatness. The Senate's deliberations "haven't been overburdened by greatness lately." Lately? Then he delivered a tribute to the Senate's "arcane rules and customs," the "seemingly eccentric practices that slow our proceedings and insist on our cooperation." The maverick was most appealing, paradoxically, when he issued a hoary ode to noble traditions, to the faith of his fathers, to the Senate, to the way it used to be—as if it ever was what it used be.

Refusing to tip his vote in advance, elevating the suspense to a level any writer would envy, he gave the dramatic thumbs-down on the Senate floor. The Republican bill was dead; the maverick lived on. Never mind that his was not a defense of Obamacare, but simply a call to dismantle Obamacare via the Senate's "regular order." Such was the McCain mystique that his own recent medical needs channeled pathos rather than hypocrisy. Americans celebrated as though the center had held.

But it has been a season of such pivotal figures, one after the other. McCain was one more figure by the thread of whose personality the American future seemed to hang. Sally Yates, James Comey, Robert Mueller, Anthony Kennedy, Ruth Bader Ginsburg. Ours *is* an era of heroic politics, or at least we make the mistake of thinking of it as such. Liberals especially have painted themselves into that corner, when in fact the real lesson of this upside-down Great Man–ism should be that a heroic politics is a broken politics.

IF GREAT MEN are obsolete among historians, so too is the asking of *what if* questions. Counterfactual histories leave no archive, yet we've been saturated with counterfactuals since Trump's election. *If only*s abound, frantic and lamenting, searching for that *one variable* that might have changed the course. These are unsatisfying because political disasters have a thousand causes. Other counterfactuals are valuable provocations. A good counterfactual can remind us that our fates are not sealed. "Bernie would've won" is such a provocation: not necessarily an I-told-you-so, but a shorthand about the recent past that suggests an actual political future. A subjunctive politics can be a hopeful politics.

No wonder we return to McCain: he was already living in an alternate history, one that was always more romantic and picturesque than ours. It was a nice alternate history to visit. As escapisms go, McCain's wasn't the worst. It had a tidy moral, like a bedtime story. Love your country, because John McCain loved your country more than you do. It also had a narrative structure: nostalgia, but with one eye trained on eulogies of the future. McCain died as he lived, preserved in the amber of the American Century. An anachronism hints that the time we're trapped in could have gone another way. It's pretty to think so. +

ACKNOWLEDGEMENTS

DONORS

Sunil Abraham
Mitzi Angel
Bobby Baird
Malavika Banerjee
Alexander Benaim
Mieke Chew & Jonathon Sturgeon
Amanda Claybaugh
Nicole Cliffe
Gabriella De Ferrari
Rimjhim Dey
Jynne Dilling Martin & Louie Saletan
John Doman
Dan Estabrook
Sarah Fan
Kelly Farber
Lauren Festa
Molly Fischer & Sam MacLaughlin
Mel Flashman
Amanda Fortini
Iris Frangou
Kathleen French
Michelle García
Amitav Ghosh & Deborah Baker
DW Gibson
Alice Gregory & Leon Neyfakh
Mark Greif
Christopher Habib
Chad Harbach
Joy Harris
Sloan Harris
Kieran Holohan

Isabel Howe
Jessica Johnson
Whitney Kassel & Josh Koppel
Denis Kelleher
Alexandra Kleeman & Alex Gilvarry
Ahmed Klink
Jennifer Krasinski
Stephanie LaCava
Katy Lederer & Ben Statz
Gary Lippman
Liese Mayer
Claire McGinnis
Marisa Meltzer
Daniel Menaker
Edward Orloff
Katha Pollitt & Steven Lukes
Sirish Rao
Bridget Read
Amy & Gregory Rowland
Jim Rutman
David Salle
Emily Searles
Gary Sernovitz
Akash Shah
David & Shelley Sonenberg
Marya Spence
Stephen Squibb
Daria Vaisman
Ryan Webb & Kris Moran
Rachel Rabbit White
Anna Wiener

Special thanks to

Lisa Borst
Jo Constantz
Sarah Gale

Emma Hager
Lizzy Harding
Hannah Kaplan

Asprey Liu
Donovan Redd
Will Tavlin

n+1 is supported, in part, by public funds from the New York State Council on the Arts and New York City Department of Cultural Affairs in partnership with the City Council.

OUR CONTRIBUTORS

George Blaustein is assistant professor of American studies at the University of Amsterdam and the author of *Nightmare Envy & Other Stories: American Culture and European Reconstruction*. His last piece for *n+1* was "The Obama Speeches" in Issue 27.

Imraan Coovadia is *n+1*'s South Africa correspondent. His sixth and most recent novel is *A Spy in Time* (Rare Bird Books, 2018). His last piece for *n+1* was "A Broken Window" in Issue 8.

Jill Crawford is a writer from Northern Ireland.

A. S. Hamrah is *n+1*'s film columnist. His first book, *The Earth Dies Streaming: Film Writing 2002–2018* was published by n+1 Books in November.

Jeanne-Marie Jackson is an assistant professor of English at Johns Hopkins University.

Pankaj Mishra's most recent book is *Age of Anger: A History of the Present*. His last piece for *n+1* was "First Love" in Issue 3.

Christina Nichol is the author of the novel *Waiting for the Electricity*. Her last piece for *n+1* was "An Account of My Hut" in Issue 31.

Meghan O'Gieblyn is the author of the essay collection *Interior States*. Her last piece for *n+1* was "Ghost in the Cloud" in Issue 28.

Barnaby Raine is a graduate student in history at Columbia University.

Lyle Jeremy Rubin is a graduate student living in New England.

Elizabeth Schambelan is a writer and editor living in New York. Her last piece for *n+1* was "League of Men" in Issue 28.

LETTERS

Correction: The printed version of Bruce Robbins's "Bad Atrocity Writing" in Issue 32 omitted a citation to the work of Gloria Fisk, a professor of English at Queens College, CUNY, whose published and unpublished writing on prolepsis and violence helped clarify the author's thinking on the subject.

In her scholarly work, Fisk observes that examples of prolepsis have increased in novelistic writing since around 1980 and notes that prolepsis lends itself particularly to the representation of violence on a massive scale (as in instances of terrorism, environmental catastrophe, mass incarceration, and genocide). She further argues that prolepsis works like ancient tragedy, to vent contemporary hopes and anxieties about the limits of political community. As Fisk writes, prolepsis "invites its witnesses to test the division between the foreign and the familiar and to reassert the difference between us and them." See "Putting Tragedy to Work for the Polis: The Rhetoric of Pity and Terror, Before and After Modernity," New Literary History 39, no. 4 (Autumn 2008): 891–902, and "Tragic Knowledge in Postmodern Novels" (PhD diss., City University of New York, 2003).

—Editors

Trapped

Dear Editors,

I'd like to respond to Jesse McCarthy's writing on the relationship between the trap, trapping, and trap music in "Notes on Trap" (Issue 32) by way of an anecdote. I know some trappers. In the car with one in Atlanta, as we drove from deal to deal, stopping occasionally to measure weight and count bills, we listened to Future's album *FUTURE*. The trapper told me this was his favorite album to listen to while trapping because he was trapping and Future was trapping.

There's a tautology implicit in his words. Trap music is trapping and trapping is trap music. Whenever someone asks a trapper to explain how trapping as an action (the closest yet totally inadequate synonym being *dealing*) relates to trapping as a musical genre, the tautology continues. Some might take it as an invitation to explain trap, but I think trappers know what they're doing when they answer this way. They're not saying, "If you don't know, now you know," but, "If you have to ask, you'll never know."

McCarthy's essay is at its best when it takes this refusal to explain for granted, understanding that trappers control just how much of trap we can know for their own purposes (safety, profit, and so on). That is, the essay shines when it inhabits the discourses of trap to better understand the subject at hand (an encounter in a store, for instance). The essay seems weakest when it fails to take the limitations of our ability to know trap seriously. At these moments, McCarthy offers definitions and analyses in terms external to the genre and makes claims about the generalizability of trap. For instance, "All these blocks, all these hoods . . . are effectively *the same.*" Never once did I feel, on that ride down Old Nat, that anywhere else in Atlanta, let alone the world, was like the south side. Thinking back on that moment now, I still can't say that I know the south side so much as that I know what a trapper showed me of his life. Taking seriously our inability to know anything other than what the trapper lets us see while still caring about those who find themselves in the trap is what seems, to me, both most thrilling and most urgent about trap. I wish only that McCarthy took the limitations of our knowledge seriously throughout.

—*Elias Rodriques*

Hello, Cold War?

Dear Editors,

It is hard to deny Aziz Rana's claim ("Goodbye, Cold War," Issue 30) that there are new openings for left influence on US domestic politics. But his main thesis about the breakdown of the cold-war paradigm seems to me wildly premature. The post-2016 "Resistance" project, as it has been molded in the hands of the Beltway's political professionals, national security establishment, and dominant media organs, has been in large part an effort to breathe new life into that old cold-war framework, fuse it to the post–September 11 war on terror project, and restore popular commitment to US global hegemony and exceptionalism. Depressingly, at least for those of us who worry about US militarism and imperialism and about the viability of left movements abroad in the face of the persistent opposition from US capital, this project appears to be quite successful.

Even putting aside the Democrats' disdainful response to the ongoing peace efforts in Korea and the party's hostile, often

hysterically paranoid stance toward Russia, the emerging neo-cold-war consensus has been something to behold. For all the intensification of anti-Russia sentiment, there has been no serious disruption in bipartisan support for the post–Iraq war project to remake the Middle East to US, Saudi, and Israeli specifications, and to combat the so-called Shi'a crescent. The hideous and cruel war in Yemen, fought by proxy by the Saudis with US logistical support, was systematically ignored by the US press for over a year, including by the main liberal cable network, MSNBC. Yet Saudi prince Mohammed bin Salman was debuted to the public with a coordinated red-carpet rollout, with the connivance and fawning assistance of major US media. Only when the war became too horrible for even the US media to ignore and bin Salman engineered a grisly murder on Turkish soil did we begin to get sustained center-left attention. I suspect this attention will be short-lived.

We also see continued support for US subversion and economic warfare against left-wing governments in Latin America. Opposition to US imperialism in Latin America on the liberal left has often been sporadic and uninterested at best, and at worst is openly or covertly supportive of capital and its imperialist imperatives. While there has been broad-based worrying on the left and center-left about the openly fascist and potentially dictatorial politics of Jair Bolsonaro, Brazil's newly elected president, the fact that Bolsonaro's associates have openly talked about cooperating with the US in defeating the Latin American left does not seem to be generating as much concern.

Meanwhile, major media gives us an endless parade of Pentagon and CIA officials to interpret world events. The most off-putting phenomenon of the past two years may well be the ongoing liberal lovefest for people like

George W. Bush, John McCain, Max Boot, William Kristol, and a whole host of icons from the cold war to the war on terror, all of them put forward as honorable defenders of the redoubtable norms and institutions of pre-Trump foreign policy. McCain's funeral was a bipartisan ritual of national mourning aimed at establishing the late senator as the eternally beating ideological heart of the US foreign policy consensus, along with its assertive militarism.

Recent years have also seen the emergence of a bipartisan consensus in favor of a new China containment policy. The Trump Administration recently labeled China a "strategic competitor." As was usual in the cold war, and throughout the history of US imperialism, this consensus is backed by the fusion of the crudely capitalist drive for accumulation and profits abroad with a certain amount of evangelical liberal zealotry

about the need to thwart alternative foreign models of progress and social organization. The need to recommit to global US military supremacy was backed up by a huge new defense bill that passed with overwhelming bipartisan support.

The picture is clear: despite the new energy on the domestic US left, the promoters of the neo-cold-war project are winning easily. There is no serious left international movement standing in the way of any part of this hegemonic and militarist project. For now, the new US left seems to have been rapidly outmaneuvered. The left might have a bit more success than the previous generation in extracting a more equitable distribution of incomes from their plutocratic bosses, but the imperatives and organizational structure of the US-led order of capital and cold-war economic and strategic competition seem unaffected. One thing we can predict with some certainty is that if these competitions produce a sequence of significant wars, as they generally do, the world's disposable working class will be the ones who feel them.

—*Dan Kervick*

Face to Face with Dystopia

Dear Editors,

As an educator at an art museum, I encourage visitors, many of whom are students, to interpret and respond to works of art during conversations in the galleries. My colleagues and I operate from the utopian assumption that an encounter with an image forms a temporary community—that every collective glance into the human past, every shared moment of recognition, gives birth to a small society. Keeping John Dewey's pedagogical theory in mind, we try to facilitate an experience with an object or an image from which the participants emerge, in some small way, better able to be people. "Works of art are the most intimate and energetic means of aiding individuals to share in the arts of living," Dewey writes in *Art as Experience*. It is the particular scrutability of objects that makes images important at all.

Rachel Ossip's thoughtful review of Hito Steyerl's *Duty Free Art* ("Ghost World," Issue 32), which addresses the role machines now play in interpreting images that would otherwise be unintelligible, seemed to describe the converse of my professional experiences. To confront the interpretation of inscrutable imagery by networks developed to identify, to censor, to surveil, and to target is to come face-to-face with dystopia. The images considered by these machines are not created by or for people (and are often never seen by people at all), but are instead activated and deployed against them—as when data from surveillance cameras tells police departments to mobilize more officers in black and brown neighborhoods. These interpretations fracture relationships, divide communities, restrict communication, and sever people from people.

It's disheartening to admit that the pace and the grim results of such interpretation far outstrips what we are able to achieve in the museum. But it is for this reason that I value Steyerl's—and Ossip's—writing: they offer us ways of understanding and examining an increasingly inscrutable moment, of seeing a way out.

—Rachel Himes